THE
PSYCHOLOGY
OF COMPUTER
PROGRAMMING

COMPUTER SCIENCE SERIES

THE PSYCHOLOGY OF COMPUTER PROGRAMMING

Gerald M. Weinberg

SCHOOL OF ADVANCED TECHNOLOGY
STATE UNIVERSITY OF NEW YORK
BINGHAMTON, NEW YORK

 VAN NOSTRAND REINHOLD COMPANY

NEW YORK   CINCINNATI   TORONTO   LONDON   MELBOURNE

Van Nostrand Reinhold Company Regional Offices:
New York   Cincinnati   Chicago   Millbrae   Dallas

Van Nostrand Reinhold Company International Offices:
London   Toronto   Melbourne

Library of Congress Catalog Card Number: 72-165813

ISBN: 0-442-29264-3

Manufactured in the United States of America

Published by Van Nostrand Reinhold Company
450 West 33rd Street, New York, N. Y. 10001

Published simultaneously in Canada by Van Nostrand Reinhold Ltd.

15   14   13   12   11   10   9   8   7   6

To my teachers, friends, students.

Preface

This book has only one major purpose—to trigger the beginning of a new field of study: computer programming as a human activity, or, in short, the psychology of computer programming. All other goals are subservient to that one. For instance, I have tried to make the book interesting and nontechnical, insofar as is possible, so as to encourage the greatest number of people to read it: not just programmers, but programming managers and others connected with programming in the many ways we are connected with programming these days. What I am trying to accomplish is to have the reader say, upon finishing the book, "Yes, programming is not just a matter of hardware and software. I shall have to look at things in a new way from now on."

Because this is a new field—a new way of looking at familiar things—it has not always been possible to support certain ideas with "scientific" evidence. Indeed, many of the views in the book are merely the author's opinions—often strong opinions, but not based on anything better than personal observation over many years. No doubt, many of these opinions are just plain wrong, as are many of the ideas supported by more evidence. But there is a world of difference between a wrong idea and a sterile one. If any reader takes issue with something expressed here, my fondest hope is that he will set up an experiment and prove me wrong.

As I hope the text demonstrates with numerous examples, our profession suffers under an enormous burden of myths and half-truths, many of which my students and I have been able to challenge with extremely simple experiments. But our resources are limited and the problem is great. There are, by various estimates, hundreds of thousands of programmers working today. If our experiences are any indication, each of them could be functioning more efficiently, with greater satisfaction, if he and his manager would only learn to look upon the programmer as a human being, rather than as another one of the machines.

I think that great strides are possible in the design of our hardware and software too, if we can adopt the psychological viewpoint. I would hope that this book would encourage our designers to add this new dimension to their design philosophy. Not that the few ideas and speculations in this book will give them all the information they need; but hopefully the book will inspire them to go to new sources for information. At the moment, programming—sophisticated as it may be from an engineering or mathematical point of view—is so crude psychologically that even the tiniest insights should help immeasurably. My own experience, and the experience of my students, in teaching, learning, and doing programming with psychological issues in mind, bears out this assertion. I hope each of my readers will try it for himself.

As will be obvious from reading it, this book represents a composite of ideas from many people, most of all my students at the IBM Systems Research Institutes in New York and Geneva and The State University of New York at Binghamton. Having had so many working programmers as students over ten years, I have been able to extend vicariously my own small experience into all sorts of programming situations which no one person could hope to experience in a lifetime. Needless to say, some of these experiences have had to be fictionalized to protect the innocent, and sometimes the guilty.

Without the many long hours of discussion with my students, without their many clever experiments, this book could never have been written. There is no sense assuming a position of false modesty by saying that all of the mistakes in the book are mine—no doubt some of the experiences related to me were distorted in one way or another. What *is* my responsibility is the acceptance of these experiences as the basis for certain ideas—just as it is the reader's responsibility to weigh each idea herein in the light of his own experiences and needs. The last thing I should wish to happen is to have anything said in this book taken as gospel—that is just the attitude we are trying to abolish. The material which follows is food for thought, not a substitute for it.

I wish to thank all of my students who have contributed so much to me personally as well as to this book, just as I wish to thank all my teachers and my friends. Teachers, friends, students—really they are all one and the same, and I hope they have found me to be so. To them the book is dedicated, not just on the dedication page, but in every sentence and paragraph. To my wife, who, in addition to her usual contribution to my life, read every page of this book from an anthropologist's point of view, I owe more than can be expressed in a mere dedication.

Gerald M. Weinberg

Suggestions for Course Use

Oscar Wilde used to claim at parties that he could discourse on any subject for half an hour without advance preparation. When challenged by a listener to speak about the Queen, he replied haughtily, "Sir, the Queen is not a subject." Even for so great a raconteur as Wilde, it is difficult to discourse on something that is not a subject, and many people are unconvinced that the psychology of computer programming is a subject. Certainly few university curricula offer such a course, so that any pioneer who wishes to inaugurate one is faced with an ardous path. A textbook, such as this one, should prove of some help, but for the first attempt at least, a number of suggestions for its use may not be presumptuous.

This book was developed in conjunction with a course titled "The Psychology of Computer Programming." The course was for graduate students in our Computer Systems program, all with some programming experience and at least one year of graduate training. It does not seem advisable to give such a course to people who are not able to write programs themselves, or who are at lower than a graduate level or a senior level with a strong major in Computer Systems or Computer Science.

The course is given in seminar form, for I am not inclined to lecture at people who know how to read. It was spread out over two semesters of two credits each, in order to give as much time as possible for students to pursue experiments of their own. Each student was required to plan and complete one small experiment, and some of them made quite significant contributions, many of which are reported in this book. The class met once a week for two hours or more, with readings in advance from this text and from some of the references to prepare for specific discussion topics.

One suggestion is in order about the readings. Since many of the works used are in obscure publications or in technical reports, we made a practice of providing Xerox copies of such readings in advance to each student. This practice seemed to encourage people to read the assignments with great regularity.

We got rather quickly into the subject of how to study programming, since few of the students had much background in behavioral sciences, let alone in behavioral science experimentation. Once this topic was covered, students were able to make a start on their projects, and we were able to proceed with the remainder of the material. Although it is not necessary that such a course require each student to experiment, when students do experiment it is important that every effort be made to get them started early.

If experimentation is not required or desired, the course would fit nicely into a one-semester pattern—either as a seminar-discussion or lecture-discussion. In any case, it is strongly recommended that at least one period per week be devoted to discussion, and the questions at the end of each chapter are intended as guides to the sort of topics that can be prepared—in notes or as an actual written assignment.

Another way this material can be used is in a one- or two-week intensive training session, as in a summer institute or in management training workshops. In such situations, experimentation is ruled out, although it is useful to perform one simple experiment in which the students are the subject so that they get the flavor of experimentation. Any one of a number of experiments suggested in the text would be suitable, but the most careful advance preparation is necessary if the time constraints are to be met. Similarly, time constraints dictate in such a class that every piece of reading material be available in one copy for each participant. Finally, if only for the necessary break in intensity, frequent discussions must be interspersed with whatever lecturing is done. Discussion will be particularly important when the class consists of experienced programmers or programming managers, for they will have as much or more to contribute than the instructors or text. The topic is so important to them, and so close to them, that with the slightest of prompting and leadership by the instructor, the success of the course is assured.

Contents

3   How Can We Study Programming?   27

II.   PROGRAMMING AS A SOCIAL ACTIVITY

4   The Programming Group   47

5   The Programming Team   67

10   Motivation, Training, and Experience   180

IV.   PROGRAMMING TOOLS

11   Programming Languages   205

12   Some Principles for Programming Language Design   217

13   Other Programming Tools   246

V.   EPILOGUE

Index   281

THE
PSYCHOLOGY
OF COMPUTER
PROGRAMMING

PART 1

PROGRAMMING AS HUMAN PERFORMANCE

The important thing is not to stop questioning. Curiosity has its own reason for existing. One cannot help but be in awe when he contemplates the mysteries of eternity, of life, of the marvelous structure of reality. It is enough if one tries to comprehend a little of this mystery every day. Never lose a holy curiosity.

Albert Einstein*

Computer programming is a human activity. One could hardly dispute this assertion, and yet, perhaps because of the emphasis placed on the machine aspects of programming, many people —many programmers—have never considered programming in this light. Among programmers, there is a certain mystique—a certain waving of the hands which takes place whenever one tries to probe the manner in which programming is done. Programming is not done in a certain way, they say, it is just *done*. Either you can program or you cannot. Some have it; some don't.

One of the corollaries of this mystique is the high salaries that must be paid to those programmers who "have it"—and even to some who

* From *Death of a Genius*, by William Miller, LIFE Magazine, May 2, 1955 © 1955 Time Inc.

don't, just on the chance that they might. Perhaps because of these high salaries, or because they cannot tolerate being at the mercy of a mystique they don't understand, computer executives have always been aware of the human element in programming. Their concern, however, has usually been with eliminating, rather than understanding, the human element.

Over the years, executives have backed their desire to eliminate programmers with staggering funds. Dozens of simplistic schemes have been heaped with money and praise on the promise—as yet not kept—of going directly from a sales proposal to a working data-processing system. But we should not chide these executives for their naiveté in assessing technical merits. We should applaud them for their sophistication in sensing the source of so many of our problems. Their touching faith in the magic of technology should serve as inspiration to those of us who daily bend our backs to the programmer's burden. Perhaps their wishes—though they can surely never be fulfilled—should give us pause—make us lift our noses from the coding pad or the terminal—and consider this human activity of ours from a human point of view.

1 ||| READING PROGRAMS

Some years ago, when COBOL was the great white programming hope, one heard much talk of the possibility of executives being able to read programs. With the perspective of time, we can see that this claim was merely intended to attract the funds of executives who hoped to free themselves from bondage to their programmers. Nobody can seriously have believed that executives could read programs. Why should they? Even programmers do not read programs.

But isn't it quite proper that only the machine should read programs? Weren't the programs written for the machine? Yes and no. Even if we were not concerned with program modification and with the interfaces between programs, reading programs might not be such a bad idea from the point of view of learning about programming.

Programming is, among other things, a kind of writing. One way to learn writing is to write, but in all other forms of writing, one also reads. We read examples—both good and bad—to facilitate learning. But how many programmers learn to write programs by reading programs? A few, but not many. And with the advent of terminals, things are getting worse, for the programmer may not even see his *own* program in a form suitable for reading. In the old days—which in computing is not so long ago—we had less easy access to machines and couldn't afford to wait for learning from actual machine runs. Turnaround was often so bad that programmers would while away the time by reading each others' programs. Some even went so far as to read programs from the program library—which in those days was still a library in the old sense of the term.

But, alas, times change. Just as television has turned the heads of the young from the old-fashioned joys of book reading, so have terminals and generally improved turnaround made the reading of programs the mark of a hopelessly old-fashioned programmer. Late at night, when the grizzled old-timer is curled up in bed with a sexy subroutine or a mystifying macro, the young blade is busily engaged in a dialogue with his terminal. No doubt it is much more thrilling to be face to face with the giant computer than merely wrapped in quiet contemplation of the work of others. But is it more edifying?

A young novelist of our time was recently asked who were his favorite authors. He responded simply that he never read novels, as his ideas were so new and superior to anyone else's that reading would only be a waste of his time. As you might expect, his work did not support his thesis. Perhaps the same could be said for some of our radical young programmers. Perhaps there is something to be gained from reading other people's programs—if only the amusement engendered by their bad examples. Perhaps if we want to understand *how* programmers program —to lift the veil of the programming mystique—we could fruitfully begin by seeing what is to be learned from the reading of programs.

AN EXAMPLE

In order to illustrate the joys and fruits of program reading, let us take a tiny example gleaned from a professional lifetime of program reading— one small program from among thousands. Suppose then that we come across the PL/I program shown in Figure 1-1. What are we to make of it?

We shall need a method of approach for reading programs, for, unlike novels, the best way to read them is not always from beginning to end. They are not even like mysteries, where we can turn to the penultimate

```
XXX: PROCEDURE OPTIONS(MAIN);
     DECLARE B(1000) FIXED(7,2),
             C FIXED(11,2),
             (I, J) FIXED BINARY;
     C = 0;
     DO I = 1 TO 10;
         GET LIST((B(J) DO J = 1 TO 1000));
         DO J = 1 TO 1000;
             C = C + B(J);
         END;
     END;
     PUT LIST('SUM IS ', C);
     END XXX;
```

Figure 1–1 A program to be read.

page for the best part—or like sexy books, which we can let fall open to the most creased pages in order to find the warmest passages. No, the good parts of a program are not found in any necessary places—although we will later see how we can discover crucial sections for such tasks as debugging and optimization. Instead, we might base our reading on a conceptual framework consisting of the *origin* of each part. In other words, as we look at each piece of code, we ask ourselves the question, "Why is this piece here?"

MACHINE LIMITATIONS

One of the reasons which account for pieces of code is that the machine on which the program is to be run is limited in some way relative to the ideal machine for the problem. In our example, we see that a total of 10,000 numbers are read into the computer and summed, but they are read in batches of 1000. As the numbers are evidently punched in PL/I LIST format, there is no reason why this division should be made, unless perhaps the total storage was limited so that all 10,000 numbers could not be stored at once. In other words, not having 40,000 bytes available, the programmer had to break up his summing into smaller sections, which led to the inclusion of an extra loop. If he had been able to store all 10,000 numbers, he might have written the program as shown in Figure 1-2.

Of course, when the programmer includes something that is intended to overcome some limitation of the machine, he rarely marks it explicitly as such. Although this omission adds to the intrigue of reading programs, it does penalize the program when, for example, it is transferred to another machine. The programmer may not even be aware that some of his coding is intended to compensate for a limitation of the machine, in which case he could hardly be expected to mark it. For instance, much programming has to be done to overcome the limited precision of our machines—or better still, the fact that they do not calculate with real numbers but only with a limited set of the rationals. Yet programmers tend to forget that these are limitations of the hardware and come to think of them as facts of life. When we include such words as REAL in our programming languages, we compound the difficulty, and make it less likely that machine designers will become aware of the difficulties this difference causes programmers.

Another area in which machine limitations are rife is intermediate storage. In the first place, we wouldn't have intermediate storage at all if we knew how to build the right kind of primary storage devices cheaply enough. But short of that Nirvana, we still have to contend with a plethora of drums, disks, tapes, and the like—all of which lead to enormous

```
XXX: PROCEDURE OPTIONS(MAIN);
    DECLARE A(10000) FIXED(7,2),
            C FIXED(11,2),
            J FIXED BINARY;
    C = 0;
    GET LIST((A(J) DO J = 1 TO 10000));
    DO J = 1 TO 10000;
        C = C + A(J);
        END;
    PUT LIST('SUM IS ', C);
    END XXX;
```

Figure 1-2   Storage limitation removed.

amounts of coding. Moreover, each device has peculiar timing characteristics, modes of addressing, and storage capacity, and we find much
programming devoted to overcoming the less-than-optimum (from the
programmer's point of view) configuration we happen to have.

LANGUAGE LIMITATIONS

But machine limitations are not our primary concern here, for we are
seeking the human underpinnings of programming. A step closer to these
underpinnings is the programming language—assuming that nobody—
but nobody—programs in machine language anymore. One of the consequences of moving up above machine language is that certain facilities
of the hardware may be lost to the user. An example of this type is the
end-of-file situation which exists in some FORTRAN systems. In these
systems, the machine is perfectly able to recognize an end-of-file and
pass control to another section of the program, but the FORTRAN language provides no such facility. Thus, the programmer has to resort to
devices such as the "end-of-file card"—an example in which both the
coding and the data have to be modified to overcome language limitations.

In our example, the language limitation is more subtle. PL/I provides
the programmer with a built-in function called SUM for taking the sum
of the elements of an array. In the original definition of the language,
however, at the time this program was written, SUM was a so-called
"mathematical" function, rather than an "arithmetic" function. What this
meant was that it assumed floating point input—and converted its input
to floating point if necessary. Aside from questions of efficiency, this
conversion could mean the loss of precision if the array—as in this example—consisted of FIXED DECIMAL numbers with fractional parts.
Many programmers were distressed to discover that pennies were being
lost when they tried to balance accounts using SUM. The resulting protest
led to a redefinition of SUM as arithmetic generic, but, in the meantime,
it could not be used successfully on a problem such as our example.
Without this language limitation, the program could have been shortened
to read as in Figure 1-3.

In this figure, we have also eliminated the OPTIONS(MAIN) on the
PROCEDURE statement, illustrating another form of language limitation—
the limitation of a particular implementation. This clumsy attribute was
only required in certain systems because of the interface with the operating system, which required that MAIN programs be handled somewhat
differently than subroutines.

Of course, PL/I is noted for its absence of silly little restrictions such as
abound in many other languages. To take just a few examples among

```
XXX:  PROCEDURE;

      DECLARE A(10000) FIXED(7,2),

            J FIXED BINARY;

      GET LIST((A(J) DO J = 1 TO 10000));

      PUT LIST('SUM IS ', SUM(A));

      END XXX;
```

Figure 1–3 Using arithmetic generic sum.

many, consider all the extra coding that has been written in FORTRAN because DO loops could not be counted backwards, because expressions could not appear as increments or bounds of an iteration, or because array subscripts had to start with one, or because only a small number of subscript expressions were possible. Still, we may not feel these limitations until they have been lifted from us, just as we often do not know we are sick until we suddenly feel better. Therefore, it is reasonable to expect that future languages will make us feel those limitations of PL/I that are not detectable today. Notice that this is a psychological question—one to which we shall have occasion to return.

PROGRAMMER LIMITATIONS

More directly psychological is the question of how much coding is done because the programmer did not have full mastery of his computer, his language, or himself. For instance, in our example, the programmer did not really understand array notation in PL/I—to the extent that he was unaware of the possibility of putting an array name in a data list in order to obtain all the elements of the array. Had he been familiar with this feature—which was, after all, even in FORTRAN—he might have written the program shown in Figure 1-4.

```
XXX: PROCEDURE;

     DECLARE A(10000) FIXED(7,2);

     GET LIST(A);   PUT LIST('SUM IS ', SUM(A));

     END XXX;
```

Figure 1–4 Increased programmer awareness.

There are, of course, programmer limitations other than merely not knowing the full power of the language—vocabulary limitations, we might say. For instance, the programmer may be unaware of certain algorithms, or he may be unable to grasp a sufficiently large portion of the problem at one time to see that certain duplications may be avoided. We shall have much to say about these and other limitations as we proceed, for these are obviously in the province of the psychology of programming.

HISTORICAL TRACES

We often find material in programs that might be accounted for under one of the above categories but is really present because of the history of the development of the program. For example, once the SUM function is changed to an arithmetic generic function, there is no longer any reason for the program in Figure 1-2 to appear. Nevertheless, things being what they are in the programming business, it is unlikely that anyone is going to delve into a working program and modify it just because the definition of the SUM function has been changed. And so, some years later, a novice programmer who is given the job of modifying this program will congratulate himself for knowing more about PL/I than the person who originally wrote this program. Since that person is probably his supervisor, an unhealthy attitude may develop—which, incidentally, is another psychological reality of programming life which we shall have to face eventually.

The prehistoric origins of certain pieces of code are almost beyond belief. In one instance, two programmers digging into one of the basic codes at the Social Security Administration discovered a curious artifact. Whenever an input card with one of several origin codes was found to have an "A" in a certain column, the "A" was transformed into a "1." This was especially curious in view of the fact that only numeric values could appear in this column—and there was a preedit program to ensure that this was so. Still, the programmers were properly reluctant to modify some coding whose purpose they did not understand, so they started an inquiry. Eventually, they turned up a solution.

Several years earlier—which means several programmer generations in some shops (which is another question of psychology, isn't it!)—one of the keypunches at one of the contributing district offices had developed a bug which caused it to punch a "1" as an "A" in just this column. Since this was before the days of the preedit program, these mispunched cards managed to penetrate the inner program and caused it to hang up. By the time the problem was detected, there were an unknown number of such cards in circulation, so the simplest course seemed to be to make a "temporary" modification to the program. Once the patch was made, it worked so well that everyone forgot about it—more psychology—and there it sat until unearthed many years later by two archeologist programmers.

Not all historic code can be so easily differentiated as these examples might imply. In particular, the larger a program grows, the more diffuse are the effects of particular historical choices made early in its life. Even the very structure of the program may be determined by the size and composition of the programming group that originally wrote it—since the work had to be divided up among a certain number of people, each of whom had certain strengths and weaknesses. Indeed, the social organization of programming groups will be an area of major interest to us.

SPECIFICATIONS

When we look at the difference between Figures 1-1 and 1-4, we might begin to believe that very little of the coding that is done in the world has much to do with the problems we are trying to solve. Everything considered, this would be a pretty fair statement of the situation—although there probably is, in almost every program, some code which actually does the work that was specified. Yet even if we succeed in extracting this kernel of the program, we must not be misled into the illusion that we could have started with this kernel as a specification and had some system take care of the other limitations. Aside from the obvious difficulties in determining a programmer's intentions when he doesn't know very much or in producing *efficient* code from a specification that is written without the slightest understanding of what computers can do, there will always remain the fact that, in most cases, we do not *know* what we want to do until we have taken a flying leap at programming it.

Specifications evolve together with programs and programmers. Writing a program is a process of *learning*—both for the programmer and the person who commissions the program. Moreover, this learning takes place in the context of a particular machine, a particular programming language, a particular programmer or programming team in a particular working environment, and a particular set of historical events that determine not just the form of the code but also *what the code does!*

In a way, the most important reason for studying the process by which programs are written by people is not to make the programs more efficient, more compact, cheaper, or more easily understood. Instead, the most important gain is the prospect of getting from our programs what we really want—rather than just whatever we can manage to produce in our fumbling, bumbling way.

SUMMARY

There are many reasons why programs are built the way they are, although we may fail to recognize the multiplicity of reasons because we usually look at code from the outside rather than by reading it. When we do read code, we find that some of it gets written because of machine limitations, some because of language limitations, some because of programmer limitations, some because of historical accidents, and some because of specifications—both essential and inessential. But for whatever reason a particular piece of code gets inserted into the final product, there are psychological aspects to that reason—which leads us to believe that studying programming as human behavior will bear numerous and not always expected fruits.

QUESTIONS

For Managers

1. If you are a first-line manager, are you capable of reading the programs written by your programmers? Or did your ability to read programs lapse with the previous generation of machines or languages? If you are capable, do you read them? If you don't, why not try it and see what you find?

2. If you are a higher-level manager, are your first-line managers capable of reading programs written by their programmers? Are you sure? Ask the programmers themselves, then answer this question again. Then find out if the first-line managers actually do read programs, even if they are capable. Our surveys indicate that nine-tenths do not, for one reason or another. Do you think it is possible for a first-line manager to know how good his programmers are or how well they are doing without occasionally reading their programs?

For Programmers

1. When was the last time you read somebody else's program? Why has it been so long? When was the last time somebody else read one of your programs and discussed it with you? Was it your manager?

2. Borrow a program from the program library or from one of your friends. Try to analyze it into pieces of code that are there for the various reasons described in the text. What did you learn from this exercise?

3. Take one of your own programs written over a month ago, and analyze it as in Question 2. What did you learn from this exercise?

BIBLIOGRAPHY

Bucholz, Werner, ed., *Planning a Computer System: Project Stretch,* New York, McGraw-Hill, 1962.
Computers too are made up of parts that get into them for various reasons. For an excellent view of how computing machines come to be the way they are, this book has not been surpassed. In addition, the book contains many insights into the question of machine limitations on programming, since Stretch was intended to be, among other things, a "programmer's machine" and thus eliminated many of the things which we take for granted on other machine designs.

PL/I Language Log, IBM Corporation, Confidential File.
This may be hard to obtain, but now that IBM is no longer solely responsible for maintaining the integrity of PL/I, it may be possible to see a copy. The Language Log is a running record of the controversies and decisions that went into the PL/I language we know today, and as such contains a marvelous education in how programming languages have been formulated. Hopefully, someone will publish parts of this Log in a suitably organized book.

Program Library of any user group or computer manufacturer. Your program library contains a wealth of information.
Patronize it!

Weinberg, G. M., *PL/I Programming: A Manual of Style,* New York, McGraw-Hill, 1970.
Read this book if you want a lot more detail on the author's ideas on how programs come to look the way they do.

Gruenberger, Fred, ed., *Fourth Generation Computers: User Requirements and Transition,* Englewood Cliffs, N.J., Prentice-Hall, 1970.
Looking to the "fourth generation" with all the wisdom garnered from the first three, several authors in this collection seem at last to be facing the problem of the psychological needs of the computer user. Murray Laver traces the ways in which designers, salesmen, and manufacturers have had more influence in the past than the people who were to use their products. Jacques Bouvard discusses the need for more user orientation in the design of systems at the software level.

2 WHAT MAKES A GOOD PROGRAM?

I f we plan to study programming as a human activity, we are going to have to develop some measures of programming performance. That is, we are going to have some idea of what we mean when we say that one programmer is better than another, or one program is better than another. Although we all have opinions on these questions, we shall find that the answers are not as simple as we might wish. For programming is not just human behavior; it is *complex* human behavior.

Consider our programming example once again. By analyzing Figure 1-1 rather thoroughly, we discover that only a small portion of it—no more than 20 percent—is directed at meeting the problem specifications. Of the other 80 percent, much, if not most, can be eliminated not by physical change but by psychological change. In fact, even the question of a limited storage could have been dealt with by an appropriate virtual machine, so that even machine limitations can be overcome by proper psychological design.

The program in Figure 1-1, though small, is typical in the percentage of coding that is actually devoted to solving the given problem. Because people do not read programs, few are aware of how common this situation is. But common it is, and it gives us much scope for improvement in our programming. Still, there is more to the question of good programming than measuring the percentage of extraneous—or at least peripheral —code. Indeed, we cannot really measure a program by itself and say whether it is good or bad.

Most programmers feel that there is such a thing as good programming. Although this feeling may be valid, it does not follow that there is such a thing as a good program. Not, at least, in the sense that we can study the program out of the context in which it was developed and in which it will be used and declare it to have a goodness of 83.72 percent.

Consider Figure 1-1. Is it a good program? It is a clumsy program, perhaps, but that is only part of the mark. After all, we only knew it was clumsy because we read it, and for the ordinary program, nobody is ever going to read it, so grace is hardly an absolute measure of program goodness. Is it an efficient program? We can hardly answer this question without knowing the machine, the compiler, and the cost situation under which it will be run. Was it done on time? What did it cost? Does it meet specifications? We cannot know these things merely by looking at the code.

In our studies of the psychology of programming, we shall be hampered by our inability to measure the goodness of programs on an absolute scale. But can we perhaps measure them on a relative scale—can we say that program A is better or worse than program B? Unfortunately, we will generally not even be able to do that, for several reasons. First of all, when is there ever another program with which to compare? And when there is, as in the case of, say, a FORTRAN compiler, how can we agree on the relative importance of the different attributes of the program. Is a compiler that quickly compiles slow code better than one that slowly compiles quick code?

But still, aren't there times when we can make a relative ranking? Isn't a compiler that quickly compiles quick code better than one that slowly compiles slow code? We have to admit that sometimes such comparisons can be made—although we must not be too hasty in making them. There are dimensions of compiler performance other than speed. There are diagnostics, scope of language covered, reliability of object code, and execution time monitoring, to mention a few. Only rarely will we find two programs so sufficiently similar that they can be compared point by point—and then find one superior on all points.

More often, then, we will be doing evaluation of programs not with respect to one another but with respect to a situation—a total situation

—in which they are developed. Looking honestly at the situation, we are never looking for the best program, seldom looking for a good one, but always looking for one that meets the requirements.

SPECIFICATIONS

Of all the requirements that we might place on a program, first and foremost is that it be correct. In other words, it should give the correct outputs for each possible input. This is what we mean when we say that a program "works," and it is often and truly said that "any program that works is better than any program that doesn't."

An example may serve to drive home this point to those whose minds are tangled in questions of efficiency and other secondary matters. A programmer was once called to Detroit to aid in the debugging of a new program—one that was to determine the parts requirements to build a certain set of automobiles. The input to the program was a deck of cards, each card representing a purchase order for an automobile, with different punches representing the different options selected by the customer. The program embodied the specifications relating the various options to the parts that would be needed. For instance, the choice of upholstery for the rear seat might be determined by such factors as body color, body style, options for deluxe or leatherette upholstery, and whether or not the car was air conditioned. The air-conditioning option is a good example of the basic complexity of the problem, for though to an untrained eye the choice of air conditioning might have no connection with the choice of rear seat upholstery, it might very well require spaces for extra ducts. In general, then, each option might have some effect on the choice of parts made, so the determination of parts requirements was an excellent job for the computer.

Unfortunately, when this programmer arrived on the scene, the basic approach to the problem had long been settled—and settled badly. Each option—as it affected each choice—was reflected as an individually programmed test and branch in the program. In a way, the program was an enormous tree, with more than 5000 branches, representing the decisions leading to part selection. Cast in this form—and with 16 programmers working at the same time—it was impossible to debug, as each and every case had to be tested separately. To test the program, a particular card would be put in and the output would be observed. When our programmer arrived, things were so bad that typical cards were calling for the production of cars with eight tires, no engine, and three sets of upholstery. In short, a disaster.

As is usual with programming disasters, nobody recognized it as such.

Instead, the whole crew had gone on double shift to get out the bugs, and new programmers, including our hero, were brought in from all over the country. Naturally, this led to worse confusion than ever, and our programmer, after a few days, determined that it was hopeless business—and in any case not reason enough to be away from his family and working night and day. He was roundly condemned for his uncooperative attitude but was allowed to leave.

While on the plane, he had his first opportunity in a week to reflect calmly. He immediately saw the error in the approach and perceived that a much better approach would be to divide the work into two phases. The main operational program would simply loop through a set of specially constructed specifications tables, so that all decisions would be made with a single test reapplied to different parts of the table. In that way, the program was at least assured to produce the right number of tires, engines, and so forth. The tables themselves would be compiled from input written in essentially the form of the engineering specifications. This would allow the engineering personnel, rather than the programmers, to check the specifications, and also permit one part of the specification to be changed without changing all parts further down a decision tree.

By the time he got off the plane, he had coded the two programs. It was a day's work to check them out, and another two days' work with the local assembly plant engineers to create the specifications in input form. After a week's testing in the plant, he was about to return to notify Detroit of the news when he got a telegram saying that the project had been cancelled—since the program was impossible to write.

After a quick call and a plane trip, he was back in Detroit with his version of the program. A demonstration to the executives convinced them that the project could continue, and then he was asked to make a presentation to the rest of the programmers. Naturally, they were a rather cool audience—a phenomenon to which we shall return in our discussions —but they sat quietly enough through his explanation of the method. Even at the end, there was a lack of questioning—until the original creator of the old system raised his hand.

"And how long does *your* program take?" he asked—emphasizing the possessive.

"That varies with the input," was the reply, "but on the average, about ten seconds per card."

"Aha," was the triumphant reply. "But *my* program takes only one second per card."

The members of the audience—who had, after all, all contributed to the one-second version—seemed relieved. But our hero, who was rather young and naive, was not put down by this remark. Instead, he calmly observed, "But your program doesn't work. If the program doesn't have to work, I can write one that takes one millisecond per card—and that's faster than our card reader."

This observation—though it undoubtedly failed to win our hero any friends—contains the fundamental truth upon which all programming evaluation must be based. If a program doesn't work, measures of efficiency, of adaptability, or of cost of production have no meaning. Still, we must be realistic and acknowledge that probably no perfect program was ever written. Every really large and significant program has "just one more bug." Thus, there are degrees of meeting specifications—of "working"—and evaluation of programs must take the type of imperfection into account.

Any compiler, for example, is going to have at least "pathological" programs which it will not compile correctly. What is pathological, however, depends to some extent on your point of view. If it happens in your program, you hardly classify it as pathological, even though thousands of other users have never encountered the bug. The producer of the compiler, however, must make some evaluation of the errors on the basis of the number of users who encounter them and how much cost they incur. This is not always done scientifically. Indeed, it often amounts to an evaluation of who shouts the loudest, or who writes to the highest executive. But whatever system is chosen, some bugs will remain, and some people will be unhappy with the same compiler that satisfies thousands.

In effect, then, there is a difference between a program written for one user and a piece of "software." When there are multiple users, there are multiple specifications. When there are multiple specifications, there are multiple definitions of when the program is working. In our discussions of programming practices, we are going to have to take into account the difference between programs developed for one user and programs developed for many. They will be evaluated differently, and they should be produced by different methods.

SCHEDULE

Even after questions of meeting specifications have been set aside, the question of efficiency is still not uppermost. One of the recurring problems in programming is meeting schedules, and a program that is late is often worthless. At the very least, we have to measure the costs of *not having* the program against any potential savings that a more efficient program would produce. In one noteworthy case, the customer of a software firm estimated that the linear programming code being developed would save more than one million dollars per month in the company's oil refining operations. Even one month's delay in schedule would result in a loss that could not be recovered if the program were run free of charge for ten years.

Losses from late delivery of programs are not always so severe, but even were the costs negligible, there seems to be, in the United States, at least, an incredible amount of annoyance when schedules are not met. In fact, the average programming manager would prefer that a project be estimated at twelve months and take twelve than that the same project be estimated at six months and take nine. This is an area where some psychological study could be rewarding, but there are indications from other situations that it is not the mean length of estimated time that annoys people but, rather, the standard deviation in the actual time taken. Thus, most people would prefer to wait a fixed ten minutes for the bus each morning than to wait one minute on four days and twenty-six minutes once a week. Even though the average wait is six minutes in the second case, the derangement caused by one long and unexpected delay more than compensates for this disadvantage.

If this observation holds true for programming, then any studies of the effect of certain programming practices should measure the effect on variability in production time—not just mean time as most studies currently do. We shall try to estimate this effect in all our subsequent discussions.

ADAPTABILITY

Having disposed of the questions of meeting specifications and schedules, we might suppose that we had finally arrived at the question of efficiency as a measure of the goodness of programs. Without begging the question of relative importance of the two factors, however, it will prove advantageous first to dispose of the factor of *adaptability* of a program. No doubt there are programs that are used once and then thrown away. No doubt there are even more programs that should be thrown away before ever being used. Nonetheless, the great majority of programs that are written, especially by professional programmers, remain in existence for a definite life span. And during that span, most of them become modified.

Few programmers of any experience would contradict the assertion that most programs are modified in their lifetime. Why, then, when we are forced to modify programs do we find it such a Herculean task that we often decide to throw them away and start over? Reading programs gives us some insight, for we rarely find a program that contains any evidence of having been written with an eye to subsequent modification. But this is only a symptom, not a disease. Why, we should ask, do programmers, who know full well that programs will inevitably be modified, write programs with no thought to such modifications? Why, indeed, do their programs sometimes look as if they had been devilishly contrived to resist modification—protected like the Pharoahs' tomb against all intruders?

There are answers to these questions, and they lie in the direction of our psychological investigations. But our job for the moment is not to answer them, but merely to raise them and remind ourselves of their importance in any discussion of what makes good programming. A related question is, of course, documentation, for why do we document a program if not to render it more easily modifiable? We would all agree that the quality of documentation and the ease of making modifications, both planned and unplanned, should count heavily in any grading of a program, or of the programmer who writes that program. We would all agree further, then, that any improvement here to be gained from psychological investigations will be well worth the effort.

But, a word of caution before we proceed to the question of efficiency. Adaptability is not free. Sometimes, to be sure, we get a program that happens to be adaptable as well as satisfactory in all other ways, but we generally pay for what we get—and often fail to get what we pay for. In his mathematical studies of genetic systems, R. A. Fisher derived a law that has often been called Fisher's Fundamental Theorem, a very significant name in view of the importance of Fisher's many other theorems. Fisher's Fundamental Theorem states—in terms appropriate to the present context—that the better adapted a system is to a particular environment, the less adaptable it is to new environments. By stretching our imagination a bit, we can see how this might apply to computer programs as well as to snails, fruit flies, and tortoises.

For a program to be efficient, it must take advantage of the peculiarities of the problem and the machine on which it is to be run. Programs that ignore the structure of the machine do so at the risk of incurring heavy cost penalties, and programmers who can exploit special situations in a problem are the ones who can speed things up and make them smaller. One peculiar example, not entirely untypical, of this type of programming was an assembly program that employed a special technique for looking up operation codes to be translated. The programmer had observed—or figured out—that there was one number which, when used to multiply the operation code bit pattern interpreted as numeric, yielded an almost solid and completely unduplicated list of addresses. Using this multiplier, he was able to effect a compact and equally fast transformation from symbolic codes to machine language.

The programmer was much congratulated for this ingenuity—the example was displayed to several generations of programmers as a prototype of the kind of work they should be doing. Sadly, however, this section of code did not have a very long life, for, as so frequently happens, the operation code repertoire of the machine was expanded. When a dozen or so codes had been added to the set, the old multiplier no longer had the same desirable properties of compactness and uniqueness. In fact, no multiplier could be found that would work in this way for the new codes.

The outcome of attempts to find a new multiplier was to abandon this special technique for a more general hash table search—one that allowed for the existence of duplicates. Unhappily, the old technique was not abandoned before a great deal of effort had been expended on the attempt to adapt it to the changed circumstances. This proved to be time wasted. In retrospect, the savings in time of the specialized technique never paid in its lifetime for the extra cost of fooling around when the new codes were added. If a general hash table method had been used in the first place, somewhat lower efficiency would have been the result; but—and this is the "but" that makes the example—the modification would have been entirely trivial. In fact, essentially no modification would have been required except the addition of the new codes to the appropriate places in the table.

This example could be supplemented with hundreds of others, but the point would be the same. When we ask for efficiency, we are often asking for "tight" coding that will be difficult to modify. In terms of higher-level languages, we often descend to the machine-language level to make a program more efficient. This loses at least one of the benefits of having the program in the higher-level language—that of transportability between machines. In fact, it has the effect of freezing us to a machine or implementation that we have admitted by our very act is unsatisfactory.

However, the same managers who scream for efficiency are the ones who tear their hair when told the cost of modifications. Conversely, the managers who ask for generalized and easily modified programs are wont to complain when they find out how slow and spacious these programs turn out to be. We must be adult about such matters: neither psychology nor magic is going to help us to achieve contradictory goals simultaneously. Asking for efficiency and adaptability in the same program is like asking for a beautiful and modest wife. Although beauty and modesty have been known to occur in the same woman, we'll probably have to settle for one or the other. At least that's better than neither.

EFFICIENCY

Measuring the true efficiency of a program is not the simple task it first seems. In the first place, efficiency is not always measured simply in terms of time on the computer, for it is often possible to trade time on the computer for time before and after the computer run. For example, a commonly used measure of the speed of a compiler is the number of cards per minute it processes. If we use this measure to compare an assembly program with, say, a FORTRAN compiler, the assembly is likely to appear more efficient, since each input card carries less information. Sometimes compilers are compared on the basis of the number of machine instructions *produced* per minute, but this measure exposes us to the danger of giving credit to a compiler simply because it is verbose in the production of object code.

A compiler, of course, is a special kind of beast anyway, since we must measure the efficiency of the code produced as well as that of the compilation process. Still, since compiler efficiency is a subject of much discussion, it may be worthwhile to pursue this example to illustrate how easily we can be misled on efficiency questions. Consider, for instance, the comparison of two compilers for the same language in terms of the "cards per minute" measure. The first pitfall here lies in the term "same language." Very few compilers handle exactly the same language, so if there is any difference between the two, we will have to adjust the efficiency obtained from cards per minute to account for the difference in value of the two languages.

The effect of slight differences in source language on compiler efficiency can be striking. Typically, if the compiler writer can choose 10 percent of the language which he will not implement, he can produce a 50 percent faster compiler. Unfortunately, *which* 10 percent is chosen differs from one machine and one compiling technique to the other, so that language designers cannot simply provide "more efficient" subsets to be implemented.

Similar improvements in efficiency are possible from similar relaxation of specifications in other areas. Indeed, if our primary concern in a particular application is efficiency, the first step should always be to look for areas in which the specifications can be changed to suit computer efficiency rather than user convenience. Of course, computer time is not the only cost element in a typical project. People time also costs money. Thus, we can leave certain crossfootings to be done by the recipient of a report, but we may only be saving computer time at the expense of executive time with paper and pencil. We may decide quite rationally to make this choice, but more often the choice is made without the executive having anything to say about it.

Trimming the external specifications can even have the opposite of the intended effect on computer time used. If, for example, a great deal of manual handling of input has been left in the system to simplify the computer run, we may find ourselves paying more in reruns than we saved in single-run efficiency. This effect is rather common when comparing two compilers which, even though they handle identical language, differ in the diagnostics and execution monitoring they produce. If we save 20 percent in raw compile time by eliminating or trimming error checking, we had better be sure that the user will not find himself making 40 percent more runs to get the same amount of information.

As hazardous as it is to make simple measures of efficiency in a single-machine, simple-scheduler environment, it is child's play compared with the difficulties of obtaining meaningful efficiency estimates in a multi-processing or multiprogramming environment. Is it better, for instance, to occupy 40K bytes of main storage for one hour or 80K bytes for 30 minutes? The answer to this question depends on the situation in the computer at the time the job is run—and may change each time the job is run. For example, one day it may be possible to add a 40K job to the machine load without affecting the performance of the other jobs by one second; yet the next day the same 40K job may lock out another job for the full hour.

Running on systems capable of dynamic load adjustment may alleviate some of the instabilities in multiprogram performance that we often see today. It may very well be that, as with schedules for programming, what the user wants is not a small mean time to execute his program but a small standard deviation, so he can plan his work reasonably. If this is true, the entire schedule from origin to destination of the work must be considered, not just the "time on the computer."

We may be moving toward a computing environment in which the best programs are those that retain the ability to be run in various sizes of main memory, on various machine configurations. Such a program may not be very efficient on any one of the configurations—considering Fisher's Fundamental Theorem applied in the inverse sense—but may lead to more consistent turnaround performance because it will never find itself waiting for just the correct slot in the day's schedule. Machines with virtual memories give us this kind of flexibility without special programming, although there are indications that performance improvements can be obtained even in this environment by taking special characteristics into account.

For instance, if we know the page size of our system, we can avoid excessive paging by tailoring our program sections to fit into single pages and not to cross page boundaries except at logical breaks in the program. If we do this, however, the program becomes somewhat less well adapted for running in a system with a different page size. Similarly, we can choose an algorithm that will require no more and no less page space than is commonly allowed by our system; but again, this kind of program will fail to take advantage of extra page space and will give the worst possible performance in a system with a smaller page space.

What all of this means is that efficiency is becoming a clouded issue in computing. Moreover, with cost per unit of computation decreasing every year and cost per unit of programming increasing, we have long since passed the point where the typical installation spends more money on programming than it does on production work. This imbalance is even more striking when all the work improperly classified as "production" is put under the proper heading of "debugging." But by any measure, the imbalance exists. And grows. And so we expect that with each passing year we will hear less and less about efficiency—and more and more about effectiveness.

SUMMARY

The question of what makes a good program is not a simple one, and may not even be a proper question. Each program has to be considered on its own merits and in relation to its own surroundings. Some of the important factors are:

1. Does the program meet specifications? Or, rather, how well does it meet specifications?
2. Is it produced on schedule, and what is the *variability* in the schedule that we can expect from particular approaches?
3. Will it be possible to change the program when conditions change? How much will it cost to make the change?
4. How efficient is the program, and what do we mean by efficiency? Are we trading efficiency in one area for inefficiency in another?

In the future, and particularly in the discussion of this book, we should refrain from using the concept "good program" or "good programmer" as if it were something universally agreed upon, or something that even *can* be universally agreed upon, or something that even *should* be universally agreed upon.

QUESTIONS

For Managers

1. On what bases do you reward programmers? Are certain of your criteria mutually contradictory, as in asking for efficient but general programs? How explicit are you with your programmers in indicating what you are looking for in their programs? Or do you just tell them that you want the programs to be fast, small, neat, easily modifiable, errorless, and done in a week?
2. How do the programs in your installation stack up on adaptability? Is

modifying programs a major expense in your installation? If so, can you see things in your programming practices—in the original goals you set—that may lead to this kind of expense?

3. How important is making the schedule in your shop? Is "a miss as good as a mile," or do you reward for consistency rather than the occasional lucky shot? Can you see how a programmer can choose an unreliable practice because it gives him the only hope of making the schedule, even though it may risk not finishing the program at all?

For Programmers

1. Do you have criteria explicitly in mind when you start on a project? Are these criteria obtained from your own impression of what is important, or do you get them from your manager? Do your criteria change as the project progresses, or do you have some device for keeping them firmly in mind?

2. How many times have you ever thought, when writing a program, of some person in the future who might modify it? How many times have you ever cursed someone whose program you were modifying?

3. Have you ever tried for "efficiency" at the expense of getting the job done? For "meeting the deadline" at the expense of doing it right?

BIBLIOGRAPHY

Fisher, Ronald A., *The Genetical Theory of Natural Selection,* New York, Dover Publications, 1958.
See particularly Chapter II for a discussion of the Fundamental Theorem of Natural Selection.

Weinberg, G. M., *PL/I Programming, A Manual of Style,* New York, McGraw-Hill, 1970.
See especially Chapter 4 on the question of the compromises among the various criteria for "good" programs.

3 HOW CAN WE STUDY PROGRAMMING?

I n the first two chapters we have tried to set the stage for a study of programming as human behavior. We showed that although programming is a form—a complex form—of human behavior, few people have studied programming from this point of view. But perhaps there is a reason why programming has not been so viewed? Perhaps programming is too complex a behavior to be studied and must remain largely a mysterious process.

Human knowledge is by necessity incomplete. We cannot know in advance what we might be able to know and what might be essentially unknowable. But of one thing we can be sure: if we do not try to find things out, we shall never succeed. To those readers who despair of success in this venture, I can only suggest that they reread the Einstein quote at the beginning of this part of the book: "The important thing is not to stop questioning."

How, then, shall we begin our questioning? Since programming is human behavior, it would seem wise to look to the sciences of human behavior for two kinds of information: results that we can apply directly to programming, and methods that we can use to get information not available directly. Of course, these methods may not be appropriate for the study of programming, and in such cases we shall have to invent new methods, something that all social scientists are doing at all times. But let us begin by seeing what types of methods are generally available to us.

INTROSPECTION

Although some modern students of human behavior tend to discredit it as nonscientific, introspection has always been the first foundation stone of their science. We may quote, for example, Sigmund Freud:*

Psychoanalysis is learnt first of all on oneself, through the study of one's own personality. This is not exactly what is meant by introspection, but it may be so described for want of a better word. There is a whole series of very common and well-known mental phenomena which can be taken as material for self-analysis when one has acquired some knowledge of the method.

Or we may quote William James,** the founder of *American* psychology:

It is in short obvious that our knowledge of our mental states infinitely exceeds our knowledge of their concomitant cerebral conditions. Without introspective analysis of the mental elements of speech, the doctrine of Aphasia, for instance, which is the most brilliant jewel in Physiology, would have been utterly impossible.

Now admittedly these are quotes from the early days of psychoanalysis and psychology, but that is precisely why their precedents are so important for us when we are embarking on the study of a new area of human behavior. Not that we intend to stop at introspection—if Freud and James had done that, their names would not be remembered today. But at the beginning of a new field or subfield, there is a great deal of information to be gleaned from the heads of people without elaborate precautions or experimental methods. What we need at the beginning are ideas as to what general directions to take, not detailed logistic plans for the journey.

What kinds of insights can introspection yield? Several examples are given in the text, but one at this point should serve to show the uses and abuses of the method. Some years ago a student of mine, in doing a classroom problem in PL/I, was having an inordinate amount of difficulty

---

* Sigmund Freud, *A General Introduction to Psychoanalysis.* By permission of Sigmund Freud Copyrights, Ltd., London England.
** Henry James, *Psychology,* Holt, Rinehart & Winston, New York.

with the statement shown in Figure 3–1. When he finally finished the program, I asked him to sit down with me and recall the thought processes —the difficulties—he had experienced with this statement.

This student came up with the following list of problems:

1. He had trouble getting the parentheses matched, because there were so many of them.
2. The original ANGLES(I) was a structure, not an array, so the compiler complained of an illegal subscript list, but he had not been able to find the problem because there were so many subscript lists.
3. When the program finally got into execution, there were these further difficulties:
   a. IND was a matrix on another page of the listing, and he had trouble finding it.
   b. Even though the parentheses were now matched, one pair was in the wrong place and was most difficult to find.
   c. The last difficulty turned out to be a problem of precision caused by capricious declaration of different data types, by the large expression, and by the division—which would not have been necessary if the two-argument form of ATAND had been used.

Now, a single case such as this contains insights into many problems in computing: the proper size of statements, the choice of data structures, the arrangement of different parts of a program, the use of parentheses rather than other techniques for decomposition, the design of compiler and execution-time diagnostics, and techniques for learning and teaching programming. None of these insights could be obtained without introspection of this sort, yet thousands of programmers each day have these same problems and simply grumble that they are having "bugs." Without the introspection, they will simply continue to have "bugs" until, in the end, the bugs will have them.

However, even though we must start with the introspection, we cannot stop there, for then we would be practicing magic or religion, not science. Based on one example such as this, we can hardly conclude such general laws as:

1. The mind cannot cope with more than five levels of parentheses.
2. Compiler diagnostics should be more explicit.
3. PL/I precision rules are too complicated to use.

```
ANGLES(I)=2*ATAND(SQRT((S-A(IND(I,1)))*(S-A(IND(I,2))))/
          (S*(S-A(IND(I,3))))));
```

Figure 3–1 A long PL/I statement.

Although each of these statements might turn out to be a "law" in the psychology of programming, writing it on the basis of a single intro-spective example hardly qualifies it as a law. To be a "law," a principle must be explored so as to set limits to its application, because all laws have limits. Indeed, the limits are usually more important to know than the laws themselves, and it is only by investigating a multitude of cases that limits can be set. Thus, without introspection, investigation would be sterile, but without investigation, introspection will be of questionable value in application.

OBSERVATION

One way to follow up introspection is by observation of what people actually do, as opposed to what they think they do. If, for instance, we want to study the question of levels of parentheses, we could observe the number of levels that other people use, and the difficulties they seem to have in using them. One of the problems with observation, how-ever, is that it tells us what people *do* do, but not necessarily what they *can* do. Thus, if we observed hundreds of programmers and never found any using more than five levels of parentheses, we could not conclude that people are *unable* to use six levels. Nevertheless, observations of this kind can lay to rest certain conjectures about what people *cannot* do, since if we find people successfully using six and more levels of parentheses, we settle the issue.

Or at least we settle *some* issue. A second problem with observation is deciding just what it is we are observing. A programmer doesn't use six levels of parentheses in just any context—there may be situations in which he really cannot use six levels successfully. Once we have observed the six levels, our work has only begun; next we have to de-limit the circumstances under which such behavior can be found and under which it cannot. How far we have to delimit depends upon the use we intend to make of the observation. For example, if we are de-signing a programming language and we would like—for reasons of efficient compilation—to limit the depth of parentheses' nesting to five, we would like to have estimates of how often somebody would be in-convenienced by not using six. We would not necessarily have to know *why* he was using six.

We must be extremely careful in making observations such as this, however, because programming is extremely complex behavior. Many languages, for instance, limit the number of dimensions that an array may have to three—not on any psychological grounds, but only on the casual observation that nobody seems to use more than three. Such an observation may be faulty for a number of reasons other than haphazardness. In the first place, if the programmer is working in a language that allows only three dimensions, we are not likely to observe more than three. Secondly, other features of the language may prevent the user from making effective use of more than three dimensions, even though the language permits them. Perhaps the printing format for higher arrays is not well chosen, or perhaps the specification of subscripts is so clumsy as to be confusing beyond three. The point, then, is that we must be most careful in trying to carry observations from one context over into another, because the contexts will always differ in several ways.

A third problem with observation is the problem of interference of the observer with the subject being observed—a kind of uncertainty principle. Here we have much to draw on from the social sciences, which have long been concerned with this problem and have extracted such phenomena as the "Hawthorne Effect." This effect was named after the Hawthorne Works of the Western Electric Company, where between 1924 and 1927 certain experiments in industrial psychology failed. They failed because no matter how conditions of work changed, productivity rose. Eventually, the experimenters came to realize that the missing factor was the pride the workers took in being subjects of all this attention. It was the act of observation itself which was producing the phenomenon being observed.

The interference of the observed and observer occurs not only in industrial psychology, of course, but in all sciences that study human behavior. The anthropolgists are constantly plagued in their field studies by the gnawing fear that the behavior being observed is that behavior appropriate for a visiting anthropologist. Through the method of "participant observation," the anthropologist tries to make himself "invisible" to the people by becoming so much a part of the culture that he is not noticed, so that the culture can go on as if no outsider were there. The method of participant observation is certainly one which can be used in the study of programming; and our students, who are often working programmers, have made good use of it in obtaining some of the data reported in this book.

Another way of being "invisible" is to observe in ways in which the people observed actually have no possibility of knowing that they are under observation. Many such methods exist, and they may all be classified under the rubric of "unobtrusive measures." There is no need for us to go into detail about such measures here, as a number of books and articles discuss not only the methods but the ethical and moral problems in using them. But we should take time to discuss one type of unobtrusive measure which is more or less unique to computer studies— the direct recording of user behavior by the computer.

In a way, any computer system that does self-accounting is doing unobtrusive observation of programming behavior. A number of explicit studies have been made, however, particularly of time-sharing systems to see how users behave at terminals. (See Sackman,* 1970, Chapter 2, for a summary of this work.) These studies have been in the main statistical, but because the computer records data in such detail, there is no reason why individual users cannot be studied, even over long periods of time. In fact, it is the enormous amount of detail that has forced most of these studies to be statistical, and one of the major problems faced by the would-be observer is what to throw away. One man sitting at a terminal for one hour generates considerably more data than a psychologist can fruitfully analyze in one hour, and when fifty users are sharing the system, the situation is certainly not improved.

However, we must not be lulled by this enormous quantity into believing that such data, by its sheer bulk, must of needs contain the *information* we want. Although it is convenient to use the normal accounting or logging information generated by a system, it will usually be necessary to provide some hardware or software to get what we are truly after in a careful study. For example, the timing information needed for accounting will usually not suffice for psychological purposes. In the first place, the units timed may not be the units we wish to study, and few systems log a time with every transaction. Secondly, the resolution level of the timing for accounting purposes may be adequate to a second or more, but for many psychological studies, we may want to get down to milliseconds.

EXPERIMENT

One way to reduce the cost of the bulk of data produced by observation is to design experiments. Through the use of experiments, fewer data can produce more information about the aspects of behavior which interest us. One of the first dangers of experiments, however, is precisely that they may be so refined that they bypass the most interesting data. The experimental situation might so constrain the subject's behavior that we will never see what we saw when observing him in a natural setting.

The constraint influencing the subject's behavior may be either planned or unplanned. To take one example, Sackman cites studies comparing on-line and batch systems where the batch system is simulated by running the jobs on-line but holding the work for a fixed period before delivery to the user. The purpose of this simulation was to ensure that the two groups of programmers were working in the same language and had the same system facilities available.

* See the bibliography at the end of the chapter.

A batch system simulated in this manner, however, may differ from a true batch system. For instance, the language used is tailored to the needs of terminal users. Some terminal-oriented system commands cannot be used, but are not replaced by batch-oriented commands. Diagnostics are oriented to terminal use, and corrective measures that might be provided in a batch system are probably not present, since it is easier for a terminal user to make his own corrections. Finally, a more subtle effect may be introduced by the very regularity of the turnaround. A normal batch system does not give jobs back precisely two hours after they are submitted, and the variance in the turnaround is a major influence on user behavior. By inadvertently eliminating the variance, the experimenters may have biased the study in one direction or the other. Only another study could tell which.

Another study! Aye, there's the rub! Studies cost money, and in programming they cost more than in other areas of human behavior. For instance, in one small study, we used one-quarter time of nine experienced programmers for three months. Their average salary was $14,000, which with modest overhead came to say, $20,000 apiece, or $1250 apiece over the course of the study. Add to this the cost of the experimenters' salaries, the computer time, and various supplies and secretarial services, and the bill comes easily to $30,000—for nine subjects.

In the classical psychological study, costs do not run so high. In the first place, computers are not used—though the modern trend is in that direction. More important, however, is that subjects are usually free. As one wag put it, "psychology is the psychology of 18-year-old college freshmen." What he meant was that the typical source of subjects is the freshman psychology course in a university, where one of the requirements for credit is participation as a subject in one experiment. Normally, such subjects are not paid at all, let alone $14,000 a year.

In selecting subjects, inadvertent constraint may slip in. Whereas psychology may be the psychology of college freshmen, the psychology of programming could easily become the psychology of programmer trainees. And for the same reason—cost. Trainees are paid less, but, more important, they are not doing anything very critical, as experienced programmers seem to be. Thus, they are far more easily obtainable for experimentation, regardless of their suitability as subjects for a particular experiment. Later on, we shall discuss the question of professional versus amateur programming, and show how this confusion has always dominated and befuddled the thinking about programming. If, in the psychological study of programming, we insist on using trainees as a matter of cost or convenience, we shall only compound these confusions and give them the weight of "scientific evidence."

Undoubtedly it will turn out that some experiments can be done equally well on trainees, but the burden of proof is on the experimenter. More often, the results obtained from trainees will be limited in their application, so that they may be useful only for the design of training programs. In one study, we tried to determine the difficulty of using OS/360 Job Control Language—then, as now, the source of many complaints. In testing the class of OS/360 beginners, we found that the difficulty did indeed exist, but more or less disappeared completely upon completion of the course of study because of the use of carefully designed exercises. If we had simply tested beginners and stopped at that, we would have indeed concluded that OS/JCL was very difficult to use, instead of the proper conclusion—that it is very difficult to *learn.* Once the learning has taken place—whether through a course or through bitter experience—JCL is no more difficult to use than any other rather rigid programming language. Although the language perhaps should be redesigned, more fruitful results would probably be obtained from improved training methods. If we had just tested experienced programmers, we might well have wondered what the fuss was all about. Only by testing both groups, or—as we did—by following a group of trainees until they became experienced, could we put the problem of JCL in the proper perspective.

Whether we use experienced programmers or trainees, however, we are always faced with another difficulty which these simple titles tend to conceal. In our study of JCL, some of the students were relative novices at programming, and others were rather old hands. All, however, were novices at JCL. Thus, if we had simply correlated our results with "years of programming" as a measure of "programming experience," we should have had no results at all. When the group was tested at the beginning of the course, experienced and inexperienced alike did poorly; at the end of the course, the groups did equally well. Thus, it was not "experience" in general that mattered in this problem, but the specific experience with JCL.

The difficulty with simple measures of experience or inexperience is illustrated by an example taken from one of Sackman's studies with "experienced" programmers. There, experience was measured, among other ways, by years of programming, ranging from 2 to 11 years. On one of the problems, the best and worst performance was obtained by the two 11-year programmers in the study. Obviously, there are factors at work other than sheer length of time in "programming." It may be that the experiences in programming are so diverse as to make length of time a fruitless measure, or it may be that people don't all learn the same things from the same experiences.

Before we leave the subject of experience and experiments, we must deal with one other problem, which is important because of a seldom-questioned view of programming—a view which this book will spend a great deal of time in questioning. That view is that programming is an individual activity, not a social activity. To the extent that experimenters have believed this, they have chosen the individual programmer—experienced or not—as the suitable object for study. But there is much evidence, as we shall see presently, to argue that the proper study of programming is done at the level of the programming social unit. Not that the individual level is unimportant, but we might start by asking why, if the average programmer spends two-thirds of his time working with other people rather than working alone (yes, it's true!), that 99 percent of the studies have been on individual programmers.

One answer, of course, is that if studying programmers is expensive, studying *groups* of programmers is extravagantly so. Moreover, not just any group of programmers will do—not, for example, a collection of trainees put into a "team." Putting a bunch of people to work on the same problem doesn't make them a team—as the sloppy performance in all-star games should teach us. And furthermore, even studying teams as they are constituted today may not be sufficient, for these are teams which have grown up in an environment pervaded by the myth that programming is the last bastion of individuality.

The neglect of social effects also casts doubt upon all individual studies, since these studies force the individual to separate himself from his normal working environment. In one of our studies, one of the programmers came to me when he had finished coding and asked who could check his work. In his home group, this was the standard practice at this point in development, but it was not allowed during the study —lest it should "invalidate" the results. Looking back, it seems that forcing programmers to work in isolation is like trying to study the swimming behavior of frogs by cutting off their legs and putting those legs in the water to watch them swim. After all, everyone knows that the frog swims with its legs, so why complicate the experiments with all the rest of the frog?

PSYCHOLOGICAL MEASUREMENT

The use of "years of programming" as a measure of "experience" is but one example of the problems of measurement faced by programming psychologists. In any observation or experiment involving human behavior, there are literally thousands, if not millions of variables, which might be measured. We can record age or agility, blink rate or birth order, cranial capacity or church preference, deductive reasoning or degrees awarded, electrocardiogram or elementary mathematics, frown rate or father's profession, gestures made or grade-point average, height or hatreds, ideas or ideals, jitteriness or jargon, kindliness or knowledge, left-handedness or latent homosexuality, mother's tidiness or muscle tension, native tongue or nervous tic, opinions held or objects touched, preferred foods or pupillary motion, questions asked or questions answered, response time or requests for assistance, source of support or slips of the tongue, time of day or tap of the foot, university degree or unconventional behavior, vocabulary or voting record, weight or wage, X-ray photographs or xenophobic index, yawns or years in college, zygosity or zodiacal sign. Surely the psychologist is the snoopiest of all the scientists.

However, that is just the problem. Of all the sciences, psychology seems to have the most possible things to measure—more than any reasonable man can comprehend. But is this surplus unique to psychology? Not really, except that psychology—and the other behavioral sciences—is in its infancy. Maxwell, the great physicist, once said, "To Measure is to Know," and his words are often taken as a motto by other sciences. What Maxwell probably meant was "To know how to measure is to know," or even better, "To know what to measure is to know." In physics, the number of possible measurements seems smaller because physicists have learned, through long experience, what is worth measuring and what is not. Knowing what is worth measuring, the physicist can narrow his experimental field to those matters. In a sense, physics is the science of those things that physicists can measure.

When we study human behavior, however, we are not blessed with this simplification. We do not define our subject by what we can measure, but by what we would like to know about—human behavior. We then must search among many possible measurements in hopes that one or a few will give us some insight which we can carry back to the problem with which we began. No clue is too tiny to be ignored in this search, no suggestion ridiculous *a priori*. Take the "zodiacal sign" we mentioned earlier. Did that stand out as the one item on the list which was not legitimate? But how do we know? Not that we are arguing for astrology, but medical scientists, for instance, have found it prudent to be a bit humble about folk medicines, and the same prudence should be exercised in the study of human behavior.

In fact, several recent studies have purported to show correlation between birth month or season and certain psychological and physical variables. Whether they prove durable observations or simply spurious is beside the point for the present argument. What is important is to see how serious workers cannot rule out any variables in advance without risk of error. And since we are working so much in the dark, we most certainly cannot afford to pass up the "folk wisdom" or our subjects, even if they ultimately prove groundless, or even outright wrong.

Folk wisdom is but one source of insight. Another is the existence of a tool presently used for some other purpose. Since the tool exists and something, at least, is known about *it,* we must allow it to influence the type of study we make. Thus, for instance, since "intelligence" tests exist, one of the first things we do is try them out on programmers, hoping to find some relationship between what they measure ("intelligence") and what we want to understand ("good programming"). If we are lucky, we will find some relationship.

The most normal course is to go the other way—from problem to tool. Sackman's work is one example of this progression—he wanted to know about the efficacy of time-sharing systems, so he constructed a number of studies and measured numerous variables. Another example is the ACM Special Interest Group on Personnel Research. This loose federation is interested mainly in programming from the point of view of management, and, more particularly, personnel management. Thus, their studies tend to be in the area of selection and training, and the things they measure reflect this interest. Much of our own interest has been in the design of programming languages, and the kinds of measurements we make are influenced as much by that interest as by anything else.

However, when you don't know very much about a subject, you don't know in advance what to measure. So your early experiments are not what they might seem to be—they are not to measure things, but to determine what can be measured and what is worth measuring. The difference here is well exemplified by the difference between the methodologists of anthropology and of sociology. The sociologist is working in his own culture, about which he assumes that he is sufficiently knowledgeable to construct, say, a questionnaire as a measuring instrument. But the anthropologist cannot use a questionnaire because he does not know what questions will be meaningful in another culture. Roughly, then, we might say that the sociologist is looking for answers and the anthropologist is looking for questions.

For the present, most of the work in the psychology of programming is going to have to be "looking for questions." Although we may use standard psychological measuring instruments—surveys, tests, and the like—we are really exploring the instruments rather than the subjects. One of the consequences of this point is that it will restrain us from publishing such specious measurements as "the correlation between test score and experience was 0.72." Although we may certainly define "test score" to whatever number of decimal places we wish, we certainly have no way of measuring "experience" to two decimal places, or even an order of magnitude. Thus, the "2" in 0.72 is of the nature of noise—and so, probably, is the "7".

We haven't the space here to survey the entire field of psychological measurement or psychological statistics, but we have given several fine references. Nobody, but nobody, should attempt to draw hard conclusions from such data as are being obtained in this field without studying the pitfalls which the behavioral scientists have already experienced. We shall have occasion to comment on specific instances as we proceed with our presentation.

USING BEHAVIORAL SCIENCE DATA

Probably the main use of previous experience in behavioral science for us is in the field of methodology, as we have discussed. Because of the nature of programming, there is not much hope that actual results can be transferred directly from other fields to ours. Our use of results has to be for insights, not for answers.

Where are we most likely to find our insights, and how? The best plan is to avoid getting fascinated with theories that are too specific, for they will ultimately turn out to be based on premises which programming does not satisfy. For example, there has been a great deal of psychological work on the subject of "problem solving" but this work in its details is not applicable to programming because the "problems" which are "solved" are simply too simple. They have had to be simple because almost all of the experimenting done in this area is based on the idea that there is one right "solution" to a "problem"—and that the psychologist knows it!

In programming, however, there is no right "solution"—we can be sure of that. But even if there were, we could be sure that we would not know it any better than our subjects. Time after time, the student or novice comes up with "solutions" which are superior in some regard to the teacher's or veteran's. Therefore we cannot draw directly on the problem-solving literature for results, but we can certainly look there for insights.

The abundance of areas from which useful insights will be available makes it mandatory to impose a certain amount of organization on our presentation. Organization can help us to remember important ideas and suggest, by defects in the structure, other areas where aid might be found. We should try, however, not to take our organization too seriously, for it is only a convenience—a tool—and not some set of truths passed down on stone tablets from the mountain top.

The social science that provides us with the most useful overall model for computer programming is anthropology. With a little artistic license and stretching of the imagination, we could imagine computer programmers as having a culture—a shared set of beliefs and activities which shape their day-to-day activities. In our study of programming, we shall first examine the "social structure" of that culture—the way programmers relate to one another and to other people who are not programmers. We shall find some surprising possibilities for improvement in this area over present practices, more even than in the second area of study—programming as an individual activity. Although stretching a bit to make the analogy, this study is related to the personality and culture studies of the anthropologist. We shall see how the individual lends his individuality to his program and how programming lends shape to the programmer himself. Whereas in the social structure discussion we shall draw heavily on social psychology, here we shall draw upon the results of individual psychology—especially the areas of problem solving and personality.

Once these two sections have prepared the way, we should be in a proper frame of mind to examine the programmer's tools—his languages, operating systems, and other devices—from a psychological point of view. These tools are the "material culture" of programming—the artifacts which the programming archeologist would find and study to understand the dead civilization of programming. Also, as programmers are not born into this culture, we shall study how they are—or should be—recruited, and how they learn this complex way of life. Here the psychology of learning—and especially language learning—shall play a large, though not exclusive, role.

Finally, as we pass successfully through all this, we may find ourselves in a sufficiently objective frame of mind to examine some of the myths of programming—the articles of programming faith. Faith, as Bertrand Russell pointed out, is the belief in something for which there is no evidence; and myths, as Ambrose Bierce once defined them, are the sacred beliefs of other people. Perhaps we shall simply carry away our old beliefs unchanged, but if just one unfounded programming myth should die as a result, this book will have been worth the effort.

SUMMARY

Because programming is such a rich and complex activity, we shall need all the richness of methods and results we can borrow from all of the behavioral sciences. But the borrowing process is not without danger, and as we prepare ourselves to make studies in the psychology of programming, we should particularly prepare ourselves to avoid the common pitfalls. Among the major problems are:

1. Using introspection without validation.
2. Using of observations on an overly narrow base.
3. Observing the wrong variables, or failing to observe the right ones.
4. Interfering with the observed phenomenon.
5. Generating too much data and not enough information.
6. Overly constraining experiments.
7. Depending excessively on trainees as subjects.
8. Failing to study group effects and group behavior.
9. Measuring what is simple to measure.
10. Using unjustified precision.
11. Transferring borrowed results to inapplicable situations.

But in any fledgling field, perhaps the greatest mistake of all is over-caution. Though we try to observe the proprieties, better to have experimented and lost than never to have experimented at all.

QUESTIONS

For Managers

1. What type of accounting system does your installation use? Do you use data from this system to evaluate programmer performance? Are the data intended for this use, and what can be done to improve the system so that it is more useful to you for this purpose?

2. Would you permit behavioral science experiments to be conducted with your experienced programmers? With your trainees? What would you do if a person objected to participating in such an experiment? What safeguards would you ask of the experimenters?

3. Do you ever read articles on psychology in such magazines as *Harvard Business Review, Reader's Digest, Playboy, Think,* or *Psychology Today?* Have you ever tried to put some of the reported results to use in your work? What kinds of experiences did you have in transferring data reported from other circumstances to the management of programmers?

For Programmers

1. When you have just found a bug, do you ever sit back and try to trace out the paths you took in your mind? Try doing this on the next bug you find, and write a brief report or outline of what you find.

2. Do you keep records on your performance? What kinds of things do you record, and how accurately do you record them? What picture do

you get from these observations which you could not get by simple reflection on what you are doing? Does your installation accounting routine ever give you insights into your behavior, or the behavior of other programmers in your installation?

3. Would you have any objections to participating in psychological experiments to study programming? What kinds of assurances would be required to overcome your objections? If you have ever participated in a psychological experiment, write a small report or outline of the most significant things you remember about the experience. Do you see any reasons why the results of the study might not be valid, or valid for programming? Were you ever shown the results of the study, or did you have the reason for the study explained to you?

BIBLIOGRAPHY

Freud, Sigmund, *A General Introduction to Psychoanalysis,* Garden City, N.Y., Doubleday, 1953.
Of great interest in and of itself, this book is also useful as a historical document on the way in which a new study of human behavior begins. Especially interesting in the present context is the way Freud has to convince his audience that the subject really exists. One of the ways he does this is through his discussion of errors—"slips of the tongue" and the like. This particular discussion is of special interest to programming people.

James, William, *Psychology,* Cleveland, The Living Library, 1948.
Certain parts of this classic by the man who was "first to extend the methods and spirit of modern science to the human mind" are outdated, but not many. As with Freud, the study of James bears many fruits for the modern student of the psychology of computer programming, and these two books might well be the proper starting place for a study of this subject, in order that historical perspective not be lost.

Brown, J. A. C., *The Social Psychology of Industry,* Baltimore, Penguin Books, 1954.
A very readable account of the practice of studying working groups, which gives a good historical view of such matters as the Hawthorne Effect. The book is recommended as an effective study for those entering the field called Industrial Psychology, which, although it may have limited relevance to work on tasks as complex as programming, must be studied by anyone seriously involved in this field. At the very least, Brown's review of the early days of the field will warn us against certain excesses to which we might otherwise be prone.

Junker, Buford H., *Field Work—An Introduction to the Social Sciences,* Chicago, University of Chicago Press, 1960.
The author claims—with probably truth—that one cannot properly appreciate field work without experiencing it. Yet by acknowledging his limitations, he does as good a job as he can at disproving that statement, and the reader can obtain some sense of the various field work methods of sociology and anthropology.

Golde, Peggy, ed., *Women in the Field,* Chicago, Aldine, 1970.
The "Women" in the title is a bit misleading, since one of the things the book

demonstrates is how little difference the gender of a fieldworker actually makes. The book can be read at several levels—either as thoroughly enjoyable anecdotal material or as a comprehensive—if not organized—survey of anthropological field method.

Hammond, Phillip E., *Sociologists at Work,* New York, Basic Books, 1964.
A collection of anecdotal material on method, like *Women in the Field,* but oriented to the sociologist rather than the anthropologist. Several of the chapters are about studies, which are in themselves of interest to the psychologist of programming: The Dynamics of Bureaucracy, Men Who Manage, and Union Democracy.

Webb, Eugine J., *et al., Unobtrusive Measures: Nonreactive Research in the Social Sciences,* Chicago, Rand McNally, 1966.
A survey of a specialized subset of psychological research techniques.

Sackman, Harold, *Man-Computer Problem Solving,* Princeton: Auerbach Publishers, 1970.
Although subtitled—Experimental Evaluation of Time-Sharing and Batch Processing—the book is the first we have on methods of psychological research in programming. As such, it is essential reading for the serious student.

Hyman, H. H., *Survey Design and Analysis,* New York, Free Press, 1955.
Possibly the best and most thorough text on the theory and practice of public opinion surveys.

Cronbach, L. J., *Essentials of Psychological Testing,* 3rd ed., New York, Harper and Row, 1970.
An elementary, but therefore useful as an introduction, account of the construction and application of psychological tests of various kinds.

Hammond, K. R., and J. E. Householder, *Introduction to the Statistical Method,* New York, Knopf, 1962.
One of the better of hundreds of books on psychological statistics, and as good as any as an introduction. Mathematically oriented programmers may be turned off by such books, which are written for the mathematically unwashed, but this one is quite palatable. In any case, it is important to know how psychologists think about quantitative data.

Morgenstern, Oskar, *On the Accuracy of Economic Observations,* Princeton, Princeton University Press, 1963.
Economics is another behavioral science, and although it does not have much direct bearing on the psychology of programming, we can learn something from its methodological problems. Morgenstern, co-inventor with John von Neumann of Game Theory, brings his steel-trap mind to the question of how good economic numbers really are. But the first half of the book is in no way really specific to economics, and should be required reading for all behavioral scientists.

Proceedings of the Nth Annual Computer Personnel Research Conference, Association for Computing Machinery, New York.
As N has grown, so has the size and scope of these conferences. So also has their availability grown, and they should be known by every researcher in this field. Even though the early issues are difficult to obtain, they are perhaps even more valuable than the later ones in that they relate the earliest struggles to come to grips with problems that are not yet nearly solved, but about which we have become a bit more sophisticated.

Parsons, Henry M., The Scope of Human Factors in Computer-Based Data Processing Systems, *Human Factors,* 12, 2 (1970), pp. 165-175.

The appearance of this article in *Human Factors* probably signals the beginning of a new interest by human factors engineers in programming, although most of the article is concerned with nonprogramming aspects of computers. Not that non-programming aspects are unimportant—far from it—but only that they are beyond the scope of this book, and would probably require three or four books to survey. The article contains no new data, but gives a few references to work already done.

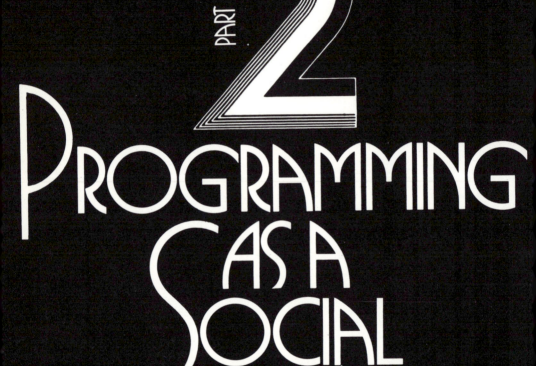

PART 2

PROGRAMMING AS A SOCIAL ACTIVITY

Having been brought up in a serf-owner's family, I entered active life, like all young men of my time, with a great deal of confidence in the necessity of commanding, ordering, scolding, punishing, and the like. But when, at an early stage, I had to manage serious enterprises and to deal with men, and when each mistake would lead at once to heavy consequences, I began to appreciate the difference between acting on the principle of command and discipline and acting on the principle of common understanding. The former works admirably in a military parade, but it is worth nothing where real life is concerned, and the aim can be achieved only through the severe effort of many converging wills.

Peter Kropotkin*

Programmers do not ordinarily work in isolation. Although an individual programmer may find himself assigned the task of writing a program, even then he has other programmers to whom he may turn for help—and who, at the same time, may be turning to him.

* Reprinted from *Memoirs of a Revolutionist*, by Peter Kropotkin. Copyright 1968. By permission of the Publisher, Horizon Press, New York.

Indeed, as we shall see, the programmer working alone is working under a serious handicap. But when working with others, many types of relationships can exist. For our purpose, we shall identify three sorts of programmer assemblage—the group, the team, and the project. Roughly speaking, the group is a collection of programmers, working in the same place, probably sharing the same machine and system, but working on separate programs, although there may be a relationship among some of the programs. A typical programming group might be found in a university computing center, an engineering firm, or wherever an "open shop" is run.

A programming team, on the other hand, is a collection of programmers who are trying to produce a single program by working together. A team might consist of from two to twelve members, though with the larger numbers the team begins to break down into two or more teams. The team may exist within a programming group or perhaps be one team of many making up a programming project. The project is a group of programmers plus their supporting activities which has probably been brought together for the purpose of producing a single integrated system, or at least a closely knit collection of programs. It will often have its own machine, plus special teams to provide systems work, standards, documentation, and other functions. It will also ordinarily have a project manager and a regular bureaucratic organization—like the Austrian army.

4 THE PROGRAMMING GROUP

The study of the programming group is important for an understanding of the other types of programming organization. Even when there is a formal organization of the programmers into teams and projects, informal connections arise much as they do in an "unstructured" group. Indeed, the first lesson we must learn from social psychology is the difference between formal and informal groups.

FORMAL AND INFORMAL ORGANIZATION

The organization chart is a nice toy for a manager, but little programming work would ever get done if interactions among programmers had to follow its narrow, straight lines. Perhaps because organization charts look much like flow diagrams, programming managers who have come up through the ranks seem to place too much confidence in them, rather than in the less formal mechanisms which they themselves used so successfully when they were in the pits. But human interactions are never narrow, never straight, and hardly ever in the directions shown an organization charts. Many serious mistakes have been made in imagining that formal structure was the only structure in an organization.

In projects, of course, much of the informal structure is determined by the structure of the work, and thus may follow organization charts more or less closely, depending on how well the project is organized. But in a computing center, even if it is completely at the service of individual programmers, an informal structure always grows to correct and complement the work of whatever formal structure exists. Sometimes, if the powers-that-be are sufficiently wise, innovations in the informal structure can be implemented formally, although not always as exact equivalents.

An example of this type took place in the computing center of a consulting engineering firm. Jobs were run on a remote batch basis, and most programmers were spread around the three buildings near to the group with which they worked. Turnaround time was irregular, and there was no reliable way to determine in advance when a job would come out. The number of the last job processed was posted on a board outside the return window, but programmers from remote offices could easily waste half an hour coming to read the board and find out that their job was not ready.

As it happened, one of the secretaries had an office whose placement permitted her to see the board out the open door, without moving from her desk. She was an attractive young thing, and one of the programmers happened to call her for a date at a time when he was waiting for a job to be returned. When they had talked for a while, she commented that he must have work to return to, but he replied that he was waiting for a job anyway. "Oh," she said innocently, "what number is it? I can see the board from here." With that remark began a service whose existence gradually became known to all the outlying programmers. It was such a good service, in fact, that the secretary soon had difficulty carrying out her other duties. In this way, this informal mechanism finally came to the attention of the administration.

Wisely acknowledging that the service could not just be cut off, the administration decided to inaugurate a special inquiry number over which one could hear a tape recording of the latest number posted. The management was even wise enough to use the secretary's old extension— although the telephone company gave some resistance before this was accomplished. Thus, a rather smooth replacement of a rather inefficient, but useful, informal service was made—with the concomitant gain in secretarial time for more conventional duties.

It should be noted, however, that the new formal system never completely replaced the old, informal one. The recordings were made more or less at intervals of thirty minutes, so that it was possible for a number to be posted on the board as much as half an hour before being noted on the telephone. For ordinary circumstances, this proved sufficient—but in a computing center, somebody always has extraordinary requirements. Thus, when a programmer was really in a hurry for a job, he would revert to the old system and call the secretary. Now, however, her workload was sufficiently decreased so as not to affect her other work, and so the system has remained unchanged, in all probability, to this day. Besides, she *enjoyed* talking to all these bright young programmers—and they, let us admit, enjoyed talking to her.

Not all conflicts between the formal and informal have such happy endings. In this case, the administration of the computing center recognized the function that the informal organization was serving; but in other cases, they might not even be aware of the existence of the function. A case in point occurred at a large university computing center. Because so many of the programmers were students who had no offices, a large common space was provided near the return window, so that the students and other users could work on their programming problems. In the adjoining room, the center provided a consulting service for difficult problems, staffed by two graduate assistants.

At one end of the common room was a collection of vending machines —coffee, coke, candy, and what-have-you. Although the room was quite large, the noise from the revelers congregating at the machines often became more than some of the workers could bear. Finally, a pair of serious-minded students appointed themselves as a committee and went to the computing center manager. He, of course, had never personally gone into the common room, so when he went to investigate their complaint, he was appalled at the goings-on at the far end. Without more than fifteen seconds of observation and consideration, he went back to his office and inaugurated action to have the machines removed to some remote spot.

The week after the machines had been removed—and signs urging quiet had been posted all around—the manager received another delegation. This one was much larger and much better organized. They had come to complain about the lack of consulting service; and, indeed, when he went to look for himself, he saw two long lines extending out of the consulting room into the common room. He spoke to the consultants to ask them why they were suddenly so slow in servicing their clients, but they told him that they were working as fast as they had ever done— if not faster. For some reason, they said, there were just a lot more people needing advice than there used to be.

The manager spent two weeks checking for a possible source of the increased load, but all courses and other users were carrying on normally.

Still, the load remained, and students were complaining that they were not able to finish their assignments. Finally, he set a graduate student in sociology to interviewing the students queued up in the consulting lines. After some time, he discovered the source of the problem. It was the vending machines!

When the vending machines had been in the common room, a large crowd always hovered around them—but not particularly for fol-de-rol, as the manager had so quickly assumed. True, they were drinking coffee and chatting, but they were chatting about their programs. The typical behavior of a student when he arrived at the computing center was to pick up his output and head for the coffee machine. There, while sipping coffee, he could have a first look at the program and also show it to his buddies who might be standing around. Since most of the student problems were similar, the chances were very high that he could find someone who knew what was wrong with his program right there at the vending machines. Through this informal organization, the formal consulting mechanism was shunted, and its load was reduced to a level it could reasonably handle.

By moving out the vending machines, the manager had broken up the focus of this informal structure and put the resulting load on his consultants. Unhappily, he could not easily believe that this was the cause of the overload, so instead of restoring the machines, he tried increasing the number of consultants. The consultants, however, complained of the trivia they were having to deal with; and eventually the consulting service was abandoned altogether, for lack of people willing to do it. When last observed, this computing center was furnishing consulting through informal channels—with students scurrying around from office to office until they could find one of the staff programmers to answer their trivial questions. Where it will all end, it's hard to say; but we can be sure that the students will always get their questions answered—at whatever the cost.

The point of these stories is that informal mechanisms always exist and it is dangerous to change things without understanding them, lest you derange some smoothly operating system which you will not be able to replace at similar cost. Many such derangements occur through a change in the physical layout of things—a change which is so common around computing centers that it will pay us to spend a few words on the relationship between physical structure and social structure.

PHYSICAL ENVIRONMENT AND SOCIAL ORGANIZATION

We all know that physical surroundings affect the quality and quantity of our work. What we are alluding to here, however, is not the effects of noise, light, heat, and other factors, which have been much studied by industrial psychologists. No doubt there are important benefits to be gained from following the design criteria developed in putting together programmers' working quarters. (Someone should definitely study the depressing effect that the all-too-common half partitions have on programmer productivity. They manage to cut off all useful communication while permitting all disturbing sound and movement to penetrate.) What we are concerned with is how the layout of work space affects the pattern of social interaction which in turn influences the work that is done.

As a simple example, consider the establishment which replaced its ancient elevators with spanking new automatic ones. This was most unfortunate for the programmers, for the old elevator operator had run an informal pickup and delivery service for them between the programming floor—the eighth—and the machine room—the basement. Of course, nobody could justify hiring a messenger just for going from the eighth floor to the basement, so the programmers lost a lot of productive time. Another function this operator served was locator of missing persons. With the machine room on one floor, keypunch room on another, and programmers' offices on a third, chances of finding a missing programmer in the first place you looked were less than fifty-fifty. The elevator operator, however, could be relied upon to know immediately on which floor a given person could be found. With these two losses—plus the loss of other services such as rerouting of misdelivered mail and relaying of important messages—the new automatic elevators proved to be a net loss, even though the elevator service itself seemed a bit faster.

Although the switch to automatic elevators is perhaps more rare, the moving of offices is an almost daily occurrence in some shops. As long as the programmers all remain together, this often has the salutary effect of making two people aware of each other's existence. In the old days, this function was often accomplished in the anteroom of the machine room, where we all queued up to take our fifteen minutes of on-line debugging. A typical conversation—circa 1956—went like this:

"What's he doing in there so long? I've got some really important work to do—but there's just one more bug."

"He's debugging FORTRAN."

"FOR-what?"

"FORTRAN. Stands for Formula Translation. They claim you'll be able to write programs as mathematical formulas and this program will translate them into machine code automatically."

"Come on. You're kidding?"

"That's what they say. As for me, I suppose it can be done, but it can't be as efficient as hand coding. It won't sell."

"Well, it's sure using a lot of machine time. He looks like he's playing the organ there, flipping those keys up and down. There ought to be a better way."

"There is."

"Yeah? What's that?"

"I'm working on it right now. We're doing it on the West Coast, but the only machine is here, so we have to come here to debug. It's called a Monitor System."

"Monitor System?"

"Yes, it's sort of an automatic operator. Takes the programmer away from the machine. For example, I've got thirty jobs here which I'm going to run in my fifteen minute shot."

"Thirty? You're pulling my leg!"

"No, I mean it. By eliminating the operator, we achieve a fantastic speedup—and eliminate set-up and tear-down time, too."

"Well, good luck. But I don't see how I'm going to debug my programs if I can't be at the console. As it is I'm going crazy waiting for these—what was that name?—FORTRAN guys. See you later. I'm up now."

A surprising amount of useful information was transmitted in this way. Operating systems eliminated this social structure in the same way as automatic elevators eliminated the other. Still, if there is a common room right next to the place where computer output is returned, useful mixing can take place there. Personalized delivery services, however, tend to isolate the programmer from this type of interaction, and terminal systems for remote-job-entry and exit may make his isolation worse. This aspect of terminal operations is probably going to be a curse, not a blessing.

ERROR AND EGO

Many programmers who have read this far will be surprised at the emphasis placed on the social interaction among programmers. Programming—perhaps more than any other profession—is an individual activity, depending on the abilities of the programmer himself, and not upon others. What difference can it make how many other programmers you run into during the day? If asked, most programmers would probably say they preferred to work alone in a place where they wouldn't be disturbed by other people.

The ideas expressed in the preceding paragraph are possibly the most formidable barrier to improved programming that we shall encounter. First of all, if this is indeed the image generally held of the programming profession, then people will be attracted to, or repelled from, entering the profession according to their preference for working alone or working with others. Social psychologists tell us that there are different personality types—something we all knew, but which is nice to have stamped with authority. Among the general personality traits is one which is measured along three "dimensions"—whether a person is "compliant," "aggressive," or "detached." The compliant type is characterized by the attitude of liking to "work with people and be helpful." The aggressive type wants to "earn money and prestige," and the detached type wants to "be left to myself to be creative."

Now, every person contains a mixture of these attitudes, but most people lean more heavily in one direction than the others. There is no doubt that the majority of people in programming today lean in the "detached" direction, both by personal choice and because hiring policies for programmers are often directed toward finding such people. And, to a great extent, this is a good choice, because a great deal of programming work is "alone and creative."

Like most good things, however, the "detachment" of programmers is often overdeveloped. Although they are *detached* from people, they are *attached* to their programs. Indeed, their programs often become extensions of themselves—a fact which is verified in the abominable practice of attaching one's name to the program itself—as in Jules' Own Version of Algol, better known as JOVIAL. But even when the program is not officially blessed with the name of its creator, programmers *know* whose program it is.

Well, what is wrong with "owning" programs? Artists "own" paintings; authors "own" books; architects "own" buildings. Don't these attributions lead to admiration and emulation of good workers by lesser ones? Isn't it useful to have an author's name on a book so we have a better idea of what to expect when we read it? And wouldn't the same apply to programs? Perhaps it would—if people read programs, but we know that they do not. Thus, the admiration of individual programmers cannot lead to an emulation of their work, but only to an affectation of their mannerisms. This is the same phenomenon we see in "art colonies," where everyone knows how to look like an artist, but few, if any, know how to paint like one.

The real difficulty with "property-oriented" programming arises from another source. When we think a painting or a novel or a building is inferior, that is a matter of taste. When we think a program is inferior—in spite of the difficulties we know lurk behind the question of "good programming"—that is a matter at least potentially susceptible to objective proof or disproof. At the very least, we can put the program on the machine and see what comes out. An artist can dismiss the opinions of a critic if they do not please him, but can a programmer dismiss the judgment of the computer?

On the surface, it *would* seem that the judgment of the computer is indisputable, and if this were truly so, the attachment of a programmer to his programs would have serious consequences for his self-image. When the computer revealed a bug in his program, the programmer would have to reason something like this:

"This program is defective. This program is part of me, an extension of myself, even carrying my name. *I* am defective."

But the very harshness of this self-judgment means that it is seldom carried out.

Starting with the work of the social psychologist Festinger, a number of interesting experiments have been performed to establish the reality of a psychological phenomenon called "cognitive dissonance." A classical experiment in cognitive dissonance goes something like this:

Two groups of subjects are asked to write an essay arguing in favor of some point with which they feel strong disagreement. One group is paid one dollar apiece to write this argument against their own opinions, the other is paid twenty dollars apiece. At the end of the experiment, the subjects are retested on their opinions of the matter. Whereas "common sense" would say that the twenty dollar subjects—having been paid more to change their minds—would be more likely to change their opinions, cognitive dissonance theory predicts that it will be the *other* group which will change the most. Dozens of experiments have confirmed the predictions of the theory.

The argument behind cognitive dissonance theory is quite simple. In the experiment just outlined, both groups of subjects have had to perform an act—writing an essay against their own opinions—which they would not under ordinary circumstances like to do. Arguing for what one does not believe is classed as "insincerity" or "hypocrisy," neither of which is highly valued in our society. Therefore, a *dissonance* situation is created. The subject's self-image as a sincere person is challenged by the objective fact of his having written the essay. Dissonance, according to the theory, is an uncomfortable and unstable state for human beings, and must therefore be quickly resolved in one way or another. To resolve a dissonance, one factor or another contributing to it must be made to yield. Which factor depends on the situation, but, generally speaking, it will *not* be the person's self-image. That manages to be preserved through the most miraculous arguments.

Now, in the experiments cited, the twenty dollar subjects have an easy resolution of their dissonance. "Of course," they can say to themselves or to anyone who might ask, "I didn't really believe those arguments. I just did it for the money." Although taking money to make such arguments is not altogether the most admirable trait, it is much better than actually holding the beliefs in question. But look at the quandry of the dollar group. Even for poor college students—and subjects in psychological experiments are almost always poor college students—one dollar is not a significant amount of money. Thus, the argument of the other group does not carry the ring of conviction for them, and the dissonance must be resolved elsewhere. For many, at least, the easiest resolution is to come to admit that there is really something to the other side of the argument after all, so that writing the essay was not hypocrisy, but simply an exercise in developing a fair and honest mind, one which is capable of seeing both sides of a question.

Another application of the theory of cognitive dissonance predicts what will happen when people have made some large commitment, such as the purchase of a car. If a man who has just purchased a Ford is given a bunch of auto advertisements to read, he spends the majority of his time reading about Fords. If it was a Chevrolet he purchased, then the Chevrolet ads capture his attention. This is an example of anticipating the possibility of dissonance and avoiding information that might create it. For if he has just purchased a Ford, he doesn't want to find out that Chevrolet is the better car, and the best way to do that is to avoid reading the Chevrolet ads. In the Ford ads, he is not likely to find anything that will convince him that he is anything but the wisest of consumers.

Now, what cognitive dissonance has to do with our programming conflict should be vividly clear. A programmer who truly sees his program as an extension of his own ego is not going to be trying to find all the errors in that program. On the contrary, he is going to be trying to prove that the program is correct—even if this means the oversight of errors which are monstrous to another eye. All programmers are familiar with the symptoms of this dissonance resolution—in others, of course. The programmer comes down the hall with his output listing and it is very thin. If he is unable to conceal the failure of his run, he makes some remark such as

"Those keypunch operators did it again."

or

"The operator put my cards in out of sequence."

or

"When are we going to get that punch fixed so it duplicates properly?"

There are thousands of variations to these plaints, but the one thing we never seem to hear is a simple

"I goofed again."

Of course, where the error is more subtle than a complete failure to get output—which can hardly be ignored—the resolution of the dissonance can be made even simpler by merely failing to see that there is an error. And let there be no mistake about it: the human eye has an almost infinite capacity for not seeing what it does not want to see. People who have specialized in debugging other people's programs can verify this assertion with literally thousands of cases. Programmers, if left to their own devices, will ignore the most glaring errors in their output—errors that anyone else can see in an instant. Thus, if we are going to attack the problem of making good programs, and if we are going to start at the fundamental level of meeting specifications, we are going to have to do something about the perfectly normal human tendency to believe that ones "own" program is correct in the face of hard physical evidence to the contrary.

EGOLESS PROGRAMMING

What is to be done about the problem of the ego in programming? A typical text on management would say that the manager should exhort all his programmers to redouble their efforts to find their errors. Perhaps he would go around asking them to show him their errors each day. This method, however, would fail by going precisely in the opposite direction to what our knowledge of psychology would dictate, for the average person is going to view such an investigation as a personal trial. Besides, not all programmers have managers—or managers who would know an error even if they saw one outlined in red.

No, the solution to this problem lies not in a direct attack—for attack can only lead to defense, and defense is what we are trying to eliminate. Instead, the problem of the ego must be overcome by a restructuring of the social environment and, through this means, a restructuring of the value system of the programmers in that environment. Before we discuss how this might be done, let us look at some examples of what has happened when it has been done—how it affects the programmers and their programs.

First of all, let no one imagine that such restructuring is the ivory tower dream of social theorists. Programming groups who have conquered the ego problem do exist and have existed from the earliest days of computing. John von Neumann himself was perhaps the first programmer to recognize his inadequacies with respect to examination of his own work. Those who knew him have said that he was constantly asserting what a lousy programmer he was, and that he incessantly pushed his programs on other people to read for errors and clumsiness. Yet the common image today of von Neumann is of the unparalleled computing genius—flawless in his every action. And indeed, there can be no doubt of von Neumann's genius. His very ability to realize his human limitations put him head and shoulders above the average programmer today.

Average people can be trained to accept their humanity—their inability to function like a machine—and to value it and work with others so as to keep it under the kind of control needed if programming is to be successful. Consider the case of Bill G. who was working in one of the early space tracking systems. His job was to write a simulator which would simulate the entire network of tracking stations and other real-time inputs. His system had to check out the rest of the system in real-time without having to have the worldwide network on-line. The heart of the simulator was to be a very small and very tight loop, consisting, in fact, of just thirteen machine instructions. Bill had worked for some time on this loop and when he finally reached the point of some confidence in it, he began looking for a critic—the standard practice in this programming group.

Bill found Marilyn B. willing to peruse his code in exchange for his returning the favor. This was nothing unusual in this group; indeed, nobody would have thought of going on the machine without such scrutiny by a second party. Whenever possible an exchange was made, so nobody would feel in the position of being criticized by someone else. But for Bill, who was well schooled in this method, the protection of an exchange was not necessary. His value system, when it came to programming, dictated that secretive, possessive programming was bad and that open, shared programming was good. Errors that might be found in code he had written—not "his" code, for that terminology was not used here—were simply facts to be exposed to investigation with an eye to future improvement, not attacks on his person.

In this particular instance, Bill had been having one of his "bad programming days." As Marilyn worked and worked over the code—as she found one error after another—he became more and more amused, rather than more and more defensive as he might have done had he been trained as so many of our programmers are. Finally, he emerged from their conference announcing to the world the startling fact that Marilyn had been able to find *seventeen* bugs in only thirteen statements. He insisted on showing everyone who would listen how this had been possible. In fact, since the very exercise had proved to him that this was not his day for coding, he simply spent the rest of the day telling and retelling the episode in all its hilarious details.

Marilyn, at the same time, did not feel any false confidence in her own work on the problem, for—she reasoned correctly—where there had been seventeen errors, there were probably a few more. In particular, she knew that after a certain amount of time working on the code, she had internalized it as much as had Bill, even though she had not written it originally. So she in turn went looking for a critic; and while Bill was giving everyone an enormous laugh at his expense, Marilyn and others managed to find three more errors before the day was over.

As an epilogue to this incident, it should be noted that when this code was finally put on the computer, no further errors were found, in spite of the most diabolical testing possible. In fact, this simulator was put into use in more than a dozen installations for real-time operations, and over a period of at least nine years no other errors were ever found. How different might have been the story had Bill felt that each error found in that code was a wound in his pride—an advertisement of his stupidity.

This incident is not an isolated case, and this group is not unique. Why, then, are such groups not more conspicuous? Why is the practice of "egoless programming" not more widespread? A number of factors might be invoked to account for the impression that such groups are rare. First of all, many of the successful software firms are based on this type of interaction, and though they will admit to it under direct questioning, they often regard this knowledge as valuable proprietary information. Secondly, groups working in this way tend to be remarkably satisfied and stable, so that the programmers we find wandering from installation to installation are not likely to have come from such a group. Moreover, these gypsy programmers—to achieve a constantly escalating salary range—must encourage the myth that the best programming is the product of genius, and nothing else.

Another reason these methods are not better known is that nobody has ever experimented on the difference in quality of work produced by this method and the method of isolated individual programmers. Some experiments have been performed on factors affecting programmer productivity, but these have suffered first of all from emphasis on the mechanical aspects of programming, not the social. For example, a study will be made comparing time sharing with batch processing or language A with language B, because someone is trying to prove that he should be allowed to develop a time-sharing system or a compiler for language B. The people who run these experiments seem to take for granted the individual nature of programming effort—for that is probably the way they have always operated. Besides, things are complicated enough working with individuals. When you compare system X and system Y and find out that 90 percent of the variance in your experiment comes from individual programmer differences, who wants to add the complication and expense of studying group performance?

An interesting anecdote—which we mentioned briefly in the chapter on methods—can be told about one of our studies that tried to assess the difference in programming results obtained when different programmers were given slightly different impressions of what they were to achieve—efficient coding or quick completion. As usual, individual subjects were employed, but one of these subjects—they were all students on a special three-month course—happened to come from a group that practiced egoless programming. At a certain point, he came to me and said that he had reached the point in his work where he needed someone to look over what he had done. As the object of the experiments was not to study differences between group work and individual work, I was forced—against my own beliefs—to request that the subject try to proceed without outside assistance, which would only add to the variance of the experiment.

As a sidelight to this incident, it should be noted that this programmer's work seemed to the evaluators to be better organized and better executed than the other four programmers working on the same problem. In discussing this question with him, he raised the point that he had worked throughout as he always did in his own group—always with an eye to making the program clear and understandable to the person or people who would ultimately have to read it. This insight indicates that all the advantages of egoless programming are not confined to the detection of errors, though that was perhaps the earliest and strongest motivation for adopting the technique. In fact, it might be useful to examine our four factors in good programming in the light of what effect this method would have on them.

For meeting specifications, the value is quite clear. On the matter of scheduling, the effect on the mean time to complete programs is not immediately evident, but the effect on the variation should be clear from our example of the bugged simulator. If it is true that programmers have bad coding days—and this seems supported from a number of sources—then a piece of code written on one of these days is going to have an extra long debugging cycle. In the case of Bill G.'s program, the twenty bugs might have taken several weeks to root out. Moreover, it seems likely that at least one of them might have survived in the system past the time when this piece was integrated with other pieces—in which case the schedule of other parts would have been adversely, or at least unpredictably, affected.

Not only is the variation in debugging time reduced, but since there is more than one person familiar with the program, it is easier to get realistic estimates on the amount of real progress that has been made. It is not necessary to rely on a single judgment—and of the person least likely to be unbiased, at that. The adaptability of programs is also improved, for we are assured that at least two people are capable of understanding the program. Under certain programming circumstances, this represents an infinite improvement. Also, the entire work is less susceptible to being disturbed if one of the involved programmers happens to be sick, or pregnant, or otherwise missing, as programmers are wont to be. This not only reduces variations in schedule, but also makes it more likely that at some time in the future, when the code must be modified, someone will be around who knows something about it.

On the question of efficiency, we can make no hard and fast statements. There certainly seems to be no reason why programs developed in this way should be *less* efficient than other programs. By having a second party look at the program, it would seem that we increase the possibility of eliminating at least the most obviously inefficient areas, although overall efficiency is usually going to be primarily influenced by the original structure chosen.

One final advantage of this method lies in the effect it has on the person reading the program of someone else, for, if we are correct in assessing the value of reading programs, he cannot help but become a better programmer for the exercise. We shall have more to say on this subject under the heading of programmer training, but it does seem that the general level of competence of such a group is likely to raise itself even in the absence of specific measures for education.

CREATING AND MAINTAINING
THE PROGRAMMING ENVIRONMENT

The question of creating such a desirable environment as we have described is different from the question of maintaining such an environment once it exists. Maintenance is by far the easier task, for converting an existing group to this philosophy will usually run against the phenomenon of "locking" or "fixation" of social structures. Fixation occurs whenever a situation creates an environment favorable for maintaining that situation. For example, an FM tuner can be designed to center itself on the strongest signal in the vicinity of the tuning knob. Once a station is captured by this device, only a very strong change can get it off, because every small tendency to change is met by a compensating action by the tuner. Such locking occurs in all sorts of systems—physiological, electronic, biological, but especially for our immediate purposes, social.

One typical computing example of social fixation is the adoption of one programming language by an installation. Once the language has been adopted, a new language has more difficulty making an entry, because with most of the people using the old language, advantages accrue to following the beaten path. If one needs advice, it is more easily found. If one needs subroutines, they are more likely to exist. Scheduling of computer runs may favor the commonly used language, keypunchers will make fewer errors punching familiar coding, and procedures for using the old language will be smoother and better developed.

In the same way that an installation fixates on a programming language, it can establish a general social environment which either encourages or discourages egoless programming. When a new programmer enters the mileu, his attitudes may be shaped by the reactions of the others already there. If he goes to somebody for advice and he is ridiculed for the stupidity of his errors, he is less likely to seek assistance the next time. If, however, someone comes to him and asks for help in looking over a program, he is flattered by the implied compliment to his ability and may not feel so threatened when he has to seek advice. To a large extent, we behave the way we see people behaving around us, so a functioning programming group will tend to socialize new members to its philosophy of programming.

Sometimes the group may have to maintain its philosophy in the face of a larger threat than the introduction of a new member or two. Adherents of the egoless programming philosophy are frequently subjected to threatening moves on the part of managers from higher levels in their organization. Managers tend to select themselves from the "aggressive" component of society and have difficulty appreciating the fact that other people do not completely share their goals of money and prestige. They are especially at a loss to understand the smooth functioning of a programming group based on mutual respect for individual talent and cooperation in the common cause. Instead, they tend to view people as working for money or under threat—as they themselves do.

A particularly pertinent example of the clash between aggressive management and a compliant-detached programming group occurred in a software section of one of the computer manufacturers. One group in the section, acting as a team, had been particularly successful at producing an entirely new system, which promised to have much market potential. The achievement of this group was so evident that the management of the company decided to give them a cash award. In typical management fashion, they gave the award to the person who had been designated as the group's manager. Imagine their bewilderment when he told them that he could not accept the award unless it was given to all.

His reaction, in view of the way the group shared its work, was perfectly correct, but was not understood by the management. Some managers thought that he was maneuvering for more money; others thought he was trying to set up a "prima donna" group. In any case, it was decided to force him to accept the award and also to break up the group—which seemed to have unhealthy ideas. He took the award and promptly split it equally among all the group members, after which the group left the company *en masse* and went to work for an independent software firm.

In this case, the group protected itself against a great outside threat by picking up and leaving. Had the management been more aware of what this group had to offer, and had they been more flexible, they might have worked out a solution that would have permitted this group to influence the work of other groups in a favorable way. But this is not easily done by managers, who tend to feel that when work gets done it is the direct result of the actions of some leader of outstanding ability. Even when the manager appreciates the work of the group, it is not consistent with his own philosophy to see the productivity of the group as a property of the group, not as a sum of the contributions of the individual members.

In one interesting case, a group of ten programmers had come to work in the programming section of a large airframe manufacturer. They had worked together in another firm for about two years, but that firm had decided to centralize its data-processing facilities on the other side of the country. These programmers had been unwilling to move. After each had received attractive offers from several firms, they decided to go with the one that would hire them all. Mass movements of groups of this type are not rare, and though management tends to see them as some sort of conspiracy, they are usually motivated more by the desire to continue receiving the fulfillment of working together than any idea of enormous material gain—such is the powerful influence of a truly receptive working environment.

Some months after this group had moved to the airframe manufacturer, their new manager happened to meet their former manager at a computer conference and asked him if he had any more people like those. Upon being told that he had the entire group, he inquired about the secret that had been used in finding these people. Their old manager could think of nothing special—one girl had been a new college graduate majoring in Italian, one man had taught mathematics in a high school for seven years, one man was a professional engineer, one girl had been a business school graduate who had worked for several years as an executive secretary and accountant. Why, he wanted to know, had the other manager asked?

"I don't know what it is," came the honestly puzzled reply, "but since those people have come to our place, I've discovered that whenever there is a job that really has to be done right and on time, I give it to one of them. And I have 300 other programmers, but if I want it done right, that's who I ask to do it. They must be some kind of geniuses." His perception was so obviously colored by what he expected to see that he could not bring himself to understand that whenever he gave a job to one member of the group, it was worked on by all of them in their usual fashion. When they tried to explain their methods to him, he understood them to be covering up the fact that a few of the members were doing all the work and carrying the others. Fortunately, he was not so rigid that he had to break up the only satisfactory operation he had merely because he didn't understand how it functioned. Unfortunately, he was unable to see how their successful methods could be transmitted to others in his group, so the group remained an isolated pocket until the time it moved on—again as a group—to a more understanding environment.

Of course, groups that follow the individualistic school of programming also have a way of preserving themselves—as did the remainder of the programming section at this airframe manufacturer. A single new member, or even a single new group within so large a group, really has no chance of converting the social system, even if he is firmly convinced of the correctness of his way of doing things. If he comes into an established group, he will probably change his ways to theirs, eventually, though after experiencing more psychological hardship than one might like. If the group is newly forming, however, as programming groups often are, and if it is forming from disparate elements, he may struggle to shape the group to his image and then leave if unsuccessful.

A case in point was Jim A., who was brought onto a newly forming project in Chicago from a programming center in New York. The group to which he was assigned was headed by two people who had been firmly brought up in the egoless programming tradition and who were determined to propagate that tradition in this project. The group consisted of these two, Jim, and four trainees. On the first day the group assembled, the group leaders began the indoctrination of the others into their method of working. It was decided at the beginning that each of the group members was to have the signature of one of the other members on his run request before going on the computer with any job. By this slightly formal method, they hoped to ensure that the group members would get in the habit of doing what they would come to do spontaneously later on.

During the meeting, Jim said nothing, but when the trainees had left, he approached the group leaders. "That's an interesting idea you have," he began, "to help those trainees learn the ropes."

"Well," it was patiently explained to him, "it's not just for the trainees. It's for all of us, so we don't start slipping into bad habits."

"You can't be serious," Jim laughed. "Why I have more than two years of experience. *I* certainly don't need anyone looking over *my* work. What could those trainees possibly teach me?"

Like most prophecies, this one had a way of fulfilling itself, and Jim managed to evade the falling of other eyes upon his sacred programs through one device or another. Before very long, his presence in the group became clearly counterproductive. As he saw the trainees advancing to do difficult and challenging assignments while he struggled on alone, he tried ridiculing them for their lack of independence and ability to think for themselves. His own programs were not up to the standard of quality which the rest of the group was producing. When the group leader finally felt forced to turn over one of his programs—which Jim claimed was debugged, or "essentially debugged"—to one of the trainees to clear up, Jim had more than he could take and resigned.

In this case, the social environment of the group had been strong enough to shape the behavior of the trainees; but it was not strong enough to counteract Jim's "two years of experience." As his personality was not strong enough to carry the group in the direction he felt was correct, the situation eventually became intolerable. Perhaps if the group leaders had been more wise and experienced, they would have excused him from the group from the beginning, but the temptation of "two years of experience" proved their undoing—as it has to many others in a business which so sorely lacks experience.

SUMMARY

The environment in which programmers work is a rich and complex environment, full of human involvement, change, and misleading appearances. To understand that environment, one must understand the difference between formal and informal structures and the many factors that shape it, ranging from the physical surroundings to the individual ego. In an ongoing programming shop, the richness of this environment gives it a self-maintaining quality which resists changes imposed from the outside—especially changes imposed without an understanding of the difference between the formal and the informal. This self-maintenance is manifest on all social levels, and is neither inherently good nor inherently bad. It is merely a fact of programming life.

QUESTIONS

For Managers

1. Do you have an organization chart showing the organization below you and around you? Try taking a copy of this chart and marking—with wiggly lines—interactions that occur in your organization. Do the wiggly lines match the straight lines? If so, get out from behind your desk and find out what is really happening out there.

2. When was the last time you moved peoples' work locations? Can you recall any changed behavior from that move which was not part of the direct intention of the move? What would you have done differently if you were planning the move now?

3. Looking back over your interactions with programmers, can you think

of things you have said that might have forced them into dissonant situations—situations in which their ego had to be defended? In those situations, was the resolution of the dissonance always in the direction you intended, or did you experience such reactions as covering up errors or schedule delays, rather than correcting for them? How could you have approached those situations so as to lessen the dissonance, or to direct the resolution of the dissonance in directions more useful to the overall goals of your organization?

4. What would you have to do to introduce egoless programming into your shop? What resistance would you expect to meet, and how would you deal with it? How long do you think it would take, and what are the chances of success?

5. What is your honest opinion of people who are not trying to "move up" in your organization, but who seem satisfied with the kind of work they do and the amount of money they get? To what extent is your view influenced by your own feelings for yourself?

For Programmers

1. If a computing center had perfectly consistent turnaround, there would be no need for an informal organization to produce information on when jobs are ready. In what other ways do the variations induced by the complexity of programming lead to the growth of informal social structures? Give some examples from your own experience.

2. If you use a terminal system regularly, how do you exchange information with other users of the terminal system? Does your terminal system have an operation which enables you to exchange messages with other terminal users? If so, how valuable is this facility for real communication, as opposed to the other methods you use?

3. Do you refer to your work as "my" program? Try passing one week without using the personal possessive in reference to programs, and take notes on the effects you observe.

4. Have you ever blamed other people for errors in "your" program? Have you ever blamed inanimate objects, such as keypunches or magnetic tapes? How many times were you right in blaming these people or things?

5. Have you ever blamed "bad luck" for errors in "your" program? How often? Are other programmers as unlucky as you? If not, why do you thinks the fates have singled you out for such ill treatment? What sort of rituals do you think you might follow to appease their anger with you?

BIBLIOGRAPHY

Lynch, Kevin, *The Image of the City,* Cambridge, M.I.T. Press, 1960.
In this small and insightful book, Lynch explores the ways in which our image of

our physical surroundings influences our lives. Although cast on the level of cities, the book contains a mine of information for anyone involved in changing or preserving the physical environment in which people work.

Wright, Frank Lloyd, *An Organic Architecture: The Architecture of Democracy,* London, Percy Lund, Humphries & Co., Ltd., 1939.

Wright, the greatest of all the American architects, expounded the theory that "form follows function"—that physical surroundings had to be planned to fit the tasks performed in them, just as a suit has to be tailored to fit its wearer. Wright's ideas may have become ossified into cliches by now, but in these times of ready-to-wear clothing and ready-to-work buildings, the sensitive manager will refresh his thinking about physical surroundings by reading a bit of Wright.

Goffman, Erving, *The Presentation of Self in Everyday Life,* Garden City, N.Y., Doubleday, 1959.

Just as workers are shaped by their physical surroundings, they are shaped by the image of the social surroundings. But working groups also tend to shape their image, which is one of the reasons why managers have such a hard time perceiving their true structure. Goffman explores the ways in which individuals and groups work at shaping the image they will present to outsiders and newcomers—something that managers and programmers alike should know.

Hall, Edward T., *The Silent Language,* Garden City, N.Y., Doubleday, 1959.

Hall takes another point of view on the image of organizations and describes how we acquire our views of the formal and informal structure of the groups in which we live. Hall's approach yields many insights into the ways programmers are socialized, and also into the ways in which we acquire specific programming practices that are never taught in courses or books.

Festinger, L. A., *A Theory of Cognitive Dissonance,* Evanston, Ill., Row, Peterson, 1957.

Festinger's work on cognitive dissonance grew out of an earlier study of what happens when a group which prophesied the end of the world saw the day arrive and the world go on. (When Prophecy Fails). Obviously, dissonance theory has a lot to say to people who work in an environment where prophecy fails each and every day—especially the prophecy that the program is sure to work this time, now that the last bug has been removed.

Haire, Mason, *Psychology in Management,* 2nd ed., New York, McGraw-Hill, 1964.

Haire's fine little book is a good starting place for managers who have a hard time understanding how nonmanagers are motivated.

Fano, R. M., and Corbato, F. J., Time-Sharing on Computers, *Scientific American,* **215** (1966), pp. 128-140.

In this popular article, the authors allow themselves the luxury of dropping some tantalizing hints about the society of users, which grows up with a particular computer system. They probably felt, however, that this was not a fit topic for a professional audience, and they never seem to have followed it up.

5 THE PROGRAMMING TEAM

The lack of experience in programming becomes more evident as the size of the system to be produced increases. Although we have seen that the programmer does not, ideally, work in isolation, even when the problem is small, there is a social difference between small programs and large ones. As long as the work of the entire group—from its purpose and general organization to the last coding detail—can be held in the mind of one person, there is no need for *coordination* of programming effort. The interaction of two programmers looking over a program that either one of them could have worked out is entirely different from the interaction of two programmers working on separate parts of a whole, which is too great for either one to produce. The difference lies in the way conflicting demands are resolved. In the first case, resolution of conflict is the thinking process of one person—aided perhaps by other people, but always under his control. In the second case, conflicting technical demands are translated into potential interpersonal conflicts, and a social mechanism must be formed to resolve them.

HOW A TEAM FORMS

A programming team, then, should be formed in response to a work requirement that cannot be met by a single person. This need relates not simply to the specifications of the work to be done, but also to the abilities of the people available to do the work and the amount of time allotted to doing it. Both factors—ability of the team members and time available—have the characteristic of requiring minima in order that the work be feasible. For example, certain programming work cannot be done by a team of trainees, no matter how large, so that doubling the number of "warm bodies"—as they are so often called in the trade— still will not get the work done. Schedule is similarly limiting—we need only cite the apocryphal experiment which tried to make a baby in one month by putting nine women to work on the job as a team.

Conceptually, there is a minimum expertise and a minimum time necessary to produce a given system. Because these quantities cannot be clearly defined—and because of the uncertainties involved in program estimation—managers often form a team which any reasonable judgment would indicate cannot perform the designated task in the allotted time. Inevitably, the team is given an extension when the time limit is reached and the reality *must* be faced. Had it been faced earlier, the work could probably have been organized differently—in recognition of the longer schedule—and thus produced, in the end, more quickly.

This far too common programming situation illustrates the complementary relationship between ability and schedule. The minimum schedule can only be achieved by putting the best team to work on the project; and the minimum work team can only be used if we are willing to let the project stretch out for a longer time. In other words, almost any program can be produced with less programming talent—if we are willing to allow a stretching of the schedule, and if we have not dropped below the minimum competence.

Such situations also illustrate an important relationship between schedule and work structure. Although we must always be on our toes against Parkinsonianism (work expands to fill the time allotted), too tight a schedule will inevitably lead to the temptation to take shortcuts. These shortcuts *might* succeed in getting the system working on time—but only if everything goes right, which it rarely does. So many failures to meet programming deadlines can be traced back to an initial schedule and plan of attack which assumed the most optimistic conditions—no days lost through illness, no machine trouble, no compiler problems, no "impossible" bugs. Because each of us has had the experience of, say, a six-month period in which everyone on the team was in top health *or* there was no machine trouble *or* there were no compiler problems *or* there were no "impossible" bugs, we can easily slip into imagining—if the price is right—that we can have a six-month period in which all of these fortunate circumstances happen at once.

If, on the other hand, we try to cover for the possibility of trouble, we have to supplement our team with extra members. Also, if the total work must be divided among more people, the amount of coordinating effort is increased relative to the total work. As a rough rule, three programmers organized into a team can do only twice the work of a single programmer of the same ability—because of time spent on coordination problems. Moreover, three groups of three programmers can do only twice the work of a single group—or four times the work of a single programmer—for the same reason. Thus, an eight-month project for a single programmer might be done in four months if we are willing to put three people to work on it or in two months if we are willing to allocate nine.

Notice that two months would probably be the minimum time for this program to be produced with programmers of this ability, for it is doubtful whether nine programmers can do *anything* useful in less than about two months, considering the time it will take them to get organized. If we have to have the program faster, we shall have to hire a better man for the job.

In any case, the basic rule for size and composition of programming teams would seem to be this—for the best programming at the least cost, give the best possible programmers you can find sufficient time so you need the smallest number of them. When you have to work faster, or with less experienced people, costs and uncertainties will rise. In any case, the worst way to do a programming project is to hire a horde of trainees and put them to work under pressure and without supervision—although this is the most common practice today.

When thrown into the breach as raw trainees, many people do not learn as effectively as they could from their programming experiences. Even the proper organization of teams for the maximum current production is not usually the best way to produce maximum *long-range* production, for to accomplish that training must be taken into account. Therefore, we may wish to place one or more relatively green programmers on a team, even though we anticipate that they will contribute little to the current effort. When the team has such members, the goal of the team becomes multiple—both production and training—and the organization of the work is affected.

In programming, the way a team organizes for work is most strongly determined by two factors—the organization of the target system and the composition of the team. Because there are frequently several ways of approaching the structure of a system but rarely more than one group of programmers available to do the work, the structure is often chosen to accommodate the strengths and weaknesses of the team members. Ideally, of course, the choice would be made the other way around—the ideal program structure would be planned and then a group would be assembled who could handle this work in an optimal way. But, given the present shortage of programming talent—or even "warm bodies"—such planning is honored more in the breach than in the observance.

As an example of the relationship between system structure and team organization, consider first Figure 5–1, which shows how a team composed of one experienced programmer and four relative trainees might organize a system. Part a shows how the program might be set up as one fairly large main program which calls upon relatively small—perhaps input-output-free—subroutines to provide some of its functions. Here,

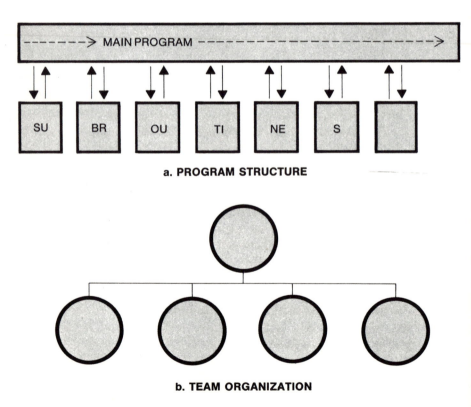

Figure 5–1 Program structure vs. team organization.

as shown in part b, the experienced programmer would act as a conventional leader of the team, programming the main section himself and allocating the subroutines to the trainees in a manner hopefully calculated to give each the experience appropriate to his level of competence.

Now consider how the same work might be organized by a team of three programmers of relatively equal experience, as shown in Figure 5–2. In part a, we see that the program is now organized into phases, one following the other, rather than into subroutines. Of course, the main program of Figure 5–1 might also have been organized into phases according to the conception of programmer leading the group, but we would probably find less interface coding in that version than in the second. On the other hand, the second group could also use subroutines within—and possibly even among—the phases, but in this situation we would be likely to find less interface material in the finished product. The structure of the programming team itself would be more a matter of communication among equals, as indicated in part b of the figure, though member II would probably spend more of his time in "teamwork" than either of the others because of the position of his section between the other two. Member II, in a situation like this, may actually have the easiest *programming* job, especially if the first and third phases take

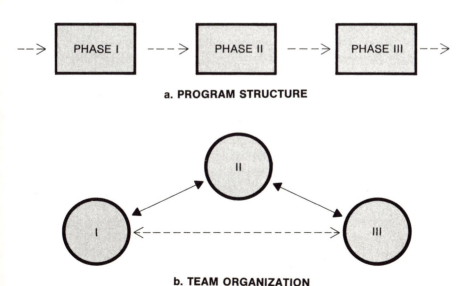

a. PROGRAM STRUCTURE

b. TEAM ORGANIZATION

Figure 5–2 Program structure vs. team organization.

care of the input and the output for the system. In his position in the structure, ability to work closely with the others is probably more important than programming ability, and he might actually be the least talented programmer—as programmer—in the group.

These structures, of course, are idealizations. They do not reflect, for example, whatever inner structure comes about because of the general programming philosophy of the larger group to which these team members belong. The organization in Figure 5–1 might in practice be far less hierarchical if the group practices egoless programming; while the team in Figure 5–2 might be far less egalitarian if its members did not. Status of members of a team evolves in a manner influenced by a number of factors, and the factor of who criticizes the work of whom is one of the strongest. Thus, if egoless programming is used, everyone in the group will have the opportunity to examine the work of everyone else at some time, thereby tending to prevent the establishment of strong hierarchy.

In programming, the status of a team member is usually strongly influenced by his abilities as perceived by the others. When programs are passed around for shared criticism, the speed at which the "cream" will come to the top is enhanced. On the other hand, if the team members work secluded in cells like monks, the reputations previously established are more likely to remain as determinants of prestige in the team—at least until it is too late to do anything about a misappraisal.

Again, the particular piece of work assigned may lend status to a team member—or take it away. Programming jobs seem to carry status just as do carpets in offices, and in organizing a team one must tread gingerly among the sensibilities of the members when passing out the work. Writing auxiliary programs, for example, such as test data generators seems to carry low prestige in some circles, perhaps because the work will not be physically present in the final system. Subroutines— though they may present far greater difficulties—are often thought to place the writer in a subservient position to the programmer who writes the routine which calls them, perhaps by analogy, to the role of the subroutine itself. These anthropomorphisms do not have to represent *rational* thinking in order to be important factors in determining team satisfaction with work assignments. They can be quite real—perhaps all the more so for being irrational.

ESTABLISHING AND ACCEPTING GOALS

Suppressed feelings by a team member about the inferiority of his assignment can be surprisingly damaging to a team effort. Egoless programming tends to moderate such feelings, since each programmer feels that he has a share in a larger part of the system. Still, if a team sets to work too quickly—before establishing a real consensus about the structure of the project and the division of work—trouble will manifest itself in one way or another.

Social psychologists have verified in other contexts that failure of one or more members to share the group goals affects the group performance—not only through that member's share but through a reduced performance on the part of the others, for they invariably perceive the division within the group or the indifference of one of the members. A rather fantastic example of the cost of achieving only a surface consensus arose in a system that was organized as shown in Figure 5–3. As we might guess from the system organization, the original team had consisted of seven relatively equal programmers, one of whom was designated to write the input/output package to provide a common interface for data which were passed from one phase to another.

This system had been in existence on the IBM 704 for about four years when it was decided to convert the 704 to a 709. From a programming point of view, the 709 was almost compatible with the 704—except for the input-output, which was entirely different. Since this system had all input-output confined to one section, a simple conversion was anticipated. The input-output routines were converted so as to use the 709 system while preserving the interface to the various phases. Once the new routines had been tested, they were mated with the old phases and all went well—until the system blew up in phase V.

The input-output routines were double-checked, and phase V was

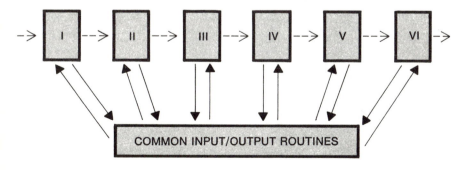

Figure 5–3 Organization of a system.

checked for any deviations from the standard interface. Absolutely nothing was found. Then phase IV was checked to see if the data it had passed on to phase V had somehow been distorted by the new system, but the output of phase IV matched the previous output for the same test bit for bit. Other theories were pursued, but several weeks went by without a clue as to what had gone wrong. In the meantime, of course, pressure was building up to remove the 704 and stop paying rental on two systems.

None of the original programmers of the system were still around, so one of them was brought in to see if he could provide a clue as to the trouble. After a day of unrewarding speculation, he was having a beer with one of the new programmers and reminiscing about the good old days when the original crew had been together. At one point, he chanced to recall that Joe R. had been very disturbed not to get the assignment of writing the input-output routines, as he thought he was much more capable than the one who got the job.

"Joe was really sore for about a week," the old-timer recalled, "but then he seemed to get over his hurt pride. He wound up doing a darn good job on his section, too."

"And which section was that?" the youngster asked, beginning to sense a wisp of suspicion.

"Section II, if I remember correctly. But why do you ask?"

The young programmer said he just had a hunch, and then excused himself to head back to the computing center. He got a listing of section II—which nobody had looked at, attention having been focused on sections IV, V, and the input-output routines—and started to go through it step by step. He didn't have far to look. Right at the beginning, the program fetched a word from the region of storage reserved for the input-output routines, which were resident in core throughout the entire run. Then phase II replaced that word with a branch to part of its own code, diverting the flow from input-output routines. At the end of its processing, it returned the saved word, leaving everything as it had been upon entry.

What had happened, of course, was that Joe—not accepting the team decision at all but merely stopping his open opposition to it—had written his own version of the input-output functions needed by his phase. He said nothing to anybody about this, but merely short-circuited part of the standard routines when his phase was in operation. When the new input-output system was created, however, the part formerly occupied by the branch was now being used to hold some variable which kept track of the position of an intermediate tape. Inasmuch as this variable was changed in the course of executing phase II, but changed back to its original value at the end, the input-output routines effectively lost track of the tape's position. Since the values on this tape were not used again until phase V, it was only then that the blowup occurred. The cost of this nonconsensus was slow in being exacted; but when its time came, it was paid, and paid handsomely.

We should stress here that the consensus we are talking about concerns the *goals* of the group, not such matters of fact as could be settled by other means. Consider, for example, the case of a team producing an on-line system for a bank. While undergoing final acceptance testing of this duplex system, they suddenly saw each on-line printer print a line of absolute garbage, right in the middle of the normal output. The two lines were identical, even though the two systems operated entirely free of influence from each other—in order to ensure that trouble in one would not affect the proper functioning of the other. Of course, the same program was used in the two systems, so all indications were that some sort of program bug existed. Indeed, it would be hard to attribute a probability to the occurrence of two machine errors in the two independent machines—they even had separate power supplies—which would lead to the same line printed at the same time on both.

One of the team members was given the job of tracing down the bug, but after a week of studying the evidence, he was no closer to the source of trouble than he had been at the start. Another team member joined him for a second week, with no better results. The scheduled date for putting the system into operation was only a week away and, since the system seemed to be operating correctly in every other aspect, a meeting was called to decide what to do about this intractable bug. The discussion among the eleven members of the team was heated, and no conclusion was reached, although one large contingent was pressing for the group to agree to label the incident as a freak—a double machine error! No amount of appeal to the statistics of the situation would sway this group from their position—for although it was physically absurd, it was psychologically satisfying. They *wanted* the system to be ready on time; and in a second meeting, they succeeded in persuading the others to sign off on the system.

The system was cut over on schedule and functioned quite well for about a week. Then, in the middle of a banking day, and just when operations were beginning to rely on it, the system just stopped—both machines at once. After about an hour, during which the bank was completely paralyzed, the system was restarted. Nobody dared to estimate how much business had been lost, but auditing the files for the effects of the restart was a gargantuan labor which stretched out over several months. In the meantime, the entire programming crew worked frantically to locate the bug before another failure might occur.

Needless to say, when the bug—a certain timing coincidence which could be expected to occur about once every week or so—was finally found, it turned out to be the same bug which had earlier caused the two garbage lines. In that case, a fortunate—or unfortunate—coincidence had permitted the system to go on essentially undamaged, but the next time it happened, things turned out rather badly.

The lesson in this example is the lesson of false consensus—that is, not an apparent consensus as in the other case, but a true consensus on a falsehood. Things are bad enough in programming without adding this type of problem, but it is a psychological problem which we shall have to face. We shall have more to say on the subject under the topic of "opinions and social pressure." For the moment, the main lesson is the difference between this kind of consensus—which stifles the healthy disagreement essential to unbiased appraisal of programming work— and consensus on the goals of the team—which smooths the way for productive functioning.

To achieve true consensus on group goals, there is no better method than having the group set the goals itself. For one thing, participating in setting the goals ensures that the goals will be more clearly under- stood. For another, it gives each group member a chance to commit himself publicly to the group's goal, and this type of public commitment— perhaps because of cognitive dissonance—has been shown to enhance goal acceptance. But participation itself, quite independent of these other factors, seems to be an important determinant in whether an individual truly accepts the working goals of the team with the pursuant increase in productivity.

To be sure, not every programming team can be permitted to set whatever goals it happens to fancy at any moment. A team is usually constituted to accomplish some task which has probably been set down before the team was even assembled. But programming tasks are not usually specified too precisely until much later than team formation, so that unless the upper management is very overbearing, much meaningful and interesting goal setting can be done by the team members in concert. The greatest danger is the manager who has come up through the programming ranks and wants to define every bit and byte before the team even sees the problem. Nothing is more sure to dampen the team enthusiasm and make them feel that they are "mere coders."

When a team does work from this sort of "bit-picking" specification, other troubles arise simply because what the group is trying to ac- complish is not clear. Precision and clarity are not the same. To be clear—and goal clarity is one of the most critical factors in goal ac- ceptance—the task outlined must be placed in a framework of the *meaning* of what is being done. The programmer wants to know *why*, not just *what*.

Problems of unclear goals become more acute when the programming team is working not to produce a specific system, but to provide some service or support function to other programming groups. At least when there is a package to produce, you can have an image of what is to be done, even if you don't understand why. But a support group must be constantly reminded of their contribution, lest they drift into doing things more concrete but less productive.

For example, many installations have a systems programming team. The tasks of such a team are rather diverse, held together by the common thread of service to the other users of the installation. We know how frequently such a team drifts off into fascinating but useless little projects simply for lack of a clear and persistent image of what they are trying to do. This tendency is exaggerated by incompetence of other users in systems matters, for they feel unable to evaluate the work being done by the systems programmers. In one case—not atypical—the three systems programmers in an installation were fascinated with the problem of producing an improved loader—possibly useful in some contexts, but definitely not in their installation. Each request from the other users for some service, such as creating a new cataloged procedure or incorporating a new system in the library, was met with the statement that it could not be done in their system. In fact, it was asserted, they could be done, but only after this new loader was finished.

The statement itself was true enough, because as long as the entire team was working on the loader, there was nobody with the competence to do these other jobs. But the loader itself had nothing to do with them, other than sucking off the labor which could have been more gainfully employed. Users were too intimidated by their own lack of knowledge of the system (most of them were not even sure what a loader was) to complain. Eventually, the whole party was broken up when someone had the nerve to call in an outside expert to do a small systems job for him. The loader never worked anyway, but a change in the system gave the team the excuse they needed; they saved face by claiming that their loader could not work under the new system.

There is no remedy for such drifting away from group goals unless there is competence in the installation to evaluate whether or not the group is working according to their mandate. Perhaps even more difficult situations arise when a group has reasonably clear goals, but has more than one at a time. In addition to the previously mentioned potential conflict between production and education as goals, other conflicts arise, for example, when a team has two distinct programs to produce. Somehow, the relative importance of the two projects must be made clear initially and must be reclarified regularly, lest the quite natural drift in favor of one or the other should occur.

Of course, it is best if each team can have a single clearly defined goal, but the world is seldom so simple. Even if the goal is a single program or subroutine, there is the possibility of conflict between emphasis on speed, space, or schedule. When a team is not fully apprised of the emphasis to be placed on each factor, the members of that team may very well be working at cross purposes. One team member may be spending most of his effort trying to save time, only to discover that this time has been squandered by another team member who was trying to compress the program into the smallest possible space. When such conflicts come out in the open—especially after the involved parties have a considerable investment in one approach or the other—serious conflicts are sure to result.

The resolution of conflicting ideas on team goals is, surprisingly, often most critical when the differing views are almost indistinguishable. Gulliver's attempts to settle the wars over which end of the egg to break are as nothing compared with the energies too often spent arguing over whether to use one subroutine with two entries or a single entry and an extra parameter. The persistence of this kind of argument among team members can reliably be taken as a sign of some deeper conflict— perhaps for "leadership" of the team—and should not be ignored simply on account of its triviality.

TEAM LEADERSHIP AND TEAM LEADERS

The word "leader," to many people, conjures up an image of Adolph Hitler sending millions of goose-stepping soldiers to their death with a tweak of his tiny moustache. And, indeed, Hitler was the "Fuhrer," or Leader, to millions of his people. But understanding such a phenomenon as Hitler would be easier under the title of "followership" than "leadership," for there is a certain type of leading which is only a crystallization of deep-seated desires shared by many onto the personality of one.

In programming, this is scarcely the type of leadership which is needed —or which would usually be tolerated. Try to imagine the reaction of a typical programming team to a supervisor standing over them with a whip or issuing commands like a lieutenant leading his squad in a charge on the enemy machine-gun emplacement. The reaction to even milder forms of authoritarian "leadership" need not be imagined, for we have numerous examples of unenlightened executives trying this approach on programmers. One typical reaction is "working to rule." One instance of working to rule occurred in a project that had a change in manager halfway through its life. The new manager was appalled at seeing some of the programmers come in to work at ten-thirty—so appalled that he didn't bother to find out that they had been working on the machine until two the previous night.

A directive was issued stating that working hours must be strictly observed, and that time-clock punching was to be enforced according to the official rules of the company. The programmers simply responded by working *exactly* the normal working hours—emptying the office precisely at five-fifteen every evening, and queueing up at the time-clock to do it. Since the project had been operating essentially on a staggered shift basis as an adaptation to limited machine time, productivity immediately fell by half. Programmers were idle during the day waiting for machine runs, and the machine closed down promptly after one shift each day.

A similar case occurred when a manager discovered that the consumption of supplies was running over budget. He immediately ordered a lock put on the supply room, with only the supply clerk having a key. The programmers responded by coming one at a time to the supply clerk all through the day, so that he had no time to perform his other duties. Finally, the manager issued a directive that supplies could only be obtained between ten and ten-thirty or three and three-thirty. This continued until he came upon one programmer staring at the wall and asked what he was doing.

"My pen ran out," was the reply, "so I have to wait until tomorrow at ten before I can write any more code."

The manager reddened noticeably. "Why don't you use a pencil?" he demanded.

"Because I always use a pen. The keypunch operators won't accept work written with a pencil. It smudges."

"Then why don't you borrow a pen?"

"But then we wouldn't be keeping accurate track of supplies usage, would we?"

Needless to say, this was not a very productive shop until the manager was promoted on to some more elevated position in the hierarchy. Of course, he might have fired the programmer for insubordination or some other such militaristic charge, but he knew very well that bad managers are easier to find than good programmers. Indeed, the chronic shortage of programmers has led to an interesting situation in the entire field with respect to programming leadership.

In studying the factors which go into the satisfaction of working groups, social scientists have isolated four major areas:

1. The material rewards and opportunities.
2. The challenge and the interest of the work itself.

3. The general conditions in the larger organization, such as employee benefits, working conditions, and organization status among similar organizations.
4. The competence of supervisors and leaders.

In programming as it is today, the first three of these wants are satisfied with such regularity that they ordinarily do not play a major role in determining programmer satisfaction. To be sure, there are instances of underpayment in this generally high-salaried profession, there are dull jobs, and there are bad companies. But these are exceptions, whereas bad supervision and leadership is more common than we would like to imagine. Thus, the attitude of a programmer toward his "superiors" is more likely to be the cause of his dissatisfaction—with consequent loss of productivity—than perhaps all the other three put together.

Leadership, in the sense that social scientists use it, means the ability to influence people. Programmers, being people who tend to value creative work and professional competence, tend to put their stock in people whom they perceive to be good at the things they do. Thus, it is easier to exert leadership over—to influence—programmers by being a soft-spoken programming wizard than by being the world's fastest-talking salesman. When nonprogramming leaders are brought in to be in charge of programming teams, trouble usually brews unless the appointed leader explicitly and implicitly recognizes his incapacity on technical matters. The very worst he can do—and this goes also for a former programmer who has lost touch with the field—is to try to match programming wits with the other members of the team. Although a team might come to respect a leader who openly admitted his programming inexperience, they could only come to ridicule one whose pretense at knowledge was revealed to be a sham.

In one case, Arnold C. was appointed to replace a promoted leader of a team within a larger project. Arnold's qualifications were mainly in the area of data-processing sales, but he affected an air of programming expertise. He even went so far as to suggest an algorithm to solve a crucial problem facing the project, although it was evident to his two most experienced team members that he didn't know what he was talking about. Instead of showing him the flaw in his scheme when he presented it to them in private, they encouraged Arnold's wish to assemble key programmers on the project to hear him present his idea. At the meeting, they gave him about five minutes to get himself solidly enmeshed in his own snare. Then they began to tear his algorithm apart —in detail as well as in grand plan. Arnold finally left the blackboard amidst the combined laughter of the assembled group, and within two months he received a requested transfer to another post.

Such problems frequently arise because the leader who is designated as such by an outside force is not capable of exerting the influence required inside the team. This "formal" or "official" leader, because he represents the goals of the outside world, is always in a precarious position, especially if he sees his job as merely "selling" or otherwise imposing the "management view" on the team. Inasmuch as this view assumes that no compromise is possible with the management, the only possible resolution of a conflict between management and the team is that the team should "give in."

Even assuming that the team could be made to give in, nobody who has ever seen the performance of a programming group which has so knuckled under would desire this result. But forced labor—to the small extent that it does work—can only be made to work with relatively immature programmers who are not aware of other possibilities, or with relatively unskilled programmers who are quite aware that other possibilities are not open to them. The typical programmer, on the other hand, is aware of other possibilities and aware of his chances of getting them. Carried to an extreme, this awareness leads to the programming type whose career is an unending succession of job changes and very little accomplishment. Normally, however, it leads to programming teams which are run more democratically than typical work teams in many other fields.

In a democratic group, leadership—or influence—is not confined to a single person, but moves around the team from member to member as the needs become compatible with his abilities or ideas. People, however, are not all created the same—even though they may all be created equal. Thus, leadership in a democratic team is never spread uniformly, but falls more on some members than others. The important factor in democratic group functioning is not that every member exerts equal leadership, but that the determinants of leadership are based on the inner realities of team life, not imposed from outside. Thus, when the team is in need of learning something, that team member who knows most about the subject may rise to a position of leader in the form of teacher of the others. Or, when the team's work enters the debugging stage, one of the members may emerge as a frequent leader because he has a peculiar talent for debugging.

A truly democratic team is marvelously adaptable to changing circumstances, and thus tends to be a more reliable production unit in the face of unanticipated difficulties. Managers, however, tend not to believe that a democratic team is superior in a crisis. For evidence, they point to the speed and determination which a centrally organized group can muster when massed behind a single leader, and they are correct—if the leader happens to be the right one for the situation. It is true that Hitler's forces, for example, won great successes under this type of command—but then it is also true that his opponents were organized under the same type of system. Perhaps Hitler was the right man at the right time—until he lost. In a democratically organized group—given, of course, sufficient talent and intelligence to draw upon—the right man can be chosen for *each* time. The Swiss, for example, *elect* a general to head their armies when war threatens. When there is no war threat, there is no general— but there are other leaders chosen according to what needs there are for leadership. The Swiss, unlike certain other countries, are not burdened by generals trying to govern the country in peacetime.

Unfortunately, no programming team can ever be completely democratic in the sense of always being able to choose the right man to lead them at each instant. For one thing, the right man may not exist in the team. For another, personality factors may intervene to preclude the selection of the correct man for the moment. Finally, the intrusion into the group of a designated leader from the outside always biases the group away from democracy.

The designated leader is a carrier of information between the team and outside forces which would like to influence the goals which the team pursues. Ideally, he would be a perfectly neutral carrier, but this never happens. His contact with the outside group gives him access to special sources of information which the others do not share, and he may use these sources as leverage to elevate himself to a stronger position of leadership. If, for example, he has been told by management that they wish a particular program to be completed in ten weeks, he might tell the group that the management has asked for eight weeks. Then, giving the appearance of winning a compromise in favor of the group's feeling that the work will take twelve weeks, he agrees to change the time to ten. The others have no way of finding out that he has used his special position to appear to be aiding the group, and his esteem as a leader may grow, even though he has been "management's boy" all along.

Of course, should the team members ever discover that he has been distorting the transmission of information from management in order to win favor for himself, he is finished as an effective leader of that team. But the temptation to be dishonest or manipulative with the team members is very great, because of the asymmetry of the designated leader's position. His work is primarily with the team, but his rewards and punishments come from the higher management. Usually, by the time a programmer consents to accept an appointment as team leader, he has acquired aspirations for a career in management. Advancement in that career is no longer dependent on his programming abilities—which have probably carried him this far—but on his ability to please management.

The shortsighted or insecure team leader may feel that the best way to please management is to promise them whatever they ask. But, ultimately, what the management wants is *kept* promises, and these can only be obtained if the team leader can win team acceptance of the promises as their goals. What the team leader must learn is that

1. Managers—no matter how hard they press for promises—really want results.
2. Results will be far more easily obtained if they are obtained in the pursuit of goals set with full team participation.

Keeping these facts in mind, the designated team leader may be able to overcome the handicap of having been designated and become a leader in his own right. He may replace the "headship" with "leadership."

We would not be completely honest, however, if we failed to admit that managers are not always aware that they want results. We frequently see a team leader removed from his post for refusing to promise achievements which his team believes are impossible. The process of replacement then goes on until management comes up with a candidate with more desire to advance himself than brains to assess the true chances of success. Unfortunately, if the project is a long one, this candidate may be promoted for his cooperativeness before the project has reached the point where management can see that his promises will not be kept. What ensues is a game of musical chairs, the object of which is not to be left in a position of responsibility at the moment the outside world becomes aware that the project has failed. This game, played over and over, has put more than one programming manager in the position he has today.

The designated team leader, however, can do no better than to resist attempts to coerce him into accepting goals his team cannot meet. Of course, he should remain receptive to new information which might change the situation—as when the management promises him additional people or a better machine schedule. He must assess for himself the chances of these promises being kept, however, for once *he* promises his managers, they are likely to forget the conditions he extracted from them. But when the management arguments turn to other factors besides the resources or the work specification, he must never let his judgment be swayed. The most typical case involves promises of special rewards if he succeeds, but he must not permit himself to confuse the value of the reward with the probability of achieving it.

When the discussions reach the stage of reward offering, there is really no strategy left to the leader but to resist. He must be willing to stake his position as designated leader on the strength of his professional judgment. If he is a good programmer himself, he is doubly strengthened in this struggle, for he has more confidence in his judgment and he knows that he will not be on the breadline if he loses this leadership post. If he doubts his own proficiency, however, he will fall easy prey to various sorts of threats veiled in a mist of wispy promises.

As an illustration of the major points of this section, consider the case of Harold M., an outstanding programmer who found himself in the position of designated leader in the squeeze. He had accepted the job of leading a team to produce a compiler by a certain date, but now management wanted to expand the specifications while retaining the same schedule. Harold discussed the matter with his team and the conclusion was reached that they could not do the work unless they got an extension of three months. When Harold carried this information back to his manager, he found that it was not accepted. When he insisted, his manager arranged a meeting among Harold, himself, and his own manager.

Harold knew from the composition of this meeting that it would be an attempt to put him in the "hot box." With this arrangement—conveniently private—Harold was supposed to get the feeling of importance in an atmosphere where threats and promises could be made but never acknowledged. But Harold had already experienced this situation often enough to anticipate each new move, and he was armed with the confidence in his own and his team's judgment. The meeting went on for some time and, with each parried thrust, the atmosphere grew hotter. Finally, it reached the stage of the ultimate threat.

"Harold," his manager began, for the manager's job was to do the dirty work and the manager's manager's job was to play the role of the benevolent father figure softening the manager's harsh threats with sweet promises. "Harold," he began again, because he had paused to pull his chair forward a significant three inches, "you're not cooperating with us. To be a manager, you have to learn to cooperate, to compromise. Perhaps you don't have what it takes to be a manager."

Harold caught the implication, and instead of letting it pass, dragged it fully into the open. "I think you may be right. Why don't you get someone else to do this job—someone who knows how to cooperate."

The manager's manager saw that Harold had been pushed over his limit and tried to swing back onto the positive tack. "But Harold," he flattered, "there isn't anyone else. You're the only one who knows how to do this job. We're depending on you."

"Then," said Harold, with a note of mock triumph in his voice, "if I'm the only one who can do the job, why don't you believe me when I tell you it can't be done in that much time?"

"Because you don't *really* understand the problem," his manager shot back, but Harold was already out of his seat and at the door.

"Look," he said, just before leaving the deadlocked meeting. "Make up your minds. If I'm the only one who understands, then I'm the only one who *really* understands and you'll have to do it my way. If not, then you won't have any trouble replacing me. It's your problem, not mine, so if you'll excuse me, I'll get back to work."

Did Harold lose his job? He didn't, in this case; but that wasn't really important, for he knew he could get another at least as good. If it had been important, he wouldn't have been able to do what he did. One of the paradoxes of leadership is simply this: only the leader who is ready to step down has a real chance of success.

THE TEAM IN CRISIS

The life cycle of a team starts with recruitment, moves through goal setting and organizing to doing the work, and finally may end with a dissolution of the team when the work is finished or with the acceptance of new goals. This path, however, is so studded with crises of one sort or another that the life story of a typical programming team would make the subject of a fairly interesting—if slightly unbelieveable—novel. Indeed, it is useful to consider the work of the team in two categories— work directed at accomplishing the team goals and work directed at maintaining the effective functioning of the team in the face of the crises it meets. To social psychologists, these activities are designated as "task-oriented" and "maintenance-oriented" and have been the subject of much research.

In certain types of groups, and often in programming teams, the group tends to choose two complementary leaders—a task-specialist who sets, allocates, and coordinates the work; and a maintenance-specialist, who irons out conflicts among group members or between individual goals and group goals. The designated leader, because of his role in carrying external goals into the group, is most often in the task-specialist position, although, as we know, he may be replaced by the group if he does not display the necessary competence. The maintenance-specialist —who will more often be the best-liked person in the group—can come from anywhere. He may not be a particularly good programmer in his own right, though he may well be. Very often, he will be a she.

In one cross-cultural study of nuclear families—father, mother, and their children—this same division into task and maintenance activities was usually found at least in the cultural ideal. In most cultures, including ours, but not in all, the ideal father was the task-specialist and the ideal mother the maintenance-specialist. Perhaps this role for a female programmer is quite a natural one in our culture. In any case, it seems quite frequent that when there is a woman on a programming team, she assumes the role of "team-mother," although no studies have been made to verify sex as a significant factor in choosing the maintenance-specialist. There have been at least several teams where one of the women was openly referred to as the "team-mother" or "den-mother," and there is the persistent joke in computing circles which defines "software" as "a girl programmer." Softness is one of the terms which has been used to characterize the maintenance task, whereas hardness seems to characterize the one who must direct the work.

Whether or not this male-female division of leadership is ultimately shown to have social-psychological validity, there is sufficient anecdotal evidence to make it a worthwhile experimental practice to place at least one woman programmer on each team, though probably not in the role of designated leader. Of course, there is no reason why a woman, as in many families, cannot take the task-specialist role; but managers should be wary of promoting a woman to be designated leader simply because she seems to be second-in-command in a team. In fact, there is no need to limit this caveat to women: if it is possible to identify the maintenance-specialist in a team, one should consider carefully before making a promotion which by its official nature may prejudice the leadership performance in that role.

The replacement of a leader—or any team member—is probably the most frequent and typical crisis in the life of a team. The effect of adding or removing a member depends quite sensitively on the group structure, and many a manager has been unpleasantly surprised at the change in performance resulting from the removal or addition of an "insignificant" group member. Of course, when higher management reaches into a team to remove a member, it is often by reason of that member's demonstrated competence, so it should not be surprising if his loss affects team performance. But not all lost performance can be attributed to the loss of individual talent—just as all team performance cannot be attributed to a simple sum of the team members' work.

The "democratically" organized team tends to be better able to withstand the shock of loss of a group member—whether by promotion, resignation, illness, death, pregnancy, or a call to the cloth. Since the work is shared among the members and since there is much communication among them, the hole left by the parting may hardly be noticed as team members step in as needed and apply the knowledge they had gained in working with the departed one. Conversely, it may prove more difficult for the democratically organized team to accept a new member, for there is no clearly delineated position in the structure for him to occupy. Paradoxically as it may seem to some, the democratically organized team may present to outsiders a rather cold and unfriendly facade, whereas the members of an authoritarian team may be most warm and friendly toward a newcomer.

In the authoritarian team, to the extent that all work is organized through and guarded exclusively by the leader, holes are left when a member leaves. Only the leader has the necessary information to make the new division of labor among the remaining members. If the leader is busy or away, the loss of a member can be a disaster.

Gaining a member, on the other hand, can be relatively simple, for the new member merely has to go to the leader to be assigned to do "this and this and that"—each of which tasks is presumably taken from some other member. Replacement of a member is probably also easier, if the new member's abilities closely match those of the old, for all that is required is a reassignment of specific tasks from one to the other. Nevertheless, we seldom find such neat one-for-one replacements, if only because the departing member knows a great deal about the project from his work on it. In the typical mismatch, the democratic team will probably be better equipped to reorganize the work to fit the realities of the situation.

Another sort of crisis appears when the team members begin to be aware that one of their number is not able to carry his share of the load. In the democratic team, the most probable outcome is a gradual shifting of the work off of this member and onto the others. If the team is more centrally organized with a strong single leader, removal of the member is more likely. This is not the whole picture, however, for by the time the trouble is recognized, removal may not solve anything, since there is not sufficient time to secure and train a replacement. In the democratic group, however, incompetence is not likely to go long unnoticed, because each member has many opportunities to review the work of each other member. Thus, only if the incompetence is really glaring is the authoritarian approach likely to prove more effective. Even then, blunt removal of an incompetent member is not likely to have the most warming effect on the team morale, for even the most incompetent member may be well liked by the others.

A member who is competent but who does not get along with the others can be an even more serious problem for the democratic group than an out-and-out incompetent. In an authoritarian group, such a member would not have much contact with others on a working basis anyway, so as long as he gets along adequately with the leader, he presents no particular problem. Indeed, some programmers prefer to work under a strong, centralized leader in order that they do not have to socialize with their fellow workers. But in a democratic team, an antisocial member cuts lines of communications and is a constant impediment to consensus in team meetings.

There are many means by which a team can "socialize" one of its members, just as there are many possible reasons for antisocial behavior. One potential source of such behavior is a team member who is indeed much more talented than the others, for he may be unable to surpress his impatience. They, on the other hand, may be unable to appreciate or implement the types of suggestions he makes. It is possible to be *too* smart for programming—if the person is not smart enough to use his intelligence to modify his social behavior and methods of communication.

George G. was a trainee who was brought into a diagnostic programming group with all signs pointing to an outstanding programming career. He had just received a Master's degree in Mathematics with honors, and only two of the other seven team members had even gone to a university. The team was working on real-time diagnostics for a military computer, and George was assigned to write the diagnostics for a high-speed drum, which was a critical part of the system. Although this was his first real program, he developed an ingenious scheme in which the program wrote all ones on the drum and then, by analyzing the patterns of zeros read back, could indicate the exact circuit that was failing.

George received high praise for this work, praise that he didn't need because he was fully aware of how superior it was to the unimaginative work of his fellows. Indeed, George lost no opportunity of telling them about their shortcomings, as reflected in the clumsiness of their program when compared with the grace of his. In a very short time, a serious crisis was brewing in the team, and several members began to look for a way to push George out—while several others, of a different bent, began to seek new positions for themselves. Then fate intervened in the form of a visit from some military brass to inspect the new hardware.

Great preparations were made for the inspection, but when the brass arrived, the computer could not be made to function. The diagnostics had all been run successfully, but the other software would not work at all. The diagnostics were rerun, but again they worked and the regular programs did not. At this point, the military was getting rather petulant, and management was growing furious. Then, somebody chanced to walk behind the main frame and noticed a cable lying loose. When he casually inquired what it was, the problem was solved. The drum had not been connected to the system!

The drum was hooked on, and the military was soothed with a fine demonstration and a lunch well oiled with martinis. Long after they were gone, however, the programmers on the team were still getting theirs back at George. He had failed to take into account the behavior of the drum interface when the drum was not on-line. The system was designed to give an interrupt if an unattached device was selected, but George had masked that off. If the interrupt was masked, a write was simply ignored and a read produced a *string of all ones.* Thus, George's marvelous program had simply indicated that all was well with the drum, even though it was not even attached.

It was a blunder that any programmer could make, and it was easily patched up. Not so George's ego, for the other programmers took every possible opportunity to rib him. Perhaps if he hadn't claimed such infallibility, his fall from the heights might not have hurt so much; but as it was, George couldn't take it. After two weeks, he simply failed to show up one Monday morning, and that was the last that anyone ever heard of George G. It was harsh, but it was effective; and the group soon returned to its former happy state—producing unimaginative, but sound, diagnostics.

Crises in a team's life need not be associated with any particular person, but may emerge at any stage in the team life as more or less normal "growth stages" or in response to changed external conditions. For example, we can expect that the formation of the team will be a critical point in its life, for it passes from a stage of no organization to some organization. Ordinarily, the team structure develops down from the top and up from the bottom, like ice cubes in a tray. This is an empirical observation, but we can guess what might be the cause, since the extremes of ability in the team will be more easily recognized and sorted out from the rest. Nevertheless, there are times when, for instance, there are two potentially powerful leaders in the same team and the formation from the top goes unresolved for a long time. Ordinarily this situation will be counterproductive, but it should be easy to avoid by selecting teams properly. It may be necessary, if there are many potentially strong leaders in a project, to make more divisions into teams than when there are few—to avoid such formation conflicts.

Who is a potentially strong leader? That depends, as we have seen, on the work demands placed on the team. Since these demands change throughout the life of the team, leaders may rise and fall. If there are personality difficulties in accepting such changes in team structure, interpersonal conflict will develop whenever a new stage of work is reached. Thus, the problems of setting the team structure are not solved once and for all soon after the formation of the team. Since we cannot predict exactly who will be the natural leader at which times, the ideal team would be chosen as much for interpersonal skills as programming skills, but this is rarely done. Thus, we usually find conflict manifested in numerous ways—but all leading to temporary decrease in productivity.

The change from phase to phase of work may be rather gradual and thus mollify the conflict arising from changing structure, especially if

there is rich interaction among team members giving many small opportunities for conflict resolution. Sometimes, however, changes come more
quickly—perhaps instigated by some outside agency or event. Typical
crisis-provoking events in the life of a programming team are machine
malperformance, machine overload, unyielding bugs in critical sections,
difficulties in system testing of two unit-tested programs, schedule
changes, arrival of new equipment, changes in higher-level management,
and changes in specifications. No wonder it seems that crisis is the
normal situation in the life of a programming team.

Two general social-psychological observations about group behavior
are especially relevant to the crisis-ridden programming team. First of all,
it has been observed that in a crisis, members of a group more readily
accept relatively strong leadership attempts. At the same time, however,
the group becomes less patient with would-be leaders if their direction
does not produce effective solutions to group problems rather quickly.
Thus, in a programming team—which is possibly in a continual crisis—
leadership patterns may be in constant flux. Because of this reshuffling,
the more difficult the task is, the more the team comes to follow those
leaders who can actually steer the team most effectively.

We can see, then, why the democratic—or perhaps we should say
"technocratic"—organization is such a natural one for a programming
team. When selecting programmers for teams, we should try to choose
people who will fit well within such a self-shifting structure—neither too
dominant nor too passive. In training our programmers, we should try to
teach them how to follow able leaders and how to grasp leadership
opportunities when they themselves are the most qualified in the group.
And during the life of a team, we should try—if we are on the outside—
not to interfere in those democratic processes which, though seemingly
traumatic for the team and its members, will in the long run lead to most
effective team functioning.

Indeed, once the team is selected and operating, the wise manager
placed above it will adopt a "hands-off" policy with regard to its internal
structure and structure change. When, as so often happens, team members come to him to lend an authoritative opinion on their side of some
argument, he would do well to follow the pattern of the old rabbi who was
sitting in his study one day when an obviously agitated man came to
see him. The man told him a long story about an argument just concluded
with his wife. When he finished his story, he insisted that the rabbi tell
him whether he or his wife had been right.

"You're right," said the rabbi, and the man left the house beaming.
Soon, however, the man's wife appeared—even more distraught than the
man had been.

"What do you mean," she insisted, "saying that my husband was right?

You haven't heard my side of the story." And she proceeded to relate her side, finishing with a demand for a new judgment.

"You're right," said the rabbi, and the wife left satisfied. The rabbi's own wife, however, was not satisfied, for she had overheard both stories and both answers.

"How can you do that?" she demanded. "You told the husband that he was right and the wife that she was right. They can't both be right."

"You're right," said the rabbi.

SUMMARY

In many programming situations, the primary working unit is a team, not an individual. Although a vast amount of experimental data about "small group behavior" has been inherited from the social psychologists, we at present have no real studies of programming teams other than highly suggestive anecdotal material. When linked with results from social psychology, this anecdotal material can give us strong impressions of the factors affecting the life and performance of a team, factors such as:

1. Variation in individual strengths and weakness.
2. The way in which goals are set.
3. The structure of the program being produced.
4. The leadership structure imposed from the outside.
5. The gender of certain members, and the attitudes of other members about that gender.
6. The communication link between the team and the rest of its environment.
7. The technical competence or incompetence of the team leader.

In viewing the anecdotal material in contrast to the experimental situations, we find there is one difference which should put us in a state of extreme caution. In the programming situations, the span of time and the complexity of the task performed are each orders of magnitude different from anything ever attempted in an experiment by social psychologists. Tasks in social psychological experiments take an hour or a day or a week. People may be able to suppress strong feelings if they know the time period will be short; on the other hand, they may not think it important to suppress what they feel, since they will never again see the people in their group. From comparisons between teams composed of strangers and teams composed of co-workers, we do know that short-term group behavior is influenced both by past experience with team members and the expectation of having to work with them in the future. Thus, meaningful experimentation on programming teams is going to be a difficult job, at best.

However, even the observations of ongoing teams in other areas will be of questionable application to programming unless they, too, involve ongoing intellectual work of great complexity, often under stress of time and strange working conditions. Here we have the advantage of several sources in which recent work has been done—such teams as are found in hospitals and research laboratories. But even here there is something that we have that they do not—that all-wise machine sitting there like a god in judgment of our work. When a patient recovers, it is the work of the doctor; when a patient dies, it is an act of God. But when a computer program doesn't work, everyone knows—and everyone knows who is to blame.

QUESTIONS

For Managers

1. Are your hiring practices such that you get more uniformity on teams than you would like? When making up teams, do you try to see that a good "mix" of people is on each one, or do you strive in the opposite direction?

2. What are your feelings and practices about putting women on teams? About making women designated team leaders? Can you back up your feelings and practices with any empirical evidence?

3. In your organization, how much decision making is left to the working team members? How much "bit-picking" is there by managers? By yourself?

4. Do you ever do things to try to inflate the appearance of your technical competence in front of the people who work for you? Describe some of these incidents, and also some incidents in which it was discovered that your technical competence was in at least one respect inferior to one of the people who work for you. What were the consequences of that discovery, and do they justify attempting to cover up?

5. In setting your own working goals, what part is set by what is passed down from above, and what part is set by what comes up from below? Are you satisfied with this arrangement, or would you like to alter it in some ways?

6. Have you ever promoted the "second-in-command" of a team to be a team leader? If so, explain your reasoning in doing so, and describe any effects you noticed afterward?

7. Have you ever been asked to serve as judge in internal team disputes? If so, describe the incident—what you did and what happened.

For Programmers

1. What part of programming work do you do best? Are you permitted to contribute that best part of your work to your team, and is it generally recognized that it is the best part of your work?

2. What part do you play in setting the goals of your team? What part would you like to play? What part would you like others to play?

3. Has your manager ever done anything to make you doubt his honesty? If so, describe the incident, what ultimately happened to your doubt, and how your work was affected.

4. Does your team have a task specialist and a maintenance specialist that you can identify? Does your team have a "team-mother?" If you are the "team-mother," describe your experiences in that role.

5. Draw a diagram or diagrams representing the structure of your team, both formally and informally. Can you relate this diagram to the structure of the program you are working on? Can you relate it to other factors?

6. Give an account of an incident in which:
   a. A team leader was changed.
   b. A member was added to your team.
   c. A member left your team.
   d. Some crisis began to affect your team socially.

Describe the reactions of the team members when the change or crisis first became known and as it happened through time. Describe any permanent changes in team behavior—either for better or worse—that came about as a result of the change or crisis.

BIBLIOGRAPHY

The reader interested in further exploration for insights from social psychology could consult any of the following books with profit:

Allport, F. H., *Social Psychology,* Boston, Houghton Mifflin, 1924.

Asch, S. E., *Social Psychology,* Englewood Cliffs, N.J., Prentice-Hall, 1952.

Lindzey, G., ed., *Handbook of Social Psychology,* Reading, Mass., Addison-Wesley, 1954.

Krech, D., R. S. Crutchfield, and E. L. Ballachey, *Individual in Society,* New York, McGraw-Hill, 1962.

Jones, E. E. and H. B. Gerard, *Foundations of Social Psychology,* New York, Wiley, 1967.

Parkinson, C. Northcote, *Parkinson's Law,* Boston, Houghton Mifflin, 1957.

Parkinson is often cited by those who fear that making a longer schedule will simply lengthen the time it takes to do a project. Those who claim him for the benefit of their pet idea should take the time to read the entire book and see what else there is to learn from it.

Kohn, Hans, *Nationalism and Liberty: The Swiss Example,* London, George Allen and Unwin Ltd., 1956.

A little introduction for those who have become disillusioned with the possibilities of democracy, those who have forgotten them, or those who never knew them in the first place. After reading the book, another step in re-education is to go there.

Mills, H. D., *Chief Programmer Teams: Techniques and Procedures,* IBM Internal Report, January 1970.

Hopefully, Mills will publish his ideas on Chief Programmer Teams in the general literature, so they can be compared, say, with the concept of egoless programming and also subject to experimental and observational tests. Briefly, the Chief Programmer Team is patterned after a "surgical team," with the master programmer replacing the master surgeon and surrounded and supported by a Backup Programmer, a Programming Librarian, and possibly additional programmers, analysts, technical writers, technicians, or other specialists. Mills claims that such an organization "permits the application of new management standards and new technical standards to programming projects," but one wonders at the validity of the analogy to surgery, which is acknowledged to be one of the most backward specialties in a backward (technologically) field. Also, anyone who has known a few surgeons personally may wonder about how great a social contribution such an organization would be—it may be fine for those who fancy themselves Chief Programmers, but what about the rest of the workers?

Mendelssohn, Kurt, A Scientist Looks at the Pyramids, *American Scientist,* V. **59,** No. 2 (March-April 1971).

Social structure has evidently always been influenced by project structure, and vice versa. In this intriguing article, Mendelssohn explores how 5000 years ago the building of the pyramids led to the invention of the state as a social structure, and how the invention of the state led to building pyramids. All project managers should take note of this message.

6 THE PROGRAMMING PROJECT

When two teams must work together to accomplish some programming end, a coordination function emerges just as it did when two programmers had to work together. New types of social relations emerge, just as they did when teams were formed from individuals. For example, two programmers now interact both as individuals and as members of different teams—so that now their team goals may differ, even if their individual goals are very similar. The success of a team member is not only measured relative to other members of his team, but also as part of his team which is measured relative to other teams. Coordination among teams now requires a second level—or higher—of leadership, and so emerges the phenomenon of leaders whose followers are not engaged in the basic work of the project, but are leaders themselves.

Many aspects of project management from a management point of view have been discussed in published books and articles, and we shall not attempt to survey the entire field. What we shall discuss in the next few sections are a few selected aspects—aspects selected for their amenity to psychological treatment and perhaps somewhat as a corrective to certain schools of programming project management thought.

STABILITY THROUGH CHANGE

One of the most intriguing characteristics of large organizations is their ability to survive over periods of time which are longer than the time that any one member remains. This characteristic is obvious in such organizations as the United States of America, for no person is known to have lived for 200 years. Thus, the United States of America cannot take its continuing identity from some person, no matter how great. Neither Washington, nor Lincoln, nor Jefferson, nor even Joe McCarthy make up the entire story of the United States of America; yet, as obvious as this seems, many managers are unable to apply the same reasoning to their programming project.

Even in a programming team, we sometimes see the survival of the team when not a single original member remains. Indeed, the ability to survive its members can be one of the strong points of a team organization, for the work to be done is not set aside if one person happens to be removed from the scene. This ability comes, of course, from the interaction among team members, because this interaction permits the goals and accomplishments of the team to be transmitted to new members and so remain when old members depart. In a sense, a programming project or team is like a river which remains the same river even though its water is undergoing constant change.

Many project managers are unable to grasp this view of a project. Their view of the project's structure is, instead, much like that of a house—a structure that might collapse should one of the beams be removed. Their actions with respect to the people in the project—especially so-called "key" people—reflect this static view, often with disastrous consequences.

Two cases should illustrate some of the consequences of this view. In one instance, Mark S. had designed the control program for an on-line system to control an industrial process. He had then been asked to stay on to implement the control program, inasmuch as he was the only person who understood the way the system was to work. Mark was not terribly happy about this assignment, for to him the design was tantamount to the implementation. He had already implemented two systems like this and did not see much challenge in implementing a third. There were sufficient differences to keep him moderately interested for a while, but this small interest was further eroded by the necessity to work in a rather remote spot—at the plant.

Mark was a city boy, yet the type of process control system he was developing had twice before required him to work in a remote location for long periods. He was, quite simply, bored. The symptoms of his boredom became manifest when he began requesting that Bob A., a programmer of rather extensive experience, be transferred from another section of the project—where he was writing certain analytical routines—to his team, which then consisted of only himself and two trainees. Bob had expressed an interest in the control program, and this had given Mark the idea to train Bob to take over his functions so that he might move back to the city.

The project manager, however, had a different view of things. He was having difficulty getting experienced people to come out in the wilds and work on the project, so he was not about to sacrifice one of his more experienced programmers to satisfy Mark's evident desire for company. Insead of adding Bob A. to the control program team, he gave Mark another trainee.

The trainee was probably the last thing Mark wanted, for he was already doing most of the work himself and carrying the other two trainees as so much excess baggage. He wanted to get done in a hurry or get replaced, and the new man seemed only to slow him down. He renewed his request for Bob A., who was also unhappy about not getting the chance he desired; but the manager was not going to give in. He recognized that Mark was a "key" man in his project and that he was unhappy, but he didn't want to go to the trouble of finding someone to replace Bob A. In order to keep Mark happy, he called him in one day and gave him a substantial raise. But before Mark had a chance to draw a single week's pay at the new rate, he had quit and gone back to the city.

Managers are quite frequently surprised to find that a programmer quits a project very soon—sometimes immediately—after getting a solid raise. It is surprising that they should be so surprised, for there are at least two good psychological reasons for this behavior. Sometimes, the programmer interprets the raise as putting extra responsibility on him, and not everyone wants extra responsibility. The programmer reasons that if he is getting more money, more work is going to be expected of him. He is already pushing himself harder than he wants to, and the raise symbolizes the straw that would break his back.

More frequently, however, the raise is interpreted as an attempt to substitute money for something the programmer really wants. Perhaps the programmer was expecting to be named team leader, but the raise indicates to him that a money reward is being given in anticipation of the team leader spot being given to someone else. In the case of Mark S., there was a correct interpretation that the raise was an attempt to avoid giving him the qualified assistant he wanted, an attempt to bind him more closely to the project. He already felt he was staying on as a favor to the manager, and since the manager had once more refused his quite reasonable request—not for immediate removal, but merely for the chance to train a replacement—he gave up.

Notice how the manager in this case, by trying to bind Mark to the project, only succeeded in pushing him out more quickly, and more expensively, than would have been necessary. After Mark left, Bob A. was in fact chosen to replace him; but as he had no training for the job, and nobody with experience to teach him, the project foundered. Finally, more than a year after the scheduled completion date, a patchwork system was put into operation, but it proved too slow to control all the variables which had been foreseen, due to inefficiencies in the control program. As a result, the anticipated savings from the system were not realized, and after about six months of operation, the entire system was discontinued.

A similar case with a different outcome should be instructive as an illustration of the concept of stability through constant change. Henry F. played a similar role to Mark S. in a project connected with the space effort. He had designed the control program and had been made team leader of a somewhat larger and better qualified team. As he began to tire of the implementation work, he filled his time by training his two best qualified team members, Mary M. and Sid B., so that they would know as much about the system as he did. The training was made simpler by the democratic organization of the team and their practice of egoless programming, but it was not encouraged by higher management.

One of the duties that Henry had often to perform was making presentations to visiting dignitaries, for this was a highly visible, high-prestige project. Henry's presentations were always well received, and the management had twice refused him to allow Mary M. to take his place on the rostrum. Finally, he told Mary to prepare a talk and then arranged to be "sick" on the day of the visit. Management was in a panic, but they had no choice but to try Mary, and she made a superb performance.

Now the managers were willing to accept Mary as a substitute leader—in fact, they began to request her services for making presentations—and Henry decided it was time to ask for a transfer to other duties. In spite of Mary's evident competence, however, Henry's manager viewed the prospect of his leaving with horror. She was good—he acknowledged that—but Henry had been the original creator of the control program concept. Besides, Mary was a woman, and though the manager had seen her make outstanding presentations, he could not believe that a woman was capable of leading the group.

Henry had been more or less prepared for this reaction, so he now brought up the name of Sid B. Unhappily, the very success of Mary M. had made it hard for the manager to believe that Sid was *also* competent to lead the group. Henry proposed that Sid be given a chance to make a presentation, but now the manager insisted that nobody but Mary would do. So, Henry arranged for *Mary* to be "sick," with the result that management finally saw the light. Henry was ready to go, and both Mary and Sid were ready—and willing—to step into his shoes. A final offer was made to give Henry a higher management position within the project, but he had his eye on something else, something which challenged his programming imagination, so he left. But, in spite of the residual fears of the management, the project went on, and to a successful conclusion.

The differences between these two cases are instructive. No single factor can account for the success of the second as against the failure of the first. Henry was more experienced in dealing with people than Mark; he was fortunate in having a team consisting of other than trainees so that a natural succession was possible without management intervention; the managers in Henry's project were more enlightened, less rigid, and perhaps under less pressure for success; and, finally, Henry was more patient and understanding of the problem as it would be seen by the management. For Mark's manager to have been successful, he would not only have had to give Mark the assistant he wanted; but he would have had to help Mark in giving that assistant the training he needed—for Mark rather enjoyed the role of indispensable man.

The lessons to be drawn from these two cases and hundreds of others like them are clear. As a project moves forward, people learn things that make them less content with limited responsibilities or—let us call a spade a spade—are simply bored with duties which they feel are beneath their capabilities. Not every programmer wants to advance to more challenging work—some will leave if pushed too fast—but for the most part, as programmers learn they become discontented unless they can apply their knowledge. Thus, to achieve a stable project over a long period of time, a manager must encourage the project to function as a sort of programmer processing plant—with a fresh supply of trainees coming in one end and a stream of experienced leaders coming out the other, with people in the middle being bumped up one position at a time by the flow.

One other lesson needs to be drawn explicitly. A project is not a house of cards which collapses when a single "key" person is removed. At least, it *should* not be; but often, when management thinks it is, the prophecy becomes self-fulfilling. That was one of the lessons in Mark's case, for if a little less reliance had been placed upon Mark, his manager might have populated his team with other than trainees. After all, even if the "key" man is as contented as a cow with his work, people are sometimes inconsiderate enough of their managers to get sick, to get drafted, or to die. No, if a manager wants to run a stable project, he would do well to follow this simple maxim:

If a programmer is indispensable, get rid of him as quickly as possible.

MEASURING PERFORMANCE

One consequence of the size of a large project is that performance becomes more difficult to measure. Part of this difficulty stems from the scale of things, which makes it impossible for a single mind to be making the judgment of all the parts. Since progress on a program is such a subjective matter, opinions would differ about the amount of progress a particular program had made, even if it were not for other effects. But we never get the opportunity to study the different views on one program. Instead, we compare and combine different people's views of different programs into some sort of picture of project progress. In making this combination, there are numerous possibilities for psychological mischief.

The numerous stages can produce interesting effects, as a result of filtering practices in a large project. An extreme example was found in a military project that involved not only programming but creation of a worldwide communication network. The programming project itself consisted of about 75 first-level people organized into twelve teams, with the twelve team leaders organized into three groups and the three group leaders reporting to one programming project manager. Within the company doing the programming, there were also projects to design and build the central computers and special hardware, so these three project managers were organized into a team under a single company project manager. The company project manager participated in a management team consisting of the project managers from the other companies and headed by an overall project manager.

Each month, by the requirements of the contract, a progress report had to be submitted to the government. Naturally, since this was an expensive project, the report had to be printed in an impressive full-color format. This meant that the final copy for the report had to be in the hands of the printer twelve days before the report deadline—the tenth of the month following the month of the report. Thus, for example, the September report had to be in the hands of the printer by September 28th—and possibly earlier if this fell on a week-end.

In order for the overall project manager to have time to review and amend the report, he had to have each company report five working days before the printer's deadline. Allowing for mailing, this meant that the September company report would have to be finished by, say, the 20th. In this particular company, the company manager needed four working days for review of his three project managers' reports. Thus, the report of the programming project had to be in by about the 15th.

Working backwards like this, we eventually reach the individual programming team, whose report had to be made about *four days before the end of the month preceding the month of the report*. Therefore, what the individual team was reporting was not *progress* for the month, but a *prediction* for the coming month. What came out the other end, however, was labeled as progress reporting, and nobody seemed to worry about the difference.

So far, none of this is particularly psychological, except for two minor factors—the willingness of people to believe something that cannot possibly be what it pretends to be and the interesting relationship between the amount of time needed for reviewing reports, the level of the reviewer, and the amount of work actually contributed. The "higher" the reviewer, the longer he insisted he must have the reports and the less he actually did with them. Not that nothing was done—quite the contrary. At each stage of the consolidation, a certain smoothing-out was made, regardless of the content of the report.

The reasoning at each stage went something like this. If a subgroup reported an abnormally high amount of progress, the reviewer would shave the amount a trifle under the assumption that it wouldn't hurt to hold a little in reserve in case their luck changed next month. If, on the other hand, little progress was reported, the reviewer would step it up by a point or two—not wanting to call attention to any weakness and resolving to look into the trouble if things persisted. Similarly, if the list of specific problems was too long, he shortened it a bit, leaving out the least important. If it was too short, he amplified some problem or other into two separate problems.

The net result of six or seven stages of such filtering was a report that monthly presented a consistent forward progress, a few areas slightly behind or slightly ahead, a few problems solved from last month, a few new problems, and a few problems still open. There was, in short, no measurable relationship between what had been reported at the bottom and what came out the top.

Of course, what went in the bottom was only a *prediction* of progress anyway, so perhaps it didn't matter what was done to it on the way up.

In fact, when one of the team leaders in the programming project happened to get hold of a final report, he saw what had happened to his information and decided not to waste his time trying to be accurate. From that point on, instead of bothering his programmers with requests for progress predictions, he just made up a set of nice looking figures in five minutes and passed it on up the line. Within a few months, the same practice had spread to the other programming teams. And so, progress reporting went on with a minimum disturbance, or relation, to actual progress.

Where did this project go wrong in its progress reporting? We can identify a number of areas. First, there is the emphasis on *reporting,* rather than on *measuring.* Even if the entire movement up the hierarchy had been speeded to five days, there still would have been no check on the meaningfulness of the initial information. And regardless of what some "management information systems" promise, garbage in *always* yields garbage out—though the converse is not necessarily true. Furthermore, the people who were supplying the intial information—the team leaders—could see that there was no check on the meaning of the information they gave. Indeed, the only time anyone ever was called to question on his predictions was when he chose some very large or small figure. In order to minimize the number of such sessions, the leaders learned to adjust their own figures to eliminate extremes.

It is a well-known psychological principle that in order to maximize the rate of learning, the subject must be fed back information on how well or poorly he is doing. What is perhaps not so well known is that people who feel that their performance is being judged but who have no adequate information on how well they are doing will *test* the system by trying certain variations. In a reporting system like this, if the people at the bottom are not fed back information based on their input, they will start to vary the input in arbitrary ways to see the effect—to get some feedback, even at the risk of it being a poor evaluation.

In this case, the team leaders were already well on the way to learning that the only important factor in their reports was that they contain nothing striking. Then, one of them chanced to see a final report, which only completed the picture that the entire reporting scheme was an exercise in futility. One additional piece of news only confirmed an already held suspicion—and at least had the advantage of saving everyone a lot of time.

From an information-theoretic point of view, this reporting system can be seen as a series of filters—each with a certain delay and each with a certain loss of information. Information, in this sense, is carried by a report to the extent that it carries surprising news. If we read in the paper that the sun came up yesterday, that conveys little information;

but if we read that the sun did not come up, a lot of information is transmitted to us because of the unexpectedness of the event. Similarly, in a progress report, the most information is carried in those items which indicate very much or very little progress. But what happens to those items?

In psychological testing, when subjects are asked to make judgments along some linear scale, very few subjects will ever choose the end points of the scale. In fact, if a discrimination of, say, five levels is desired, a seven or nine point scale will usually be used and the end points—if they are chosen at all—are lumped in with extremes closer to the center. This effect is probably related to what we see in the filtering of the report at each stage, with each editor softening the harsh extremes left over by the last.

The extremes in this case, however, are relative to what has been left in by the previous editor, so the report moves more and more toward the center in each of its figures. In doing so, however, it is filtering out precisely the information it is supposedly designed to reveal. Is there not some way this filtering can be defeated?

To answer that question, we must identify the psychological source of the tendency to move the extremes toward the middle. One possibility is cognitive dissonance. To the extent that a manager believes that good management creates a smoothly running operation, he is likely to find fluctuations in performance inconsistent with this managerial image. From there it is a small step to believing that the fluctuations are simply misjudgments on the part of the people who are "too close to the situation to get the big picture".

Another possibility—not excluding the cognitive dissonance idea—is implied or inferred pressure from higher up. Pressure from higher up is classically recognized by management manuals as both the way to get work done and the way to destroy a reporting system. What a manager must learn to do is to motivate people to modify the way they work or the rate at which they work, not motivate them to conceal what they are doing. Therefore, he has to reward an accurate reporting of good work. Since the person doing the reporting is usually the one responsible for the work being reported, it is difficult, if not impossible, to reward him for accurate reporting at the same time he is being reprimanded for poor performance. Inasmuch as the hierarchical system of organization requires this confusion of goals for its managers, we generally see that reporting systems in this type of organization move further and further away from meaningfulness as time goes on.

Even where the project is not organized hierarchically, pressure to modify judgments of progress can come from other sources, particularly from colleagues. In a classical series of experiments, Asch demonstrated how people could be made to modify their judgment of the relative lengths of two lines simply by the pressure of knowing the opinions of others. In a typical experiment, six "subjects" sit behind a table and are asked to state which of two straight lines on a card is the longer. The only true subject is seated perhaps in the second-to-last position, and the others are told secretly what answers to give. After a few rounds of correct answers, all the "subjects" preceding the true subject say that the shorter line is the longer. This creates a pressure on the subject, who can see that they are wrong but would have to contradict them all if he is to assert the facts of the matter.

Some people, it is found, never yield to these pressures, but most do. As we might expect, more yield when the lines are close in length—but some even yield when the longer is three times as long as the shorter. Moreover, when interviewed, they *believe* in the judgments they made, as we might expect from dissonance theory.

There are many variants to these social pressure experiments, and it would pay the programming manager to study them. For our present purposes, however, it is sufficient to notice how opinions on concrete matters can be easily influenced by the announced opinions of others, and how the influence becomes more effective as the judgment becomes more difficult. Under the circumstances, it is easy to see how such a difficult and subjective judgment as the progress on a programming project could come under the influence of one's peers—either in a meeting or through reading their reports.

One other relevant result of these experiments is the effect on judgment when the pressure for the wrong selection is not unanimous. If, for example, the second "subject" is instructed to make the correct choice when all the others choose the wrong one, almost all influence of the wrong group on the true subject disappears. In other words, the presence of even a single "ally" gives many a man the courage to see things as they really are.

A striking example of this effect occurred in one project where the system testing of six subsystems together was to begin the following week on a machine that was located across the country—so that a crew of eight people would have to be supported on expenses while the testing was going on. At the final meeting of the six team leaders with their manager before system testing, a review was made of progress. Everyone agreed that all was on schedule and that the system testing crew could be sent out and set up in their hotel. After discussing various technicalities and logistic problems, the manager prepared to wind up the meeting.

"Just one more check," he said, "before we adjourn. Does anyone see any delay in having his part done by next week?"

There was a silence, which the manager allowed to prolong itself for a full sixty seconds. Finally, one of the team leaders made a slight movement of his hand, almost as if he didn't wish it to be noticed. But the manager picked it up. "George. Do you have a problem?"

George squirmed. "Just a little one."

"How little?"

"A slight delay."

"How long?"

"Umm. Maybe six weeks."

The room exploded. "Six weeks?" they all shouted at once. "How can you sit there through the whole meeting and not say anything when we're getting ready for system test and you're *six weeks* behind schedule?"

The manager calmed down the other team leaders and congratulated George on having the courage to admit his difficulties before they had gone to the expense of setting up their system test crew in a hotel. After some discussion, he persuaded George to try and get his part ready in four weeks and set a new system test schedule. Then, the manager was about to adjourn once more, but once more he asked for any further problems.

"Well," one of the other leaders put in reluctantly. "If George gets four extra weeks, I think my group should too."

"You mean," asked the manager, "that you're not ready either."

"Not exactly."

"How much not exactly?"

"I guess about six weeks. But we'll try to do it in four."

Eventually, with the floodgates thus opened, it turned out that *every* one of the six parts was behind schedule. And yet, if George hadn't taken the first step to admitting what they all knew, the meeting might have closed without a single hint of the trouble, and a fruitless system testing effort would have begun at enormous expense.

Recognizing that even a single ally can provide a safety valve to release the social pressure to produce conforming opinions, some programming projects have established a "devil's advocate" system for their management meetings. In a typical situation, a technical staff assistant to the project manager assumes this role. In every meeting, it is his duty to raise all possible negative points to opinions which all the others seem to share. By thus expressing disagreement with the group, he provides an anchor point for anyone whose lurking doubts were being restrained by the difficulty of being one against many.

Because the role of devil's advocate is institutionalized, the pressure on him is less than it is on any other member of the group who is first to express a dissenting opinion. Nevertheless, the official devil's advocate may find himself under increasing social pressure as time goes on, for the others will have difficulty in remembering that he is acting officially and is not necessarily against the others all the time. If this happens, his ability to play the role effectively may diminish just at the time when it should be increasing. Some projects attempt to avoid this personalizing of the devil's advocate role by rotating the position among the various leaders from one meeting or one report to the next. In this way, they each have the opportunity to learn that taking the negative point of view is not necessarily a negative activity.

PROJECT STRUCTURE

If a programming project is going to overcome the psychological pitfalls inherent in progress evaluation, some sort of separation between doing the work and evaluating it is essential. Probably the most serious weakness of the hierarchical organization lies in its inability to achieve this separation, because the lines of control for doing the work are simply the lines of progress reporting run in reverse. Such a system, as we have seen, generally leads to a deterioration in the quality of information communicated through it. In order to combat this deterioration, deviations from a simple hierarchic structure begin to emerge.

Many projects have a standards group whose principal duty is not production, but evaluation of the production of other groups. When the testing stage is reached, the standards group—or part of it—may become responsible for system testing, or a system testing group may have existed from the beginning. Special groups also arise for functions other than the evaluation of progress—a library group, a hardware group, a group of documentation specialists, or a systems programming group responsible for all the service programs used by the project. One type of group, which is particularly useful in projects of a high degree of visibility, is the public relations group, whose activities shield the other groups from daily interference from inquisitive outsiders. Finally, various groups may be set up for special projects of limited duration.

For instance, if there is a bug in the system which ordinary methods do not find, a special task force may be set up to root it out. To be able to establish such temporary groups, the project manager must preserve a certain amount of "slack" in the project, so that people can be extracted and used to plug the leak. No project, no matter how carefully planned, can anticipate all contingencies and set up groups in advance to meet them. Thus, the typical project may expect to experience several reorganizations throughout its lifetime.

When a reorganization is made, it sometimes reveals more worms than lifting a large flat rock. People refuse to move from one group to another, to work with a certain person or on a certain job. Others insist that they must continue working with a certain person, or on a certain job, or that they must go to a different group. Essentially, all these problems stem from a division of loyalties, much like the problems arising from an individual going to work on a team.

Each person working on a team within a project has come to accept certain of the team goals as his own. But when the team is specialized, its goals do not necessarily coincide with the overall goals of the project, or with the goals of another team. These conflicts are invariably manifest in some sort of social relations. For example, certain group tasks are considered less prestigious, more menial, than others. A documentation group, for example, is often looked down upon by members of working programming teams—with the result that the documenters become defensive and clannish, avoiding contacts with other team members as much as possible. But, unfortunately, avoidance of others is precisely what we do not want in a documentation team.

Managers are not guiltless in encouraging this type of division in a project. In the first place, they may simply have their own prejudices and permit them to become reified in the project structure. In one large project, the manager was telling some visitors about the training program they had, in order to demonstrate that he understood the concept of stability through change. He showed the visitors a list of the new trainees arranged by their final evaluation scores, and called their attention to the fine scores they "all" had achieved.

"But," asked one of the visitors, "what about these three at the bottom? Their scores seem to be way below the others."

"Oh, that," shrugged the manager. "That's nothing. They're going into the documentation group, so it's nothing to worry about."

Can we be surprised if the other groups hold a low opinion of the documenters and do not want to cooperate with them?

Any testing group is also put into a difficult relationship with other groups, because it is their job to criticize. One of our students who was working in a program testing group did a study of social interactions between members of her group and of the group whose programs they were testing. Although their offices were intermingled, there was almost no social interaction between them. Members of each group did not lunch or take coffee with members of the other, nor did they do even such simple things as borrow pencils or paper clips from one another. In conversations among members of a group, members of the other group were typically characterized as unintelligent, unfriendly, and unfair.

To some extent, this attitude of mutual dislike was encouraged by the management, for when this student tried to arrange a party for the two groups, she met with strong management resistance on the grounds that it was not "healthy" for these two groups to become very close. When she explained that she wanted the party just to test this assumption for her class in the psychology of computer programming, she was reluctantly given permission. The party was held under the pretext of a celebration of the successful completion of testing of a major piece of the project. In the week before the project, social contacts increased between the groups, and the party itself was a great success. Afterward, according to her observations, the two groups seemed to be able to carry out their mutual work with more personal contact and less traffic in recriminating memoranda.

We have no way of measuring whether or not this improved social climate led to better or worse work between these two groups. However, we do know through our experiences with egoless programming that there is no particular reason why your friend cannot also be your sternest critic. We could certainly use controlled experiments on this question. In the meantime, it probably is a good idea for a project manager not to foster conflict between groups whose work brings them into some sort of natural conflict.

Another natural conflict which arises in projects cuts horizontally instead of vertically—tending to separate the management from the working programmers. This conflict arises over the setting of goals, for project goals are not simply the sum of individual team goals. Typically, goals are set from the top down, with major decisions having been made before most of the teams have even been put together. Such a structure does not encourage democratic goal-setting within the teams, and it may therefore be difficult to get the programmers to have loyalty to the project as well as to their own group.

Many of these problems can be overcome if the management of the project can see the operation as a machine for getting the project done, rather than as a pyramid to be climbed for the satisfaction of their personal ambitions. In an engine, for example, the valves are not the "boss" of the cylinders, nor is the crankshaft the "boss" of the valves. The hierarchical organization, which so many of our projects seem to emulate, comes to us not from the observation of successful machines or natural systems, but from the nineteenth century successes of the Austrian Army. Yet it would be difficult to imagine two groups which differ more than a bunch of privates and a bunch of programmers.

In the army—old-fashioned style—every footsoldier was considered interchangeable with every other. The hierarchical organization, then, was conceived as the structure that could give the fastest and most direct coordination between these interchangeable parts. But a programming project is not a battle, regardless of appearances. There is no need for quite the speed of communication which is necessary under field conditions, nor are the things to be communicated so simple that they can be barked over a two-way radio with shells bursting in the background. What is needed in a programming project is slow, careful communication among teams of people doing very different, highly specialized tasks. Moreover, the programmer is not drafted into his job, and he is not subject to courts-martial if his program does not meet specifications. And finally, there is no danger to the officers of being hit by enemy fire or being shot in the back by their own men, so there is really no excuse for not getting down in the trenches once in a while with the troops.

COMMON SOCIAL PROBLEMS OF LARGE PROJECTS

The remoteness of the project leadership from the workers is the source of many social problems in large projects. There are, within a programming team, only two roles to fill—the programmer and the leader of programmers. Within the project, however, there emerges a third role, the leader of leaders, or nth-level manager. The differences between first-level and nth-level managers are significant, for the first-level manager maintains at least some contact with the actual work being done, and the nth-level manager only sees the work indirectly, through other managers.

Even though the nth-level manager may have originally been a programmer, which is rare enough, he has almost certainly lost any programming ability by the time he reaches these heights. Given the rapid change of programming techniques and hardware, the higher-level manager becomes obsolete even if he retains the skills he originally had and keeps them sharply honed, for those languages and those machines are no longer in use. In a small survey of working programmers, only 15 percent of the first-line managers were thought to be as skillful as the programmers themselves, and none of the higher-level managers. Some of the programmers commented that a higher-level manager sometimes came around and looked at what they were doing, but that his attempts to look knowing were perfectly transparent to the programmers. Nobody, of course, was going to risk challenging his manager's manager, but after he left, all would have a good chuckle at his expense.

Whenever a supervisor is responsible for work he does not understand, he begins to reward workers not for work, but for the *appearance* of work. Programmers who arrive early in the morning are thought to be better programmers than ones who are seen to arrive after official starting time. Programmers who work late, however, may not be rewarded because the manager is not likely to see that they are working late. Programmers who are observed talking to others are not considered to be working, because the manager has an image that programming work involves the solitary thinker scratching out secret messages to the computer.

But what else can a manager do? Since the results of programming work will not be available for many months, he cannot just wait to see whose programs run and whose don't—even if he could tell the difference. Probably the best thing the manager can do is to rely on his first-level managers, and to insist that they actually observe the work—yes, even going so far as reading the programs. Lurking around and dropping in on the programmers to give them the impression that he is watching isn't going to fool anybody.

One programmer we interviewed told us that he had "earned" a fat raise by preparing a program that produced some output that the project manager thought he understood. When the project manager dropped into his office, the programmer took out this program to show him, and asked his advice on how to handle a certain situation. The manager gave him some advice—which would have been worthless even if the program had been part of the system they were producing—and left beaming. A few days later, the programmer made a point of thanking the manager in the lunch room, in front of his lower-level managers; and a few days after that, he got his raise.

Being thanked for some technical advice must have elevated the status of the project manager in the eyes of his fellows, for such direct performances are rare for managers. At the working level, status is largely determined by the ability to perform technical tasks—such as legendary feats of debugging. But for the manager, such avenues to earning status are not normally open, though he may often bore everybody by recalling the good old days when they were. As he climbs the management ladder, it becomes less and less easy for him to establish his technical superiority, so he comes to rely more and more on symbols of status to give him his authority.

Status symbols are always amusing—to anyone outside the system. Within programming, some special status symbols not found in other professions are worth mentioning even though the subject is well-treated elsewhere. For instance, we have a card file in the office. At certain low levels, the card file is a positive status symbol over ordinary programmers, because it implies that its owner cannot leave his important programs unguarded. At higher levels, of course, the card file must be removed, lest the observer should think that one was too close to the actual programming. In shops which run a closed machine room, anyone with permission to enter the machine room is obviously more important than anyone who does not—though usually it is safest to give such permission only to those high enough so that they really have no business being there. Where access to the machine room is not the issue, priority of running jobs may be, especially if each person's priority is listed—in descending order—in a conspicuous place. It must be tremendously satisfying to the project manager to know that his job would be run ahead of everyone else's—if he ever had one.

Lately, the terminal has become the number one status symbol for programming managers. No matter how short of terminals the poor workers may be, the project manager must have his terminal by his side for all his guests to see. What he uses it for is rarely known, or at least is a well-guarded secret. What the casual visitor usually sees is a hoked-up demonstration or a game of Nim or Spacewar, depending on the type of terminal. One of the most beautiful of such demonstrations consisted of displaying a PERT chart of some project function on the CRT. When the manager pushed a button, the critical path in the chart was illuminated with greater brightness than the other paths. Then, by pointing the light pen at one of the nodes, a deletion was made and the new chart was displayed. One more button push and the new critical path was illuminated. This demonstration never failed to impress visitors with the great control the manager had over his project. Of course, it was a complete fake—all four patterns were prestored in the system, and they were the *only* four patterns available.

One of the classic status symbols from which programming managers are not exempt is the secretary or the administrative assistant. The difference between these two titles is that secretaries are always female, and administrative assistants may be of either gender. The prettiest secretary may be a status symbol—though an ugly one may be taken as indicating that one's status is so high that one rates a *competent* secretary.

This association of women with the menial tasks of an office and of good looks with poor brains is the source of one of the more serious social problems in large projects—the sex problem. One of the women in our class undertook to study the attitudes about women programmers of men in her project. The picture that emerged from this survey was of men (especially the older ones) who plastered over their insecurities by belittling the women who were involved in professional work. Women working as secretaries did not come in for this abuse—presumably, they "knew their place." But anything the women programmers did was interpreted in the worst possible light.

For example, if a woman was seen talking to another woman, the tendency was to call it "gossip." If a woman talked to a man, it was "flirting". But when men talked to men, there was no special name—it was just "business," even when the business was baseball, basketball, or bowling. In one section of the project, there were only two women, and they had been put into the same team because the manager thought they would "like each other's company." Whenever the manager saw the team leader, he would ask how "they" were doing. Everyone understood who "they" were.

Most men, of course, will dismiss these observations as not being serious. "Of course men talk about women in those ways, but a little friendly joking never hurt anybody." Even the women who are not professionally involved tend to support the system by taking every opportunity to express disbelief that other women could "do such complicated things" —meaning, "compete with men." But to the women involved, the matter is deadly serious—though they are not about to let any curious male know about it. In many projects, women are systematically excluded from management positions, or management positions above the first level. Thus, a woman who has such aspirations knows that her future is limited as long as she stays on this project—not a very healthy way to inspire participation.

To be sure, male managers can offer all sorts of rationalizations for such policies, but such rationalizations accompany any prejudice. Individual cases can be called upon to support each erroneous belief, but that is true of any prejudice, too. Anybody who thinks Scotsmen are cheap can point to an example of a Scot who saved little pieces of string; anyone who thinks Sicilians are gangsters can show you a newspaper clipping to "prove" his case; and any manager who won't promote a woman can point to a case where a woman was promoted and then left to have a baby or to follow her husband to his new job. And, of course, if a woman doesn't have babies or follow her husband, he says, "What kind of a woman is she?"

Each prejudice has its price. In a programming project, the exclusion of anyone from any position on any basis besides lack of competence robs the project of the best possible performance. Moreover, once one faction begins to feel that they are being judged differently from others, they will begin to act differently. Although prejudices against other groups can also be serious matters, the prejudice against women is so common in programming that it merits special attention. Possibly the greatest single action to relieve the shortage of programming and programming management talent would be to start treating women as true equals—if indeed they are only that.

SUMMARY

At the end of 1969, the second NATO conference on Software Engineering was held, and the tone was already much changed from the one held the previous year. *People* were beginning to come into the picture, and the reason is not hard to find in the proceedings. We may quote this comment from Joel Aron as most clearly representing the problem:

> We made a study of about a dozen projects, though not in a very formal manner. However, our results were convincing enough to us to set up a course on programming systems management.
>
> The nature of the study was "Why do our projects succeed or fail?" We took as "successful" a project that met its requirements on schedule within the budgeted dollars and satisfied the customer. On this basis, out of 10 or 12 projects that we examined, we had one success and a whole lot of failures.
>
> We analyzed the reasons for failure, as given to us by the project managers, and by people who had performed previous evaluations of the projects. They gave various reasons behind the failure of the projects, *virtually all of which were essentially management failures.* We ran into problems because we didn't know how to manage what we had, not because we lacked the techniques themselves. (Emphasis added.)

Over the years, I have had the opportunity to work with Joel Aron as he has crusaded to get people to believe what he says about programming projects. The sad part of it is that most of the computing fraternity remains unconvinced. On the very next page of the proceedings, C. A. R. Hoare, a very brilliant man, says:

> Basically all problems are technical. If you know what you want to do and you have the necessary technical background, there is no point in making a great management problem out of it. Obviously a certain amount of resource control and personnel work have to go on but that's all.

Hoare is right, in a certain sense, but it doesn't work out that way. People are trying to cope with problems they don't understand, and those they don't know they don't understand—in itself a failure of management. We have tried to show how a project can go down the drain even when it does have the technical capability—for if people remain as unconvinced as Mr. Hoare, there will be no fruitful study in this area. The picture is only sketched in broad outline with a few anecdotal details, but it must be filled in, or we must stop trying to do programming projects until it is.

QUESTIONS

For Managers

1. How long have you been in charge of your present group? How many of the original people remain? Make a list of the people who have left and give the reasons for their departure. What sort of provisions do you make for this kind of turnover?

2. Have you ever had someone quit soon after a promotion or a raise? Was the promotion or raise a substitute for something you would not or could not give that person? What reasons were given for quitting, and what do you think the real reasons were?

3. Do you have an indispensable woman or man working for you? If so, what would you do if she or he got killed or was sick for six months?

4. In what ways do you modify information as it passes you on its way up through your organization? What does your manager do to reward you or punish you for accurate information?

5. Which do you reward most, accurate information or pleasing information? Do your programmers know what the information you require is used for? Do they see the final reports which are the destination of their information? If not, why not?

6. At your next management meeting, try to play devil's advocate on some point on which there is otherwise common agreement. Record the pressures you feel, and the reactions of those trying to bring you into line by other than rational arguments.

7. Do you favor certain of your teams as being more important? Do you see certain of the teams as more prestigious than others? Which of your teams have the greatest morale problems?

8. Do you encourage competition between groups with conflicting interests in order to stimulate production? How can you measure whether or not this strategy is working?

9. Look around your office and make a list of the status symbols you find there. If you can't find any, go to some other manager's office and make a list of *his* status symbols. Then go back to your office and try to make another list.

10. Are women in your organization treated any differently than men? In what situations, and for what reasons? Are the women in your organization contributing less than the men, or don't you know?

For Programmers

1. Have you ever felt that you were being forced into staying in a position that you wanted to leave? What methods were used to force you? How did it affect your work in that position?

2. Have you ever been given money as a substitute for something else you wanted, such as a different job, more help, better access to the machine, or different working hours? Did the money satisfy you so that you no longer wanted the other thing?

3. Are you indispensable in your position? If so, what are you doing about it, making yourself more or less indispensable?

4. Do you know what happens to your progress reports or time sheets? Do you ever wonder? Do you ever ask?

5. Have you ever yielded to group or managerial pressure against your best technical judgment? Describe the situation and the consequences.

6. From the point of view of prestige, how do you rate the following types of assignments, and why?
   a. Documentation
   b. Program library work
   c. System testing
   d. Progress reporting
   e. Standards work
   f. Diagnostic programming
   g. Education

7. What status symbols do you have in your office? See Manager's question 9.

8. What is the attitude toward women in your organization? If you are a woman, what does that attitude do to you and your work?

BIBLIOGRAPHY

Naur, Peter, and Brian Randell, eds., Software Engineering, *NATO Science Committee Report,* January 1969.

Buxton, J. N., and Brian Randell, eds., Software Engineering Techniques, *NATO Science Commitee Report,* April 1970.
These two conferences brought together some of the leaders of the international programming community to discuss problems of controlling software projects. Although the reports cannot be expected to capture the full vitality of the conferences, the editors have done a fine job, and there is much information on software engineering to be gleaned from them—although there is not nearly enough from the point of view of the behavioral sciences.

Asch, S. E., Studies of Independence and Submission to Group Pressure: I. A Minority of One Against a Unanimous Majority, *Psychological Monographs,* **7,** Series No. 416, 1956.
This is the classical and original work on opinions and social pressure, and it should be required reading for all technical people.

Kantowitz, Leo, *Women and the Law: The Unfinished Revolution,* Albuquerque, University of New Mexico Press, 1969.
A fine antidote for those who feel that women are treated equally with men in the United States, as seen through the codification of laws over time.

Friedan, Betty, *The Feminine Mystique,* New York, Norton, 1963.
One of the first of the new "women's liberation" books, giving the way our world looks to a woman who has her wits about her and her consciousness raised.

Gagne, Robert M., ed., *Psychological Principles in System Development,* New York, Holt, Rinehart, and Winston, 1962.
This book is a good job documentation of the "Systems Development" movement of the fifties, which was largely a baby of the military, through such agencies as

RAND and SDC, with some participation from the universities. It is not clear that the "movement" was ever very successful at accomplishing anything but getting large grants of money from the government, and certainly its influence on non-military work has so far been rather small. The level of work in the collection is uneven, ranging from superficial platitudes to detailed system diagrams and photographs, and there is much overlap. The "psychological" aspect is largely concerned with how to view people as components in complex system—the human engineering approach and the personnel approach. There is really nothing of value on computer programming as such, and the main interest in this book is discovering why this approach does not succeed in programming.

Meyer, Marshall W., Automation and Bureaucratic Structure, *American Journal of Sociology* **74,** 3(1968), pp. 256-264.

This study, which is a survey of 254 departments of finance at state, county, and city levels, shows the differences in structure between the data-processing sections and the other parts of the organization. Among other things, first-line supervisors supervise more people, and higher-level ones fewer people, giving a narrow organization with a wide bottom. This expansion of the span of control at the lowest level and extension of the number of levels to reach the top is just what we don't need in computer programming, where first-line managers already don't know enough about what their people are doing, and communication up the tree is already too slow and unreliable.

PART 3

PROGRAMMING
AS AN
INDIVIDUAL
ACTIVITY

> I have in mind the only liberty worthy of that name, liberty consisting in the full development of all the material, intellectual, and moral powers latent in every man; a liberty which does not recognize any other restrictions but those which are traced by the laws of our own nature, which, properly speaking, is tantamount to saying that there is no restriction at all. . . .
>
> Mikhail Bakunin*

At the beginning of this book, we set out to account for some of the variation in programming performance among different programmers. We have seen that much of that variance can be accounted for by social factors—much more than we might have believed from casual considerations. But, no matter how much variance is attributable to social factors, there will always remain a residue. No matter how similar the structure of two programming groups might be, they will produce different finished products. In this section, we shall try to account for some of those differences by examining factors centering in and around the individual.

How shall we proceed? Although little psychological research has been done directly on programmers doing programming, we could imagine that a psychological study had been done and think about how we would analyze it to account for differences in performance by different subjects.

The first thing an experimental psychologist would ask is "Did all subjects do the same task?" Even in a carefully controlled experiment, there are many differences that might creep into what the subjects were doing, or thought they were doing. Moreover, if we want to compare two different experiments, we are obliged to look first for any difference in task before we can draw meaningful conclusions. Certainly in programming, where every task is different from every other in a multitude of ways, our first investigations would have to be into task differences.

The next thing a psychologist would consider would depend on the object of his experiment. If he were trying to measure individual differences, he would concentrate on keeping all aspects of the environment as constant as possible so that they could be excluded from consideration. He would not, for example, give a test to some subjects in an air-conditioned room and others in a room that was overheated, for the room temperature could easily be a more dominant influence on performance than the individual differences he was trying to measure.

But if the psychologist were trying to measure the effect of temperature on performance, he would make exactly this kind of variation. Instead of holding the environmental variables constant, he would try to hold individual differences down to a minimum. To do this, he might try giving the same test many times to the same individuals—although he would then have to contend with learning effects, something we, too, must consider.

In any case, we are interested in *both* the effects of environment and the differences among individuals, so the order in which we consider them is not really important—as long as we give both their due.

In the following chapters, we have broken down the factors which, in sum, constitute what psychologists call "individual variations." That is, if two people are given the identical task to perform in the identical environment (which is, we all realize, an impossibility; yet it is a necessary conceptual fiction), the differences in the way they behave can be attributed to one or more of these factors. The individual variations that interest us may be further subdivided into the general categories of "personality," "intelligence," and "training" or "experience."

7 VARIATIONS IN THE PROGRAMMING TASK

"**P**rogramming"—like "loving"—is a single word that encompasses an infinitude of activities. A high school student fiddling around with a BASIC terminal is programming, but so is an engineer trying to produce the tightest possible microprogram for a special-purpose on-line computer. Is there anything in common between these two activities besides their name?

The programming literature usually assumes that there *is* something in common between the activities of the high-school student and the engineer, and this assumption is probably correct, as far as it goes. But perhaps much of the difficulty in trying to account for differences in programming performance arises from a lack of refinement in our classification of the activities called programming. After all, we could create a theory of economic activity by flying over the United States at 5000 meters, but we couldn't say much more than that "everybody is driving around

121

in all directions." To account for more details of behavior, we would have to get closer to the ground, and this is what we shall have to do if we want to remove some of the mystery from programming.

PROFESSIONAL VERSUS AMATEUR PROGRAMMING

The high school student and the engineer represent two ends of a rich spectrum of programmers. These ends may or may not be different, but nothing antagonizes the professional programmer more than to hear an amateur—having just completed a six-statement program in BASIC to find roots of a quadratic eqaution—discourse on the theory and practice of programming. We know well, of course, that this vehemence could be a symptom of *lack* of any difference between the two activities, for such a lack would put the professional in a much diminished stature. Although some professional programmers may indeed be no more than hacks camouflaged by esoteric obscurities and some amateurs might be able to gain a deep appreciation of programming through the writing of a single short program, there *is* a difference.

Perhaps the deepest differences emanate from differences in the ultimate user of the program. Almost invariably, the sole intended user of an amateur's program is the amateur himself, whereas the professional is writing programs which other people will use. To be sure, the professional oftentimes finds himself writing a program for his own use—to generate test data or to evaluate the performance of an untried algorithm, to name but two instances. And, indeed, when doing this kind of work, the professional commonly slips into amateurish practices. But the main thrust of his work is directed toward use of the program by other people, and this simple fact conditions his work in a number of ways.

Because the amateur will be the user of his own program, he has the choice of doing his thinking either before or after programming. Consider, for example, a student who wants to write a program to find roots of quadratic equations. Ideally, he is sitting at a terminal, for terminals are well suited to post-programming thought. He decides that he will probably need some input. This requires that he choose some names for variables. Here the small size of the program and its complete isolation from other programs give him a big boost—without his awareness, of course—for he may choose whatever names first come to mind, such as a, b, and c. In simply following the notation of high school algebra, he does not think at all about possible conflicts with other symbols, standards which must be observed, or even with declaration of attributes. No, he merely types something like

GET LIST (A, B, C);

After adding some other program parts in a similar way, he will be ready to try his program. Upon initiation of processing, the terminal will pause in request for data. Since it is his own program, he does not need any prompting about what data are expected at this time, so he has saved at least such coding as a preliminary

PUT LIST ('ENTER A, B, AND C');

He also knows the order in which things are required, and the simplified input system of his language permits him to enter his data in such diverse forms as

1 2 3

1,2,3

1, 2, 3

1.0, 2.0, 3.0

1E0, 2.0E+0, .3E+1

Moreover, if he should happen to slip and enter

1A, 2, 3

the system will reject the first value without his having had to program an error-handling routine or document the reasons why such a data item is rejected. He knows what is expected, for he wrote the program.

Even more subtle problems can be handled for him because he can think *after* programming. When he enters such a case as 1, 2, 3, he will probably find that some later statement coughs up the data because he will be trying to take a square root of a negative number ($b^2 - 4ac$). He gets the diagnostic automatically—without any forethought or foreprogramming —and probably realizes rather quickly what the problem is. He may then simply decide that he doesn't want complex roots anyway, in which case the problem disappears by definition. Only when the programmer himself is defining the problem is this sort of simplification possible, for the professional programmer would at least have had to leave the terminal and find someone to authorize a change or clarification of specifications.

If the amateur does decide that he needs complex roots, his task is still much simpler than that of the professional in making the necessary modifications. Even when he has finished the program, his job remains simpler, for when he is finished, he merely has to forget about it. The professional, on the other hand, has to put it into a neat package and send it out into the cold world—from which it may return to him bearing caustic comments, comments whose sense has to be considered for subsequent modifications. A true professional, of course, would have constructed the program in such a way that modifications will not be overly involved—but that was another thing he had to think about when writing.

Even if the program is not intended for other eyes at all, the professional cannot quite forget about it in the same way as the amateur. For instance, if the program is just stored in the terminal system, the user will eventually receive notification to clean up his storage. The professional has to recall each of the programs in his library, for some will still be needed. The amateur, however, probably has only one program, so he instructs the system to erase it—or lets the erasure be done automatically by default. But woebetide the professional who lets the system erase his library! No, he must drop what he is doing and check his long library list before the deadline comes around, or all his work will be gone with the wind.

Many years ago, when programming systems were rudimentary, the difference between the professional and amateur was not nearly so pronounced. Today, however, so many of the things that amateurs want to do have been made implicit in our systems that the gulf is a wide—and widening—one. Paradoxically, however, as the gulf has widened, the amateurs have become less and less aware of it, for they have become less and less aware of what the system is doing for them. Just as a good manager faces the problem that his employees are unaware of his management, so does the systems designer suffer because the better his system does its job, the less its users know of its existence.

And speaking of managers, they can be the most amateur of amateurs when it comes to programming. A few years ago, one firm decided to try to give its executives a course that would make them appreciate the problems of their professional programmers. Inasmuch as these were *executives,* each was assigned a professional programmer as "assistant" for the duration of the course, the climax of which was a problem which each executive had to program "for himself."

To enhance the executives' appreciation for the problems faced by programmers, this work session was interrupted by frequent trivial phone calls, meetings, and small changes in specifications. The executives got the point—that executives could increase programmer productivity by "sheltering" their staff rather than being the major source of disturbance. But they also took away another—deeper rooted—idea. After all, in spite of all these disturbances, they *had* managed to get their program working, hadn't they? Sure, they had a little help from their "assistants," but not much, really. So, if they could get a program done on time, why couldn't their programmers? And what was so hard about programming, anyway, if they could master it in a week?

This entire impression was based on a combination of illusions of the same sort that make any amateur unable to appreciate the abyss which separates him from the professional. First, there was the semantic illusion which equates the "program" they wrote—a trivial problem involving compound interest calculation which could have been better solved using a log table or slide rule—with the "programs" written by their staff—operating systems, compilers, utilities, and the like. Second, there was the illusion that their assistants were "not helping them much"—an illusion based on a lack of understanding of the complexities of programming—the very complexities which the assistants were supposed to shield them from lest they take away a bad feeling about programming engendered by being unable to complete their little problem. And so, the very efforts directed at giving the executives a better appreciation for the problems of the programmer resulted in precisely the opposite effect.

Better appreciation of programming by managers is needed: a case in point is the fact that a manager could even begin to believe that he could learn in a week what the professional has learned through years of experience. Indeed, it is a homily that the difference between the professional and the amateur programmer lies in the superior past experience of the professional. But one could also contend that an equally important difference lies not in the programs each has *previously* written, but in those he will write *in the future.* The amateur, being committed to the results of the particular program for his own purposes, is looking for a way to get the job done. If he runs into difficulty, all he wants is to surmount it—the manner of doing so is of little consequence. Not so, however, for the professional. He may well be aware of numerous ways of circumnavigating the problem at hand. He may even employ one of them for the immediate purpose of getting the job done. But his work does not stop there; it begins there. It begins because he must *understand* why he did not understand, in order that he may prepare himself for the programs he may someday write which will require that understanding.

The amateur, then, is learning about his *problem,* and any learning about programming he does may be a nice frill or may be a nasty impediment to him. The professional, conversely, is learning about his *profession*—programming—and the problem being programmed is only one incidental step in his process of development.

The other side of this observation is that the professional never quite takes any problem as seriously as does the amateur. He has had bugs before, and he will have them again. This difference in attitude is a source of constant friction between the two types: the professional is very tired and a bit irritated by the unending stream of amateurs waving their printouts in his face and condemning the machine, the operator, the system, the keypuncher, the language, or the government. The amateur, on the other hand, can see that the professional does not even *care* that his means and standard deviations are not going to be ready in time for inclusion in the proceedings of the conference.

WHAT THE PROGRAMMER IS TRYING TO DO

There is an asymmetry in the relationship between amateur and professional programmers, because the one cannot appreciate the complexities that the other faces. Nonetheless, the professional often commits the error of deriding the work of the amateur for not being sufficiently professional; and this error is much less excusable than that made by the amateur in underestimating the distance between himself and the professional. The professional, if he is truly professional, should know better, whereas the amateur cannot. The amateur may fail to program an elaborate error-handling routine because he doesn't know how or doesn't even know what an error-handling routine *is*. But then, why should he know, if he doesn't need one? Isn't it much worse for the professional to insist on treating a tiny one-time program for personal use as if it were an operating system intended to be used by thousands of people for five or ten years?

Programs, like any other man-made objects, are designed—or should be designed—with a definite lifespan and scope of application in mind. Like the "Deacon's Masterpiece," which was "built in such a logical way it ran a hundred years to the day," a program should have neither over-designed or underdesigned parts. Yet it is an occupational disease of programmers to spend more time on those program parts that present, for some reason, the most intellectual challenge rather than on those that require the most work.

A case in point is the semi-professional programmer who was commissioned by a physics professor to write a program to find the inverses of some matrices. As there were too many matrices to keep in storage at once, he needed a routine for reading them from tape one at a time for processing. He had little experience with input-output programming, so he decided that this would be a good chance to learn something, and he set out to get some advice.

"How can I program the input from tape so as to buffer the input from processing?" he asked a somewhat more professional colleague. Being somewhat more professional, the colleague didn't answer the question, but put one of his own.

"*Why* do you want to buffer the input?"

"To save time, of course."

"Have you estimated *how much* time you will save?"

"Not exactly, but it will be a lot, because there are a lot of matrices."

"*How many?*"

"I don't know exactly. A lot."

"*Approximately* how many?"

"Maybe a hundred."

"Good. And *how large* are they?"

"Ten by ten."

The colleague did a quick calculation on the blackboard which showed that these matrices would require about one minute to read.

"See," said the semi-pro, in triumph. "That's a lot of time."

"Perhaps—or perhaps not. *How many times* will you run this program?"

"What do you mean?"

"I mean, if you write a buffering routine, you're going to have to test it, and I doubt if you can do that with less than one minute of machine time. So if you only have one set of matrices, I'd advise you to forget it. Just the computer time in testing will cost more than you could possibly save—not to speak of your time."

"But you don't understand," said the semi-pro, who was not willing to see his chance of writing a new and interesting program slip away. "This has got to be an *efficient* program!"

His colleague should have been discouraged by this response, but could not stop himself from trying to rephrase the arguments. But, alas, it was all in vain, and the next time he chanced to see his friend—which was the next semester—he was still having problems getting his buffering routines working. The poor physics professor, still waiting for his matrices, was completely unaware of what was going on—but was mildly flattered that his programming problem had proved so complex.

The moral of this tale—and a hundred others like it—is that each program has an appropriate level of care and sophistication dependent on the uses to which it will be put. Working above that level is, a way, even less professional than working below it. If we are to know whether an individual programmer is doing a good job, we shall have to know whether or not he is working on the proper level for his problem. The same talents or personality that make a person an excellent amateur programmer may make him singularly unsuited for being a professional one; but the lack of ability to adjust his working behavior to the problem at hand will always make him unsuited.

Usually, though, the programmer fails to adjust his activities to the problem at hand because he does not know what the problem at hand is. That is, he *assumes* that certain things are wanted—perhaps on the basis of what he knows how to do, or on the basis of what was wanted in the last job he programmed—but he never finds out what was wanted until the job is finished. Working for buffering is not a bad thing in itself, but only in terms of what a particular program is going to be used for. If the matrices were 100 by 100, and if there were going to be thousands of them, the goat of our last tale could have been a hero.

There have been very few studies of programming performance, but what few there have been all seem to have suffered from a lack of appreciation for the problem of ambiguous programming objectives. It is not enough to give a carefully selected bunch of programmers the same problem to work on and then measure their "performance." Any psychologist knows that subjects must be given explicit instructions on what they are to try to achieve, and that even that is not enough in most cases. For instance, if we are given a list of words to match with their synonyms, are we supposed to work for speed or for accuracy? And if the psychologist tells us to be as fast as we can, do we really follow that instruction at the risk of making truly careless errors? Well, that depends on a number of factors—because some people are inherently more meticulous than others. Psychologists lose many nights of sleep over such questions, and perhaps programmers and their managers should share a bit of that concern.

In order to test for the influence of assumed goals on programming preformance, we conducted a small experiment. Four programmers were asked to work on the same problem—a nontrivial one which would take perhaps one-fifth of their time for ten weeks. Although the problem specifications were otherwise as identical as a Xerox machine could make them, two of the programmers were given a last page which differed from the last page given to the other two. For one pair, the last page read as follows:

Your objective on this project should be to get a fully debugged program which is as efficient as possible, in the sense of using the least CPU time possible. You may use as much core storage as needed, up to 128K. Although you are not working for fast completion of the project, you should plan to reach the final test level by the end of the ninth week.

For the other pair, the last page read as follows:

Your objective on this project should be to get a fully debugged program in as short a time as possible without considering the efficiency in speed or space of the program insofar as those factors will slow down the completion of the program. However, you should not spend any more time on the project than the normal work load allotted (one-fifth time). You must, however, keep the program size less than 128K.

By making the instructions explicit, we hoped to measure the type of variation attributable to different understandings of the objectives of the project. None of the programmers knew that the others were working toward different objectives. At the end of the project, however, the difference in performance between the pairs was striking. Those who were asked to complete the program as quickly as possible used, on the average, only two-fifths of the machine time and one-third of the individual time used by the other group. Their finished programs, on the other hand, were, on the average, about ten times slower! (See Figure 7-1, "Index Problem.")

This experiment was repeated with another group of programmers and a different type of program, but one designed to be about equally complex. Here the possibilities for spectacular savings were not so great, but again the "fast-completion" group averaged two-fifths the machine time and one-third the individual time used by the other group. The "efficiency" group, in this case, achieved about 50 percent more speed in their programs. (See Figure 7-1, "File Problem.")

This pair of experiments gives a nice contrast, for it shows that the gains to be had from striving for efficiency depend on the type of problem as much as anything else. Thus, we could never make a general statement about how much effort toward efficiency is justified, even if we were equally interested in efficiency on all problems. But the important result from the experiments is that a large proportion of the variance between

	INDEX PROBLEM		FILE PROBLEM	
	MEAN # OF RUNS	MEAN EXECUTION TIME	MEAN # OF RUNS	MEAN EXECUTION TIME
EFFICIENT PROGRAM	78	1	60	1
FAST PROGRAMMING	30.5	10	27	2

Figure 7–1 Effect of environment on performance.

programmers on any job can be attributed to a different conception of what is to be done.

When we investigated in more detail the source of added machine time and programmer time for the "efficiency" groups, we found that much of it could be accounted for in the way the programmers reacted to unanticipated difficulties. In the "fast-completion" group, when some method was not working out, it was simply dropped and another one was substituted; but when the "efficiency" programmers had trouble, they were loath to change their approach because they would then have to sacrifice some efficiency. Thus, though two programmers in different groups might have started out with the same method in mind, the "fast-completion" programmer wound up with something rather different—but he did finish while the other was still struggling.

It is also important to notice that the source of the difficulty is more or less irrelevant to this result. In one case, for instance, a compiler bug caused trouble with a feature that was critical to one of the possible approaches to a problem. Although both groups encountered the same bug and neither could do anything about it, the "fast-completion" group dropped the approach long before they ever found out that it was a compiler bug, and the others stuck with it until the bitter end, only to have to drop it when the source of the difficulty was uncovered. Although this turn of events may have been "unfair" to this group, it was nothing that does not happen thousands of times a day in computing centers all over the world. From a psychological point of view, the lesson is clear. The same objective event (a compiler bug, a difficult algorithm, or what-have-you) affects a project in different ways according to the objectives—even though they be unstated—of the project. Therefore, if we are to measure programmer performance, or language performance, or operating system performance, or anything else, we must be sure that everybody is truly working on the same problem.

In real life, of course, we do not usually have more than one group working on "the same" program at a time. Thus, we may not be aware that the group is working toward a different set of objectives than, say, their manager thinks they have. Consequently, unless we take precautions to see that *all* the objectives are communicated—and remain communicated—we should not be surprised when the program does not meet schedules or runs inefficiently, or uses too much storage, or what-have-you.

But let's back off a moment, for "real life" is never so simple. There is a certain danger in communicating objectives: objectives can change estimates! In our experiment, after we had found the effect of instructions on performance, we went back and checked the estimates given by each programmer. The programmers had estimated number of batch runs and number of elapsed days to complete each project, and the comparison of

	RUNS		DAYS		
	ESTIMATED	ACTUAL	ESTIMATED	ACTUAL	% LATE
EFFICIENT PROGRAM	22	69	48	76	75
FAST PROGRAMMING	39	29	68	65	25

Figure 7–2   Effect of environment on estimating.

their actual and estimated runs and days is shown in Figure 7-2. It is easy to see what happened. Those who were instructed to finish as fast as possible were motivated to be far more conservative in their estimates of time to completion, and they actually performed much better than their estimates and much better than the other group—even though the other group had been much more optimistic in their estimating.

One interesting sidelight is that there was one person who absolutely refused to make a time estimate, and he was in the group asked to do the job as quickly as possible. He was also the only one who got appendicitis in the middle of the project (though fortunately he was a fifth person in that group). Programming managers should take a long, hard look at this figure before they set down the goals for their next project. If a goal is set explicitly, there are two effects: programmers work toward that goal at the possible expense of another goal, and programmers will be far more conservative (or accurate) in estimating how well they will meet the goal. Estimates on goals not emphasized will probably be completely unreliable, both because they are not made carefully and because they are not important enough to resist being sacrificed to other goals. Unfortunately, this modification of estimates was not anticipated by the experimenters, so we neglected to ask the programmers to estimate the efficiency of their programs, but it seems reasonable that the same type of result would have obtained—but reversed for the two groups.

Should this result prove general, it would clarify somewhat the mysteries of Parkinson's Law and might thereby relieve the nightmares of numerous managers. When Parkinson said that "work expands to fill the time allotted," he was making us aware that the very existence of schedule goals can influence the rate of work. But now we see that the very existence of schedule *as a goal* can influence "the time allotted." The reason work can expand to fill the time allotted is the existence of other goals whose importance relative to scheduling is not made clear. Perhaps we might follow this line of reasoning and begin to understand what fallacies underly the generally accepted conclusion that programming projects can never be done on time.

STAGES OF PROGRAMMING WORK

Another fallacy which we shall have to lay to rest is that "programming" is some sort of uniform effort requiring a set of uniform talents. For the professional, at least, the job of getting from specifications to delivered program demands various kinds of work, which, in turn, demand various talents.

In a properly organized project, not every programmer need have all of the talents required to produce complete programs, since work may be allocated according to individual abilities. Indeed, it may be that suitability for work in one stage of programming makes one more or less unsuited for work in another. The job of system design calls for an eye which never loses sight of the forest, whereas the job of debugging may require that every tree—even every branch or leaf—be seen with utmost clarity. The job of coding often requires squeezing out every drop of redundancy, and the job of documentation may require that simple sentences be plumped up to paragraph size.

Just as a successful programmer may become a failure when moved into a management position, so may a successful designer become a handicap when the time comes to debug a system. On the other hand, the man who might have helped us most in debugging may have been pushed out of the project during the design phase because his peculiar talents were neither needed nor appreciated at that time. If we are to ensure that the proper talents are available when needed, we shall have to classify the work that programmers do into somewhat more refined categories than the simple term "programming" covers.

Programming is often described as a process moving from problem definition through analysis to flow diagramming, then coding, followed by testing, and finishing with documentation. Although this rough view contains some truth, it distorts the truth in several ways. First of all, the actual sequence is not so fixed, because, for example, documentation may precede testing, coding, flow diagramming, and even analysis. Secondly, not all steps need be present, as when we are recoding a program for a new machine or language. Thirdly, it need not be a *sequence* at all—and, in actual practice, rarely is. Who has not experienced a problem definition that changes as discoveries are made in analysis, flow diagramming, coding, testing, and documentation? Or who has ever seen a flow diagram that remains unmodified throughout the coding—or code that remains unmodified throughout testing?

If we are to study programming from a psychological point of view, we must decompose these complex activities into simpler ones—that we have established. And yet, because of the cyclic, or iterative, nature of the programming process, even such a decomposition as we have made above is too refined. These divisions lack sharp boundaries, or perhaps have no boundaries at all. To be sure, if we ask a programmer what he is doing, he will say "coding" or "debugging" without any hesitation. Moreover, the system of "progress reporting," which is in effect in most installations, tends to force people to put their work in sharper categories than really exist. In this way, people are led to believe in the reality of the categories they write on their time sheets each week.

To take a specific example, consider a project which has a set date when each of the activities will be completed. As the date for problem definition approaches, great haste is evident in the preparation of "problem definitions." At the required date, all the definitions are in the hands of the project manager—but that does not mean that the project is defined. All it means is that the definitions are in the hands of the project manager.

Now that definition is formally finished, analysis starts. If, perhaps because of the hasty definition process, some flaw is discovered in the definition at this point, one of two things will happen. First—and worst—the flaw may be covered up, under the belief that the definition is now fixed. Second, the definition may be changed—probably informally in most cases, but with the time and effort required being charged against "analysis." And so the project goes on, from category to category without ever a backward step—or so it seems to the project manager. His model of how a programming project is done has been superimposed on the project itself, and he never becomes aware that things are not so simple. It all makes for a very neat accounting system, but it will never do for an understanding of the psychological processes underlying success or failure of the project.

Even if it really were possible to force a programming project into sharply defined stages, it might not be a good idea to do so. The programmers on a project constitute mixed talents, some of which are better suited for one type of work than another. If only one type of work is being done at a time, certain talents are going to be underexploited at that moment. Moreover, even for the individual programmer working alone, it may be a good idea deliberately to break up the work so that different parts are in different stages at any one time. Why? Because the progress of the work is likely to be more uniform and less dependent on day-to-day variations in the programming environment or in the programmer's own temperament.

Consider, for example, the idea that not every day is a good one for coding. If we are coding and become aware that we are muddling about—taking four steps backward for each three forward—it would be a good idea to put aside the coding for some other activity requiring a different set of skills and perhaps a different frame of mind, such as documentation. But if the only work being done at the moment is coding, there is no escape from coding except by escape from the program altogether. Since we can seldom afford to drop work altogether—or at least to be *seen* dropping work altogether—we would then have to try coding anyway, in spite of our best knowledge of ourselves.

The external environment also varies from day to day. If, for instance, the computer is down for installation of some new equipment or for fixing some hardware bug, machine testing must cease altogether. If all that is going on at the moment is machine testing, then progress grinds to a frustrating halt. If there are a number of phases in progress at once, we merely turn to some other activity.

Another consequence of "lock-step" programming is that, at any given moment, certain facilities are likely to be overloaded at the same time that others are lying fallow. Program testing makes the biggest demands on machine time, and if everyone is testing at the same time, the machine may be overloaded. Documentation puts a big load on the secretarial staff: the same secretaries who were idly waiting for work while the machine was overloaded with testing runs now find themselves swamped with typing and such as everyone starts to document at the same time. And because certain people in the project are specialists in certain phases of programming, they, too, are alternately idle and swamped.

The ideal project design, then, would avoid having all its parts in the same stage of programming at the same time. However, if one were to believe typical management texts, one would get precisely the opposite impression. What saves us, more often than not, is the lack of true boundaries between these stages, so that a little debugging is already going on during problem definition and a little problem definition is still going on during debugging. The same kind of "smearing" is done by the good programmer—whether consciously or unconsciously—so that when he runs into an obstacle in one area of activity he switches to another. Indeed, one mark of a poor programmer is that he can be found sitting around doing nothing whenever there is machine trouble and he cannot get his programs run. If he can't do the one thing scheduled for today, he is lost.

Of course, not everybody is equally good at all things, and we like to work on the things we do best. The widespread inability to write plain English, for instance, no doubt explains why documentation is a universal festering sore. Even when there is nothing else to do, doing documentation is never a voluntary alternative. We can try to arrange the work of our project so that each person specializes in what he does best, but this approach has at least two drawbacks. First of all, we probably will find nobody to do the documentation work; and, second, nobody will learn very much.

We can, on the other hand, maximize the rate of learning by assigning each programmer to be a specialist in that part of the work he does *least well*. In this way, also, we can ensure that each one will jump at the opportunity to switch to some other task when he runs into a snag.

The multiplicity of different types of work under the rubric of "programming" also accounts for a certain exaggeration in psychological studies of programming. If we test for performance on a small programming project, the results are likely to be dominated by performance on one phase of the work. For instance, in a problem which emphasizes painstaking attention to detail, certain programmers will show a marked superiority to others. The situation might reverse itself if the problem posed required the ability to sit back and take the broad view of things; therefore we could well have two studies which showed thirty-to-one differences in performance.

When we put these same programmers on a somewhat larger problem, however, we may see these extreme differences reduced, for each type of programmer now finds some parts that are suited to him and some parts that are not. With larger problems then—such as we reported in the previous section—we will more likely find differences of two-or three-to-one. Even these differences, moreover, are no longer attributable to differences among the programmers, but to certain external factors, in many cases. Not that the programmers do not differ, but simply that these differences average out over a project that requires all sorts of attitudes and skills.

All the same, there is a certain truth in the thirty-to-one ratio, if we but knew how to exploit it. This ratio *is* probably representative of the differences in ability among programmers—*in different stages of program-*

ming work. Thus, a project that can divide the effort not into programs but into types of work might realize gains in productivity of this magnitude. Notice that this is precisely what happens when egoless programming is practiced; and as long as programmers "own" programs rather than, possibly, "owning" programming *stages,* we are not going to realize these potential gains.

With this argument, then, we come the full circle, back to the attempt to isolate the truly different kinds of activity that programmers do. Even acknowledging the fuzzy boundaries between the classical divisions, we will be able to do some fruitful subdividing as we go along. For example, consider the testing stage. We can immediately isolate at least three different activities (from a psychological point of view), which are lumped under this single title:

1. Detecting the presence of errors.
2. Locating errors which are known to exist.
3. Correcting errors that have been found.

In a very broad way, we can see that these three activities could require different combinations of skills and personality traits. To detect errors, the programmer must have a conniving mind, one that delights in uncovering flaws where beauty and perfection were once thought to lie. Perhaps a touch of paranoia helps—the kind of thinking that automatically conjures up the worst imaginable case.

For locating errors, however, we want a person who has the persistence of a mother-in-law and the collecting instincts of a pack rat. In one project, for instance, a bug in the operating system was known to exist for six months before it was finally tracked down by one programmer who had saved every dump taken in that period—three nine-foot stacks of paper! Late at night he could be found poring over his dumps—searching, groping, rummaging about for some slight clue that would have escaped the eye of a Sherlock Holmes. Months went by, and then, in one dump, a single bit which didn't seem *quite* right. Back he went through all the other dumps, until he had ferreted out two more cases, then five, then a dozen out of the hundreds. These twelve cases he arranged on a large table, first in one pattern, then another, until some threads of connection became visible.

By this time, his mind was so specialized to the cases at hand that it was fruitless for him to try to explain his hypothesis to anyone else. It seemed to him that one of the data channels—when certain conditions were just right—was picking up a bit in one of the positions of its address register, thus causing a single character to be stored out of its regular sequence. Since this error usually occurred in the middle of a large data block, the stray character was usually wiped out by subsequent characters in the block, but in a few cases—the twelve—the character was found just past the end of the block. He tried to convince the engineers, but they would not listen. Programmers always say that there are machine errors. So, finally, he constructed a program that would force the channel into just the right circumstances with an increased frequency. Then, when he made the error occur with more regularity, he was able to define the circumstances with enough precision to find on the schematic exactly the circuit card that must be in error. The engineers were impressed with his diligence, so they finally granted him a test of the card—and found that he was right!

Such programming sleuths are not rewarded for their discoveries with the fame of a Pasteur or a Salk. Nonetheless, they are satisfied—beyond the comprehension of ordinary men—with the work itself. And yet, such a bug-finding genius may be rather inept at correcting a bug once it has been found—indeed, the found bug has lost its interest for him. If forced to make the correction, he will, more often than not, introduce a much cruder bug in its place, or else create a clumsy and inefficient patch. For corrections that fit into a program with a certain elegance, another type of programmer is needed.

Correcting errors in other peoples' programs requires a sense of fitness and proportion, plus an extensive repertoire of tricks for one machine or language. The "patcher," in other words, must have a "synthetic" mind, as opposed to the "analytical" mind of the "bug-finder." To be sure, the same person *could* excel at both of these tasks, but we are more likely to find that a team can do a far better job than any of its members—if they have the sense and humility to recognize their talents and shortcomings.

SUMMARY

Programming is not an undifferentiated mass. Software designers often forget that professionals need different types of tools than do amateurs. Managers often forget that programming work breaks up into stages, and not very neatly or linearly at that. And programmers themselves often forget that they are trying to do different things with different programs.

The variegated nature of programming leads to confusion and complication in the work of software designers, managers, and programmers. But most important for us, it leads to confusion and complication in the psychological study of programming. Just as we could not say in absolute terms what is a "good program," we cannot say what is a "good programmer," "a good programming manager," or, for that matter, "a good piece of software." As a result, we shall be forced to elevate the discussion of programming by lowering the level of discourse: we shall only be able to make conclusions of general validity if we get down to much more detail than is usually found in discussions of "what makes a good programmer." And perhaps we shall find that what makes a good programmer is much like what makes a good friendship—a mutual recognition and encouragement of individuality.

QUESTIONS

For Managers

1. Have you ever had an "executive" programming course? Describe what you did, and how it relates to the job of the professional programmer. Also describe any practices in the course which misled you as to the nature of programming.

2. How do you estimate the complexity of a programming assignment? By examining the specifications? By listening to what the assigned programmer tells you? By taking several informed opinions?

3. How explicit are your assignments in terms of the relative importance of the following?
   a. Schedule
   b. Specifications
   c. Speed
   d. Space
   e. Documentation
   f. Other factors

4. Describe the sequence of work planned for your current project. Is the actual work proceeding according to the original scheme? Do you expect it to continue in this manner?

5. How close is your progress reporting scheme to the reality of the programming work that goes on? What checks do you have to find out if it corresponds to reality? Does your scheme achieve correspondence to reality by forcing programmers to work in patterns that conform to the scheme rather than to the needs of their current task?

6. What steps do you take as manager to level the load on critical facilities?

For Programmers

1. Are you a professional programmer? What is it that makes you a professional programmer?

2. Make a list of things that your software does for you that fifteen years ago you would have had to do for yourself. Or don't you know anything about what software was like fifteen years ago? Do you think a professional should know something about the history of his profession?

3. Is your programming a balanced effort, or do you tend to favor the work you like best? What steps are you taking to improve your performance in those areas where you are weak or where you dislike the work? Or, alternatively, what steps are you taking to see that you can work most in those areas where you excel?

4. What are the objectives on your current project? Make a list of them, in order of importance, and ask your manager if he will make a similar list without seeing yours. Then compare the lists, and report on the differences.

5. What do you do when the machine is down for a day or more, so that you cannot make any debugging runs?

6. Which of the following do you do best?
   a. Detect subtle errors in output.
   b. Locate errors in the code, once they have been detected.
   c. Choose corrections that are simple and effective.

What do you do to overcome your deficiencies in the other two areas?

BIBLIOGRAPHY

Rosen, S., ed., *Programming Systems and Languages,* New York, McGraw-Hill, 1967.
Rosen has collected and annotated most of the important original papers on computer software, particularly languages and compilers. The collection can be used by the beginning professional programmer to get a sense of what has brought his profession to the point in which he finds it today.

Sammet, Jean E., *Programming Languages: History and Fundamentals,* Englewood Cliffs, N.J., Prentice-Hall, 1969.
Whereas Rosen goes back to the original papers, Sammet tries to give the sense of history by bringing all work, major and minor, into one coherent pattern. Her approach is valuable for two reasons. First, in attempting to bring pattern to this potpourri, she succeeds in displaying how rich and complex the pattern of programming work really is. The second value to this approach is related to the first, for a collection such as Rosen's of only the best and most successful work tends to give the impression that there was much less experimenting going on. Sammet successfully captures the flavor of trial and error (more error than trial) which has dominated software development. Of course, even she fails to capture the flavor of all the errors which were (happily) never published. I can think of one, called MYSTIC, which was so bad that it should be resurrected for the educational purposes that only a horrible example can serve.

Metzger, Phillip W., *Programming Project Management Guide,* IBM Federal Systems Division, April 1970.

Lecht, Charles P., *The Management of Computer Programming Projects,* American Management Association, Inc., 1967.
These two documents represent a fair sample of the management school of programming project management. Metzger's book is a guide for an IBM internal course on programming project management—a course originated by Al Pietra-

santa and Joel Aron, and one of the original guides. The Lecht volume is the effort of the American Management Association on the same subject. Both volumes contain useful information, as well as management pep-talk. The vantage point they take, however, is well characterized by this sentence taken from the last page of the Metzger collection:

"You know, it's no crime to want to work in some field other than management." You almost expect the next sentence to read: "Why some of my best friends aren't managers." Given this elitist undercurrent in the thought of managers—or, to be more precise, of the staff people who prepare courses for managers—is it any wonder that the typical project management view of programming is rather remote from the individuality of the programmer and his task?

Williams, R. J., *Biochemical Individuality,* New York, Wiley, 1956.
Williams' highly individual book on individuality at the physical level should be required reading for all those who suffer from the illusion that "all programmers look alike." Can we really comprehend that some people have three kidneys and some have one and then still believe that each programmer should take the same amount of time to do the same job?

Tyler, L. E., *The Psychology of Human Differences,* 3rd ed., New York, Appleton-Century-Crofts, 1965.
Tyler does for man at the psychological level what Williams does at the physical level. Is it a coincidence that both of these books saw the light in 1956, the year FORTRAN was born?

8 PERSONALITY FACTORS

In one sense, the concept of *personality* encompasses all the individual variations we find among people. Even to the most casual observer of human behavior, it is evident that intelligence and education affect personality. When we use the term "personality" in the sense of the previous sentence, we mean the totality of personal characteristics by which we ordinarily identify people—a kind of summary of the person. In this sense, one's personality is one's identity, a concept which is neatly illustrated by a study done in one computing installation.

The Mad Bomber

In a remote batch environment, the operators in the machine room may rarely, if ever, interact directly with the programmers whose jobs they run. Under the circumstances, we might expect that operators will not know much about the personalities of their programmers, but this is not the case. Personality, being the totality of factors contributing to our individuality, is displayed in everything we do or say. In particular, it is reflected in our programs, and, even more particularly, in how those programs look to the machine operators.

The chief systems programmer, who, by the nature of his duties, was in face-to-face contact with both programmers and operators, had observed that the operators often had disparaging comments to make about certain programmers. As he was attending our seminar on "The Psychology of Computer Programming," he decided to study these comments with an eye to correlating them with specific programming practices. His most interesting findings, however, had to do with the personalities of two of the programmers.

Of the seventy or so programmers using this machine, these two stood out in the comments of all the operators. Even operators who worked on different shifts and therefore had no opportunity to discuss such matters agreed that these two programmers were worse than any of the others. Upon further investigation, the chief systems programmer found that these opinions had been formed largely on the basis of the abnormal terminations—dumps and "bomb-outs" of the entire system. Such abnormal terminations were extremely rare events—except for the work of these two individuals—and they were also most annoying to the operators. As there were no regular channels by which the operators could communicate with these programmers, they could only curse among themselves each time a "bomb-out" occurred.

The systems programmer began to save examples of these disaster situations, and after he had gathered enough to form a definite pattern, he interviewed each of the two programmers. The first one, he discovered, was an engineer who had no programming training whatsoever. His engineering group was highly dependent on the results from a single program. This program had been left in charge of the engineer when the original programmer had left. Not knowing anything about programming —and being too shy to ask for help—he ran the program on a trial-and-error basis, changing now one card, then another, until he got the results he wanted. In the process, he was giving the operators fits, though he was, quite naturally, unaware of any disturbance.

The second programmer—the worst offender of the two, and affectionately known among the operators as "the mad bomber"—turned out to be a rather different case. Not only did he have programming experience—he had fifteen years of it. In that decade and a half, he had —according to him—programmed eleven different machines in fourteen different languages. Moreover, he was—again according to him—an expert in all of them. Small wonder his programs bombed the system: they were far too abstruse to be understood by mere operators or to be handled by some operating system which he himself had not written.

The number of times this expert's programs bombed the system had evidently been magnified by a factor of three or more by the simple expedient of resubmitting the offending decks without change. According to him, the probability was so small that his programs could be wrong that it wasn't worth his precious time to look at them until they had been rejected three times in a row. At that point he would stomp into some other programmer's office and demand to know why the system was not working properly.

Even after his errors had been patiently pointed out to him, the bombing was not finished. In one example, found by the systems programmer, the bomber had made an error in job control in the first step of a three-step job. After having been shown the error and how to correct it, he resubmitted the job only to have it bomb the system once again. Back it went for another bombing, and another, after which he had the same error pointed out in the *second* step of the job! And even that was not enough. The whole cycle was repeated for the third step, which—as we might have guessed—contained precisely the same error.

Both of these cases are archetypical examples of how personality affects programming performance, although the personalities in the two cases are as different as a mouse and a lion. The engineer's bombing problems were solved by sending him to a programming course—giving him the aid he was too shy to request for himself. For the "expert," however, education was no solution. Inasmuch as he held an absolute faith that he knew everything about programming—or at least everything worth knowing—he could not be convinced to attend a course or even to listen to the advice and counsel of anyone else. Eventually, his problem was "solved" by permitting him to take his services elsewhere, and, for all we know, the "mad bomber" still lives today.

PERSONALITY CHANGES

Although there exists no universally accepted definition of personality, we can take the following* as a good working model for our study of personality as it affects—and is affected by—programming:

Personality is the integration of all of an individual's characteristics into a unique organization that determines, and is modified by, his attempts at adaptations to his continually changing environment.

* D. Krech, R. S. Crutchfield and N. Livson, *Elements of Psychology*, 2nd ed., New York, Knopf, 1969.

The first thing in this definition that may surprise some readers is the clear statement that personality is not fixed. Nevertheless, there is a certain enduring quality to personality, and therefore personality does not change when there is no reason for it to change, although it may sometimes seem that way. For instance, a relatively mild-mannered and amiable programmer began to shun his fellow workers and to react rather testily to attempts to help him in his work. Such behavioral changes often arise quite slowly, and considerable time may elapse before we recognize the change. Sometimes, in fact, the condition engendering them is a transient one, and the behavior change reverses itself before we have had time to identify it as a "change in personality." But when a change persists, there is always a reason behind it, although the reason may not be related in any direct way to the actual behavior.

In our example, the change in the mild-mannered programmer came to the attention of his manager through the complaints of other programmers. In an interview, the programmer acknowledged that he had noticed a change in his behavior, but was at a loss to account for it. The manager speculated on the cause, but had no more success than the man himself. After a few weeks, however, this programmer had to leave work early with a racking toothache. Upon visiting a dentist—something he had failed to do for several years—he was informed that four of his teeth were so badly infected that they would have to come out immediately. Within a week after the extractions, his former sweet self had emerged, the source of his transformation having been the debilitating effect of the infection upon his health.

Unfortunately, it is easier to identify the source of a personality change after the fact than before. We cannot conclude that whenever a friendly person turns unfriendly he should have a few teeth removed. The same personality change could have come about from any number of causes—physical, mental, or strictly external to the man himself. In one instance, a man attending programming school was doing very poorly, in spite of the fine recommendations he had brought with him from his home office. The director of the school was about to fail him and send him home, but first took the trouble to take the man to lunch to give him a chance to account for himself. Not until dessert was served did the poor student reveal the fact that his wife—1500 miles away—was dying of cancer. Going to the school had represented an important opportunity for his advancement, and his wife had insisted that he go. But, though he tried to fulfill her wishes, he was unable to concentrate on study. Not wishing to earn special favors for himself, he had not told anyone at the school of the situation. Were it not for the director's patience, he would have been sent home in disgrace for no more of a crime than being distraught over his wife's dying.

Situations such as our last two examples present a grave moral dilemma for a manager, at least in our society where one's "private life" is not supposed to enter into office affairs or be examined by one's manager. However, since there is no way to determine from the symptoms whether the cause lies in the office or out, a manager has no choice but to try to understand behavior that is disruptive to the work at hand. If the source of trouble does lie in the office, it may prove an easy matter to rectify. Perhaps the programmer does not get along with his office mate. Unless he is unable to get along with *any* office mate, the "personality" problem can be erased by a change of venue.

Even if the source of difficulty cannot be so trivially removed, an adjustment may at least alleviate the problem. For example, if a programmer has become irascible in his dealings with the machine operators, it may be a result of pressures put on him to complete a troublesome program whose bugs he cannot locate. If he tends to be an assertive person, he may be unwilling to admit that he is having trouble at all, much less to seek assistance. Prohibiting him from entering the machine room will only eliminate the symptom, and his trouble will shortly manifest itself somewhere else. If the true source of difficulty can be detected, he may be given assistance without his having to admit that he is in trouble. He may be annoyed at this impugning of his programming ability, but once the bug is found, he will probably soon forget it. We all feel, at times, that a strong medicine is worse than the disease, but at least its effects are over sooner.

In all of these cases, no effective action can be taken to correct or adjust for a personality problem without uncovering its true source. Psychological awareness can help in locating the source of such a problem, but psychology has not developed to the point—and never will—that it can be used for diagnoses without the aid of the person himself. Nobody can tell from watching a man work that his wife has cancer, or that his teeth hurt, or that he fears he will not meet his deadline. No manager will be successful if he tries to make psychological judgments of people on the basis of external symptoms. But, if he takes those symptoms as indicators to attain further information before taking action—information which can only be obtained, if at all, through the people themselves—his actions are quite likely to be rewarded with success.

PERSONALITY INVARIANTS

If personality "is modified by . . . attempts at adaptation," we can use personality changes as signals that a person's environment has changed. But changes in personality—although they may represent extremely serious situations—are not that frequent. What may be of more concern in the long run is the way in which a programmer's more or less invariant personality affects his work as a programmer.

One popular view of personality—popular both with psychologists and with the man in the street—is that personality may be characterized by a collection of *traits*. This person is said to be "conservative, stable, and shrewd," and another is described as "shy but imaginative." The intuitive appeal of such descriptions is compelling, and we might be tempted to try describing the traits that make up the "ideal programmer personality type." Because of the variety of situations that are subsumed under the name of "programming," the best we can hope for is a relation between certain traits and certain types of programming work.

We need not discuss the various "trait theories," for we are not seeking such exactitude, even if it existed in the theories. Also, if the theories are controversial, or inexact, that need not mean that they are not suggestive. For example, one pair of traits often used is "trusting-suspicious," and we might ask ourselves at which end of the spectrum it is best for a programmer to be. Clearly, when one is debugging, it is best to be suspicious, almost to the point of paranoia. On the other hand, in any work with other people, it is best to have a certain amount of trust, for people who are not trusted are not trustworthy. In some situations, however, these two needs come into conflict. If a programmer works in a "product test" group, he *must* be suspicious of other people's programs. If someone tells him, "Don't bother to check that. I fixed it up and checked it myself," his impulse as a trusting person is to believe, and the requirements of his job are to be suspicious.

The product test programmer, then, is in a quandary, but how serious this quandary is depends on his other personality traits. If he has a great need to be liked, it will bother him to have to seem to show unfriendliness by calling someone's word into question. But, if he is of more independent mien, or even a bit antagonistic to other people, suspecting others' statements about their programs may not bother him a bit. Thus, all other things being equal, certain people will find the job of product test programmer easier psychologically.

As usual, all other things are never really equal. Such personality traits as emotional stability or instability will affect how well a person can tolerate being in any paradoxical position for an extended period. Because the period of time is important, a manager can, by changing work assignments more frequently, relax the stringent personality requirements that might otherwise be necessary for the job of product test programmer. This type of alternation of jobs is accomplished automatically through egoless programming, for no person is subjected to unrelenting assault on his particular personality—the type of assault that forces people into "attempts at adaptation."

Through egoless programming, then, we sacrifice the possibility of having each person *always* in the job for which his personality best suits him, yielding, in this way, some potential efficiency for security and stability. Moreover, the full potential for efficiency may not be lost, since we are not likely to have had the perfect mix of personalities in the first place. Then, too, "wearing the other man's moccasins" has always been a good way to develop the personality trait of tolerance.

Attempts to place each person in the job best suited to his personality are subject to failure from another direction. Personality is not simply a single surface layer, but runs through many layers. Identical surface layers may conceal rather different—even quite opposite—interiors. A "friendly" person may seem that way because he is anxious to present a good impression of himself in a situation where he is insecure; or, his friendliness may be a manifestation of his complete relaxation in the situation. Evidently, we must be more than a little cautious in inferring the inner layers of personality from simple observations of the outer.

Another factor that distorts our perception of someone's personality is that many people tend to show a different face to people in authority than to their associates or to their employees. Also, many people behave differently with people for other reasons, such as sex or age. An amusing instance illustrating this principle occurred late one night in the test cell of a computer manufacturer where a programming team was testing a new machine. At about two in the morning, a plant guard discovered the team at work, and he became quite upset and a little arrogant as he explained to the group that women were not permitted to work in the plant after midnight. One of the three young men in the group rose to the defense of his manager—the one female among the four of them.

"You mean there are no circumstances under which a woman can work here after midnight?" he demanded.

"None," was the reply, clothed in tones of authority. "You'll have to get out of here immediately. I'll escort you to the exit."

"But we have permission of the plant manager. We must work at night because the machine is not available during the day."

The mention of the plant manager introduced a faint note of uncertainty in the guard's answer: "The only time a woman can work here after midnight is when a manager is present." Then, surveying the four members of the team and reassuring himself that not one was over thirty, he regained his positive voice. "But there is no manager here, is there?"

At this point, the female member of the team stepped forward and with her most seductive smile and managerial manner of speaking said, "But *I* am the manager of this group."

The guard's confusion was so great that he lost control of his jaw, which simply hung open for a few moments while he considered the implications of a *woman,* a *young* woman, an *attractive* woman, being a manager. When he regained his composure, his voice was soft and subservient. "Oh, I see. I beg your pardon, ma'am. I'm sorry I disturbed you. If you'd like, I'll come around here every hour or so and see if things are all right."

Sensing his discomfort, she, too, softened her tone to one of managerial largesse. "That won't be necessary, I'm sure. But thank you for offering. We appreciate the job you're doing." It was a clear dismissal, and he understood it, turning around without another sound and walking off into the dark recesses of the empty test cells. If he had had a tail, it would have been between his legs.

Now, a plant guard is not a programmer and may not be as familiar as programmers with the common programming situation of women, young women, or even attractive young women in positions of authority. Nonetheless, programmers as well as plant guards have personalities—personalities that change their external appearance in response to the perceived social roles of the people around them. We should not be surprised, then, when a manager is unable to understand why a programmer who, with him, seems the very model of friendly, quiet cooperation is, with his co-workers, aggressive, noisy, and generally difficult to get along with.

CRITICAL PERSONALITY TRAITS

Measuring personality is difficult, and matching personalities to job descriptions is perhaps even impossible; but isn't there some way we can select those people whose personalities suit them for programming? After all, if personality is important for programming, we cannot just give up without trying. Perhaps we can gain something from consideration of extreme cases, even if we cannot do very much with the general case.

The nature of the way that personality interacts with programming success is subtle, but we probably can make some assertions about how personality traits may lead to programming *failure*. Although the average programming manager would say that intelligence is more important than personality in programming success, very few could cite cases of people who turned out not to be intelligent enough to program, but everyone knows of cases of people who were not temperamentally suited to the programmer's job. It is in this sense that we can assert that personality is more important than intelligence in programming.

If we look more deeply into the observed dominance of personality factors in programmer failures, we can easily understand why we are more likely to make a personality mistake in hiring a programmer than an intelligence mistake. In the first place, there is an enormous amount of *preselection* of people, which places limits on who is likely to be making application for a programming job—even as a programming trainee. Part of the preselection is imposed in explicit hiring policies, such as requiring a college degree, or even a degree in specific fields. Possibly even more important is the self-selection that takes place because the uninitiated believe that programming requires "a lot of math." Not too many years ago, the external perception of programming was so distorted that young men were advised to "study electronics" if they expressed an interest in working with computers. Young women, of course, were automatically excluded by this criterion, for young women did not study to be "engineers."

Whatever the faults of this preselection in excluding people who might have made great success as programmers, it does have the effect of largely eliminating people of below-average intelligence. Such people, if they had presented themselves for jobs as programmers in great numbers, might have failed in great numbers, making us feel a need to measure intelligence of programmer applicants. But is there no comparable selection process on the basis of personality, as well? No doubt there is, but personality has many more dimensions than intelligence—although intelligence is not by any means measurable by a simple score on an IQ or programmer's aptitude test. Thus, selection on a personality basis is not likely to produce such uniform results with respect to the needs of programming. Moreover, even if the schools, say, did make a personality selection as strong as an intelligence selection (and, make no mistake, school success involves a large element of personality), personality is more changeable than intelligence.

In fact, one of the few really reliable things psychologists can say about these two aspects of a person is that intelligence is much less responsive to environment than is personality. Marriage, for example, is not likely to have a measurable effect on a college graduate's intelligence, but it will most assuredly provoke personality changes that can be perceived even by the untrained eye. Thus, a man who was a frivolous playboy in his fraternity days might well surprise us with the conscientious programming job he now does; but if he was unable to write a simple declarative sentence in college, marriage and family will probably not help one bit.

What traits, then, would give an indication of potential failure in a programmer? We can speak on this subject only from anecdotal material, for there have as yet been no formal studies of this question. Nevertheless, we can probably say with assurance that someone without the *ability to tolerate stressful situations* for a period of a week or more is not good programmer material—given the realities of programming work today. We are speaking of professional programming, of course—where the work and schedules are imposed from the outside. Amateur programming is not such a stressful pastime, possibly because one's entire career does not seem dependent on finding a particular bug by next Thursday.

Because of the diversity of programming work, people who are not in some measure *adaptable to rapid change* will probably have trouble as professional programmers. It is unlikely that a programmer will go through a month—not to speak of an entire career—without having to face the psychological shock of having his work pulled out from under him, or at least changed sufficiently so that his previous efforts become garbage.

And speaking of garbage, one of the most easily identifiable personality needs in programming is a modicum of *neatness*. We are not speaking here of personal grooming, though in one case a programmer actually smelled so bad that nobody could sit next to him long enough to look at his listings. What we mean is a slight compulsion to keep one's papers in order, without which the computer's paper-generating capacity inexorably leads to grief. One computing center selects its programmer trainees by giving a test and choosing the candidate who turns in the neatest paper, not the one with the highest score.

Another essential personality factor in programming is at least a small dose of *humility*. Without humility, a programmer is foredoomed to the classic pattern of Greek drama: success leading to overconfidence *(hubris)* leading to blind self-destruction. Sophocles himself could not frame a better plot (to reveal the inadequacy of our powers) than that of the programmer learning a few simple techniques, feeling that he is an expert, and then being crushed by the irresistible power of the computer (the *Deus ex Machina*).

The other side of the coin of humility is *assertiveness,* or force of character. A programmer's job is to get things done, and getting things done sometimes requires moving around obstacles, jumping over them, or simply knocking them down. The humble person is acutely aware of the ways in which he may be wrong; his critical mind tends to dominate his force of character. Now, although it is true that force of character without a critical mind is like a steam boiler without a safety valve, a critical mind without force of character is like a safety valve without a steam boiler. There is no danger of explosion, but then there is no possibility of getting any work done, either.

We have some empirical evidence from an unexpected source on the question of humility versus assertiveness in programming. In perusing the data from our study designed to test the effect of instructions, we plotted the lengths of time each programmer spent studying his runs from the batch system. When length of study period was plotted against frequency, we found we had two distinct types of graph, as shown in

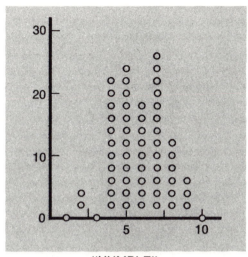

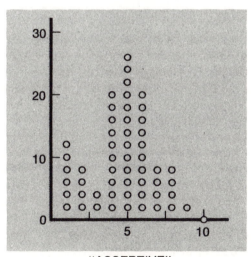

Frequency of work periods plotted against log base 2 of period length in minutes (e.g., 1 means 1 minute, 2 means 2 minutes, 3 means 4 minutes, and 5 means 16 minutes)

Figure 8–1 Two programmer personalities.

Figure 8–1. The top graph shows only one peak in the plot of frequency versus logarithm of time period, and the second shows this peak with another peak added at the low end. This second peak is a preponderance of one-, two-, or three-minute work intervals, which we were able to track down to corrections of careless coding or keypunching errors.

We took the trouble to look for such a pattern in other work, particularly when we were studying errors in PL/I syntax. Previously, we had overlooked this pattern because we only asked the programmers in the syntax study to turn in runs with errors. When we started collecting all runs, as we had in the "instructions" study, we saw the same pattern in a different way. Certain programmers, once they got out their original syntax errors, essentially *never* made another syntax error. As they made their modifications, one or two at a time, they carefully and methodically checked and punched them so that every run after the first few was free of syntax errors. The other programmers, however, and they formed about one-third in this group, consistently fell into a pattern of hasty changes so that two runs were almost invariably required to make a single correction. After the first run, the programmer would make a one- or two-minute work period to fix the syntax error he would not have made in the first place had he been inclined to a more humble view of his abilities.

In Figure 8–1, we have taken the liberty of labeling the one graph "humble" and the other "assertive." Although the patterns are definitely there, and although they are stable patterns (the same programmer does the same thing on different programs), we really cannot yet say that these patterns correspond to the traits "humble" and "assertive" as measured by some standard psychological testing instrument. This is a clear area for further research—research that will be important, for example, not only in the selection and training of programmers, but in the design and evaluation of on-line systems. We might conjecture here that "humble" programmers perform much better in batch environments, and "assertive" ones will be more likely to shine on-line, where their assertiveness will not be severely penalized, and their willingness to push ahead will blast them through problems that will leave the "humble" programmer just gaping at the terminal.

Last among the essential personality traits for programming, we might list *sense of humor*. The computer "doth make fools of us all," so that any fool without the ability to share a laugh on himself will be unable to tolerate programming for long. It has been said with great perspicacity that the Programmer's National Anthem is "aaaaahhhhh." When we finally see the light, we see how once again we have fallen into some foolish assumption, some oafish practice, or some witless blunder. Only by singing the second stanza, "ha ha ha ha ha," can we long endure the role of the clown.

PERSONALITY TESTING

The impressionistic picture we have painted of the ideal programming personality—ideal by virtue of exclusion of extreme traits that should lead to failure—is not the usual one of a "rigid" person. There seems to be some current folk wisdom which imagines that, because programmers work with rigorous machines, they must themselves be rigid. In effect, the opposite is true, for since the machine is so inflexible, the programmer must be flexible enough to supply the elasticity needed in matching any system's abilities to real world needs. Is it possible, then, that we could introduce some system of personality testing to help us overcome our folk prejudice in the selection of programmers or programmer trainees?

There exist today a number of "personality tests," some of which have been used on occasion to aid in the selection of people as potential programmers. A number of these have been developed for, and used primarily in, the detection of personality disorders—the famous Rorschach Ink Blot Test, the Thematic Apperception Test (TAT), and the Minnesota Multiphasic Personality Inventory (MMPI). The MMPI, for instance, was developed on the basis of empirical information arising in part from a study of institutionalized psychotics, since their personality characteristics had supposedly been well determined by trained psychologists and psychiatrists. "Normal" people were also used, but the main thrust of the MMPI was to aid in diagnosis of mental illness, not in differentiating among various "normal" personality types or traits.

Naturally, we feel that mentally ill people are not what we are looking for when we hire programmers—although there are no empirical data to support or contradict that view. The question of whether to use this type of test for hiring programmers, however, is not one of effectiveness or appropriateness, but simply one of the ethics of normal hiring practices. Is it appropriate to give tests for mental illness to anyone applying for any kind of job?

The answer to this last question is not limited to programming, so we shall sidestep the ethical issues involved. But what about personality tests that have been devised as a way of selecting people for jobs or even for careers? A typical examination of this type is the Strong Vocational Interest Blank. (Strong is the name of a man, not an adjective suggesting that the test measures strong interests.) In tests such as this, interpretations are based on a comparison of "scores" with sets of scores obtained from people already in various professions. Thus, if a career counselor had given this test to a high school student, he would compare the student's score, or profile, with profiles considered "typical" of various professions. The counselor tries to determine the professions that most resemble the student in profile, and then, presumably, he recommends that the student choose his career from among that set.

In hiring, of course, the employer is usually interested in one or, at most, a few types of work. By comparing the applicant with each appropriate profile, he may make a judgment as to whether or not that applicant possesses a suitable personality for the job. Now, how suitable is this procedure likely to be, given what we know about the relationship of personality to programming?

The first weakness of this procedure is that there may be no profile for the group called "programmers." A number of firms have used the Strong test for selecting programmers in the absence of programmer profiles by making a judgment that a programmer is "like" a mathematician, engineer, writer, or what have you. Since the basis for these judgments is pure speculation, such selection procedures could have been equaled by throwing dice. Throwing dice, however, does not have the right sound to it. A personnel manager can say, "We use the Strong Vocational Interest Blank to help us select programmers." This will certainly impress his manager more than saying, "We throw dice to help us select programmers."

Now, however, we have a profile for programmers (Perry and Cannon, 1966)—and if personnel managers actually use it as intended, something better than dice-throwing might be accomplished, though there are many reasons for doubting it. For instance, which type of programmer are we talking about? Or will we have separate profiles for systems programmer, applications programmer, product test programmer, maintenance programmer, and so forth?

Even assuming that the profiles are available with sufficient resolution of job descriptions, do they really reflect what we want? After all, these profiles are obtained by testing people already in the profession, not the people we would necessarily want to be in it if we knew what we wanted. For old, established, and stable professions, it may be valid to assume that people in the profession are, by and large, the ones who should be in it—even though they may have been steered there by the Strong Vocational Interest Blank, completing the cycle of a self-fulfilling prophecy. But surely we are not in that advanced state of knowledge about programming as yet. There is, on the contrary, reason to believe that employers, at least, are not at all satisfied with the average programmer they employ. Why then should this group be used as a template into which all programming applicants must fit?

One other point deserves mention in this regard—the question of "cheating." Essentially all psychological tests—certainly including all the personality tests—assume that the psychologists who made the tests are smarter than the people who take them. Indeed, if we were to take a personality inventory of people who are attracted to psychological testing as a profession, we should probably find that these people generally hold themselves to be smarter than other people. Perhaps it could not be otherwise, for how would they get evidence to the contrary? But just because they believe they are smarter does not mean that they are smarter.

In a way, a personality test is an intelligence test—a matching of wits with the person who made the test. Suppose, for example, an applicant for a programming job takes a test where he is asked to agree or disagree with the statement, "When I concentrate too hard on a problem, I often get a headache, which keeps me from working." Anyone who would be stupid enough to answer "agree" to that statement probably isn't smart enough to be much of a programmer. As we know, applicants for programming jobs are likely to be a rather clever bunch, so we can assume that a great deal of "cheating" will take place if they are given such tests. But that should not worry us, for if they cheat successfully, they are probably going to have a number of the critical personality traits we desire—adaptability to sense the direction of the test, ability to tolerate the stress of being examined by someone they don't know under assumptions they cannot challenge, assertiveness to do something about it, and sense of humor enough to enjoy the challenge.

Psychological testers, of course, will deny the possibility of such cheating, or at least pooh-pooh its importance or frequency. But cheating *is* practiced among programmers. One large company had hired a psychological consulting firm to derive a personality profile for them to use in the hiring of programmers. As usual, the profile was to be based on a group of people who already were programmers in this company—with the added feature that only the acknowledged "best" programmers in the company were to be used (although it is not at all clear that we want a programming staff composed entirely of "best" programmers).

The programmers to be tested for creating the standard were chosen by the criterion of having been selected to attend a company-wide programmers' meeting. A few hours were set aside for the administration of the tests, but when the psychologist arrived at the testing room, he discovered that there were 60 people to be tested instead of the 30 he had anticipated. He did not have enough test blanks, but since this particular personality inventory was in two parts, the problem was solved by having half do part A first and half do part B. At the conclusion of the first half of the session, the papers were exchanged and the psychologist addressed the group with the standard instructions, terminating with the perfunctory question, "Are there any questions?" To his utter astonishment—since the group had already completed one-half of the test, one of the programmers raised his hand.

When the psychologist regained his composure enough to call on the questioner, he got the perfectly straight-faced query, "Are we supposed to use the same personality on this half as we used on the other?"

The psychologist, who did not seem to be as adaptable in the face of stress as the average programmer, turned red in the face, then sputtered for a while before he managed to say in his most kindergarten-condescending tone, "You're supposed to answer the questions *honestly,* to the best of your ability."

"What kind of fools do you take us for?" was the reply from another of the programmers, at which point the whole room broke up in waves of conspiratorial laughter.

PERSONALITY TESTING OF PROGRAMMERS

With all of these cautions about personality tests in mind, we may look at some of the results of personality testing of programmers. David B. Mayer (1968) has provided a useful survey of some of the results with the Strong Vocational Interest Blank and other testing instruments, and the reader with a stronger interest in the Strong Interest Blank than we shall satisfy should look there for further illumination. Mayer first appropriately cautions that the author of this instrument *does not claim that it predicts performances on the job.* What it does is to elicit information regarding the person's interests. The relationship of a person's interests to the kind of job he does is left to the user to decide.

Mayer points out that the Strong Blank did show certain differences between the programmers tested and the general population, and he offered a few selected examples of the type likely to catch the public interest. For instance, more programmers "like conservative people" and fewer "like progressive people" than do people in the general population. After arousing the reader's interest with such titillating examples, Mayer lowers the boom. He asks, "Can we look at individual items in the SVIB to see if these indicate anything in regard to the general interest pattern that should be the pattern of a successful programmer? The answer to this is a decided NO."

Why is Mayer so emphatic in rejecting this kind of game with individual Strong items? Because, in the first place, the instrument was only intended to be used with an analysis of the entire pattern of 400 responses. To make such an analysis, one would have to use a scoring key worked out on the basis of a large sample, such as that developed by Perry (1966). Perry's scoring key for programmers is not available for all users of the Strong Vocational Interest Blank, but as of 1968, at least, a survey of organizations revealed that none of them were using Strong, the only personality test of any kind for which a programmer scoring then existed.

Other tests in the personality and interest area which were in slight use at the time Mayer made his survey were the Thurstone Temperament Schedule, the Activity Vector Analysis, and the Kuder Preference Test, although only about 10 or 15 out of 282 organizations were using any such tests. In view of our reservations on the use of these tests in programming, it seems that many companies have made a wise decision in waiting for much further work before plunging into personality testing of their programmer applicants.

Even given the existence of valid testing instruments for testing interest and personality, the personnel manager would be faced with the nontrivial problem of which tests to use for which purposes and in what order—and what to do with the results once he had them. Since tests cost money to administer and to have scored, the burden of proof of usefulness rests on those who propose that a test be used in preference to simpler, more intuitive methods. Mayer refers to an "X-factor which can be extracted from simple interviews, and which he suspects is related to aptitude. My own interviewing experience tends to weight my "X-factor" more to personality items, as we have discussed. To be worth its cost, a psychological testing instrument is going to have to do better than X-factors—demonstrably better.

Along this line, it may be appropriate to cite the classical, though perhaps apocryphal, story of one of the largest efforts ever made to select people on the basis of psychological tests. During World War II, the United States Army was faced with the problem of fighting on widely different fronts, and they soon discovered that some men performed very poorly in tropical areas and others performed very poorly in wintry climes. In an effort to preselect soldiers for one theater of operation or another, a large study was commissioned, and hundreds of questions were tested for correlation with battlefield performance. At the end of this effort—which coincided with the end of the war and was thus too late to be effective—only one question turned out to have significant correlation with climatic influence on fighting behavior. And what was that question? Simply this: "Which do you like better, hot weather or cold?" Has anyone ever thought of asking applicants whether or not they *like* programming?

SUMMARY

Because of the complex nature of the programming task, the programmer's personality—his individuality and identity—are far more important factors in his success than is usually recognized. Nevertheless, personality tests have not been used successfully for selecting programmers who will become good programmers. Part of the failure may be attributed to the inadequacies of the tests, part to the inadequacies of our understanding of programming itself, and part to the inadequacy of our knowledge of which personality factors play what role in which part of the programming process.

All the same, there seems to be evidence that critical personality factors can be isolated and associated with particular programming tasks—at least in the sense of their possession rendering one incapable of performing that task well. Consequently, attention to the subject of personality should make substantial contributions to increased programmer performance—whether that attention is paid by a psychological researcher, a manager, or the programmer himself.

QUESTIONS

For Managers

1. Have you ever had an employee display a sudden change in personality? What did you do about it, and what would you do differently today in the same situation?

2. What personality traits do you look for in selecting your programmers? What personality traits do you regard as favorable when evaluating your programmers? Are they the same traits, and if not, why not?

3. Does your organization use personality tests in selecting programmers? If so, are the people (including yourself) who use these tests properly trained in their interpretation? Are you aware of any validation of the effectiveness of these tests for selecting programmers? Have you attempted any validation within your organization, or for your own information?

For Programmers

1. What single personality factor do you feel is most useful to you as a programmer? Do you feel that this factor was important to your employer when he hired you for the job?

2. What single personality factor do you feel is most harmful to you in performing your job as a programmer? Was this factor considered

when you were hired? What are you doing to diminish the effect this factor has on your performance?

3. Ask some of your coworkers to answer Questions 1 and 2 for you. Do they give the same answers as you gave for yourself, or did you learn something about yourself as seen by your fellow workers? What do you intend to do about it?

BIBLIOGRAPHY

Mayer, David B., and A. W. Stalnaker, Use of Psychological Tests in the Selection of Computer Personnel, *SHARE/GUIDE Presentation,* October, 1968.
This survey was adapted from a tutorial presentation given at the Fifth Annual Conference on Computer Personnel Research sponsored by the ACM special interest group in personnel research—SIG/CPR. The paper gives a good review of the work of that group since its founding in 1962, and has a good bibliography.

Perry, D. K., and W. M. Cannon, A Vocational Interest Scale for Computer Programmers—Final Report, *Proceedings of the Fourth Annual Computer Personnel Research Conference,* Association for Computing Machinery, New York, 1966, pp. 61-82.

Cronbach, L. J., *Essentials of Psychological Testing,* 3rd ed., New York, Harper, 1970.
A serious review of testing.

Wernick, Robert, *They've Got Your Number,* New York, Norton, 1956.
A nonserious, and therefore very serious, review of testing.

Cronbach, Lee J., and Goldine C. Gleser, *Psychological Tests and Personnel Decisions,* 2nd ed., Urbana, University of Illinois Press, 1965.
Even given the correct application and analysis of a psychological test, the manager is faced with making a personnel decision which is not uniquely determined by the test outcome. Or, alternatively, he must decide which tests to give, and whether to test at all. These are not easy decisions, and there are no magic answers, but this book takes a hard, and often mathematical, look at some of the problems.

Hall, C. S., and G. Lindzey, *Theories of Personality,* 2nd ed., New York, Wiley, 1970.
There are rather many theories of personality, each of which, no doubt, contains more than a grain of truth and more than a gram of insights for the programmer and programming manager. Hall and Lindzey give fair descriptions and critical analyses of twelve of the most prominent personality theories, and their book seems a good place to start exploring this field for the nonpsychologist.

White, R. H., *Lives in Progress: A study of the Natural Growth of Personality.* 2nd ed., New York, Holt, Rinehart and Winston, 1966.
Much of the work on the development of personality has concentrated on the growing child, which is not much use to us until the time comes when we start recruiting child programmers. White, however, is interested in the development of personality in adults. Since he picks up his cases starting about at college graduation—the time when many programmers are taking their first jobs—this book is of more than average interest to programming managers.

White, R. W., *The Abnormal Personality,* 3rd ed., New York, Ronald, 1964.

To discourage programming managers from being so quick to label as "crazy" people whose personalities they do not understand, White has written this careful textbook, giving a number of cases of people outside the "normal" range of personalities. Books such as these, as opposed to overpopularized accounts of management "psychology," are needed to subdue the instant psychotherapy movement.

9 INTELLIGENCE, OR PROBLEM-SOLVING ABILITY

Working with programmers, as we have seen, is working with people that are above average in intelligence. Although no formal study has been reported on the subject, we could make a fair guess that the average programmer's IQ is well above the average even of college graduates, and that the more successful programmers, by and large, have an even higher average IQ. Not, of course, that intelligence is all there is to the matter—we have long since disposed of that fallacy. But since above-average intelligence is something most programmers possess, we are sure to understand programming better if we look at it in the context of how programming work is affected by intelligence, whatever that may be.

PSYCHOLOGICAL SET

For certain types of error location activities, psychological *set* proves a major impediment. Numerous experiments have confirmed that the eye has a tendency to see what it expects to see. For instance, when looking rapidly over lists of words, a subject may encounter a "word" which is actually not a word at all, such as "dack." The first influence of set can be seen in the fact that the subject sees this nonword as a word, for he finds it among words and thus has a predisposition, or set, to see it as a word. Secondly, if the subject has been told that the words in the list have to do with "animals or birds," he is quite likely to read "dack" as "duck." If, on the other hand, he has been told the words have to do with "means of transportation," he will much more often read it as "deck" or "dock."

Anyone who has ever tried proofreading is aware of this type of set phenomenon, and anyone who has ever tried to locate a mispunched word in a computer program is more than just aware—he is scarred. In such tasks as proofreading, it is hard to measure the difficulty in overcoming the effects of set, for texts that are sufficiently perfect to serve as standards and sufficiently difficult to simulate actual conditions are difficult to obtain. Not so in computer programs, for the computer provides an automatic testing ground for the efficacy of proofreading.

The testing that a computer can provide for this type of error in its own programs has quite a range of subtlety and power. On the simple end of the range lie the tests for unrecognizable syntax, misspelled keywords, and ill-formed constants. The type of cross-checking provided by symbol tables, cross-reference lists, and flow analyses go one step deeper, but are still essentially static. Dynamic checking for uninitialized variables, flow-tracing, and subroutine call-tracing contribute to cleaning up such typographical errors as may have sifted through the other levels. Nevertheless, no automatic system can be guaranteed to locate all such errors, and we may expect certain improvements by attention to psychological facts when the programs are written or languages are designed.

Related to the concept of "set" is the concept of "distance." Not all misreadings are equally likely, regardless of the set of the reader. Thus, "daxk" is less likely to be mistaken for "duck" than was "dack," because the reader will have to make two letter transformations instead of one. In information theory, two "messages"—which may be taken to be strings of bits—have a "distance" that can be obtained by counting the number of bit positions in which they differ. The importance of this measure is that it indicates the number of bits that would have to be changed to transform the one message into the other—as might happen if noise were present in the transmission.

For the symbols of a programming language, just as for the words in a natural language, such a simple measure of "distance" can only be taken as a first approximation to the likelihood that one symbol will not be mistaken for another. For instance, psychological tests have shown a tendency for initial and final letters to be more significant in making distinctions. Thus, "gucr" would be much less likely to be seen as "duck" than would "daxk," even though they each differ in exactly two letters from "duck." Moreover, each pair of symbols cannot be assumed to be the same distance apart as each other pair. Although the exact relationship must depend upon the typescript used, letter pairs such as "x" and "k" would seem to be more readily confounded than such pairs as "x" and "o."

One of the first lessons the novice programmer learns is to make careful distinction between his handwritten "zero" and "oh," if someone else is keying his program. Most programmers, unfortunately, never advance much beyond this point in developing habits that will facilitate the conquest of set as a programming hazard. For example, no matter how carefully one writes the zero in the symbol "STOP," it will be mistaken for an "oh" all along the line. The psychological distance between "STOP" and "STOP" is so slight—because of the similarity of the zero and oh, the middle position of the single differing letter, and the set *within* the symbol which strongly biases us toward the English word—that the programmer who habitually makes such choices is headed for certain disaster.

No doubt, the rather extensive success of automatic methods of detecting such errors has lulled many programmers into carelessness when choosing symbols. Nonetheless, there will always be some situations in which the compiler or interpreter cannot make a sensible conclusion that there is an error. In one case, a programmer had used both the symbols "SYSTSTS" and "SYSSTSTS" in the same code and only discovered that one had been substituted for the other after hundreds of hours of erroneous simulations had been run, a book had been published containing these results, and several systems had been misdesigned on the basis of their errors. All this could have been avoided if he had adopted the practice of keeping a minimum distance of two (dissimilar) characters between his symbols, and perhaps ensuring that at least one of these differences was at the beginning or end.

Mnemonic symbols are particularly susceptible of inducing a torpor in the program reader. Mnemonic symbols expose us to misreading for several reasons:

1. They tend to make programs seem "sensible" by their satisfaction of our general set toward sense over nonsense.
2. They play upon our tendency to believe in the name, rather than the denotation of the name. Who would believe that the symbol "FIVE"

denoted a value of 4? But it did, in one case where the programmer had to modify his code and didn't have time to change all references to "FIVE." He did, however, have time to rerun the program—after having taken much time to locate the source of difficulty.

3. They tend to give something less than an optimal "distance" pattern. English words, for example, are not random collections of letters. Some patterns such as consonant-vowel-consonant, or consonant-vowel-vowel-consonant, tend to occur more frequently. Even worse, there are homographs such as "LEAD" and "LEAD," which might pop up in the same program from two different origins.

4. Optimal distance is further reduced because of regularities in the way we abbreviate, leading to such ambiguities as "PEND," for a record that is held in pending status, and "PEND," short for "end of part P."

We cannot abandon the subject of set errors without a comment on comments. The whole idea of a comment is to prepare the mind of the reader for a proper interpretation of the instruction or statement to which it is appended. If the code to which the comment refers is correct, the comment could be useful in this way; but if it happens to be incorrect, the set which the comment lends will only make it less likely that the error will be detected.

This effect of comments on interpretation of erroneous code can be measured quite nicely in an experiment in which several versions of the same code are produced, one with correct comments, one with one or two incorrect comments, and one with perhaps no comments at all (Okimoto, 1970). For certain types of code, at least, correct interpretation of what the program does can be obtained more reliably and faster without any comments at all. Correct comments, if well constructed, reduce errors when compared with cases in which incorrect or misleading comments are used. Nevertheless, many experienced programmers make a habit of covering all comments when scrutinizing a program listing for errors, thus reducing set which, though helpful to understanding a correct program, only complicates the already impossible job of debugging.

SOME DIMENSIONS OF PROBLEM SOLVING

In psychology, "set" is usually considered part of the study of "perception" rather than part of "intelligence." Yet it should be clear from the preceding section that set phenomena can influence behavior which we would surely label "problem solving." Of course, even before the question of problem solving comes the question of problem *avoiding*. As we saw, numerous techniques exist whereby a programmer can avoid the problems of set altogether in certain situations. Considered in the abstract, a programmer who avoids a problem altogether is more "intelligent" than one who brings it upon himself, whether or not he ultimately "solves" it.

However, abstract ideas about intelligence rarely fall into accord with our beliefs about concrete situations. Lacking any objective measure, we often judge how difficult a program is by how hard a programmer works on it. Using this sort of measure, we can easily fall into believing that the worst programmers are the best—because they work so hard at it. A case in point was a programmer who worked 14 hours a day, seven days a week, for eight weeks to get a small program running in a new installation. For his efforts, his company gave him an award for exceptional service. Shortly thereafter, another programmer (for the first had been promoted to a management position as an additional reward) was given the job of making some additions to this program. He found that the program was such a confusing mess that it was easier to rewrite it than to try and modify it.

The rewriting and debugging took exactly one week, working normal hours. Even considering that writing a program for the second time is far easier than writing it the first, the difference is significant. Moreover, the new program ran eight times faster than the old, took half the storage, and was half as many lines of coding. Clearly, the first programmer had been rewarded for making a mountain out of a molehill. The discovery of this misapplication of management largesse then led to a severe drop in morale in this programming group.

Problem-avoiding behavior, then, is intelligent behavior at its highest, although not very intelligent if one is trying to attract the eye of a poorly trained manager. It will always be difficult to appreciate how much trouble we are *not* having, just as it will always be difficult to appreciate a really good job for problem solving. Once the problem solution has been shown, it is easy to forget the puzzlement that existed before it was solved. For one thing, one of the most common reasons for problem difficulty is the overlooking of some factor. Once we have discovered or been told that this factor is significant, working out the solution is trivial. If we present the problem to someone else, we will usually present him with that factor, which immediately solves nine-tenths of the problem for him. He cannot imagine why we had such trouble, and soon we begin to wonder ourselves.

Overlooking a factor in a problem is just one special case of assumptions leading us astray. We assume that a certain factor is not important—probably without even thinking about it in any conscious manner. We are led similarly astray by assuming that a certain factor *is* important, when it has no significance for the problem at hand. People who spend much time debugging other people's programs soon learn not to listen to explanations before tackling the problem, for these explanations tend to put the listener on the same false track of assumptions that prevented the speaker from finding the bug for himself.

Psychological set, of course, is another form of making assumptions. Although the assumptions may be buried more deeply in this case, they have the same effect on problem solving. Could we not say, then, that the first rule of problem solving is "don't make assumptions"?

We could say that, but we would be precisely wrong. If we are to be successful at solving problems, we *must* make assumptions. If we really faced each problem as entirely new, it would be impossible to improve our problem-solving performance. The set we have, for example, which enables us to read a misprint as if it were correct, is a most valuable asset—in most situations. Only when we are proofreading, something few of us spend much time doing, does this particular set cause trouble. Intelligent behavior, then, does not consist in eschewing assumptions, but in being sufficiently flexible to manipulate assumptions as the occasion demands. In other words, being intelligent is not having some magic formula which one can apply to every problem. It is, rather, having a number of "formulas" and not being so much in love with one that it cannot be dropped for another.

Before we leave the topic of adaptability in problem solving for closer examination of some of the "formulas" which are selectively applied by the successful problem solver, we must lay to rest one more fallacy about intelligence. Intelligence, however it is ultimately defined, is, at best, a statistical concept. We cannot ever hope to measure intelligence by performance on one particular problem, for there are as many non-intelligent reasons for getting the "right" solution as there are intelligent reasons for getting the "wrong" solution. Indeed, the explanations for success given by some programmers bring to mind the story of the village idiot who won the monthly lottery. When asked to explain how he picked the winning number, he said, "Well, my lucky number is seven, and this was the seventh lottery this year, so I multiplied seven times seven and got the winning number—63."

And, when someone tried to tell him that seven times seven was forty-nine, he merely answered with disdain, "Oh, you're just jealous"—which, of course, was true.

FACETS OF PROGRAMMING INTELLIGENCE

Adaptability, then, is required for all sorts of intelligent behavior. Behavior which, though mental, only requires carrying out a set of fixed rules is not properly considered intelligent. It might better be carried out by machines than by people. Not that carrying out a set of fixed rules cannot be an important *part* of intelligent behavior. On the contrary, a programmer who cannot add two numbers together without extraordinary difficulty is heavily handicapped in the race for better problem solving, unless, of course, he turns his handicap into an asset by developing shortcuts that bypass the arithmetic he cannot do.

To a great extent, problem-solving technique is idiosyncratic, if only because certain people can do certain things better than others. Each person, if he is intelligent, tends to look for methods of solution that depend on his best qualities and avoid his weakest. As a specific example of such a quality, consider the facet of memory.

There is no doubt that memory is one of the most important aspects of intelligence for a programmer—if he can but harness it. Memory helps a programmer in many ways, not the least of which is by enabling him to "work" on problems when he does not have all his papers in front of him. Consider this anecdote related by a programmer about how he solved a problem while lying in bed:

The problem was given to me by a programmer I encountered yesterday morning at the computing center. He said he had the problem since last April (it is now January). The problem was not very serious, but it had puzzled him on and off since then, and everything he tried failed to work. It was a PL/I program, and the trouble was in the format of the output. He had established an ON ENDPAGE unit, but it only worked at the end of the first page and when it was raised by SIGNAL. After the first page, the listing just went on from page to page without producing the headings he wanted.

I checked the PAGESIZE he was using, and his job control cards—to see if he had some strange carriage control situation. I checked the position of the ON-unit, but obviously it was executing once. Were there any switches in it? Nothing. The only unusual thing I found was that he had used a PUT SKIP to print the heading, not a PUT PAGE as I ordinarily do. I pointed out to him that this explained why the heading he had printed failed to go on the top of the page. But, after testing a number of other hypotheses, I knew I wasn't going to find the major trouble. I showed him how he could get the right output, using a test of LINENO to raise ENDPAGE. That satisfied him, but I knew I couldn't put my mind at rest until I understood what was happening.

I put the problem out of my mind, but when I went to bed last night, my mind seemed clear, so I decided to work on it as I lay there. I reconstructed the whole situation mentally—the coding and the output. When my eyes are closed and I am in a quiet place, I can call up the picture of any program I am currently working on—even one like this, which I had seen only once. I scanned the output in my mind and tried to imagine what kind of program would produce this output. After reviewing my hypotheses from the morning and rejecting each on carefully considered grounds, I decided to look for something new.

The strange element, I felt in scanning over the program, was the PUT SKIP in the ON-unit. This stood out in my image the more frequently I scanned it, for I never did that. Never? In that case, perhaps it was causing the difference. But why would starting a page in a different way cause the end of the page to be missed? Well, how is the end of a page detected? By being so many lines from the top. But how is the top determined? I realized I didn't know that answer precisely, so I speculated on possible alternatives. By this time, I knew I was on the right path, and I simply considered each alternative in turn, imagining the action each would produce in this program.

Finally, when I worked through the action under the hypothesis that only PAGE (or possibly LINE, which did not apply in this case) could start a new page, I realized the problem. PUT SKIP in the ON-unit did not start a new page—the line number simply kept increasing and no new end of page was ever reached because no new page had ever been started. Satisfied that I had solved the problem, I went immediately to sleep. This morning, I made this test case to demonstrate my conjecture, and you can see that it is precisely as I say.

Without the aid of a fine memory, this programmer might never have solved this problem—and learned something new—because he might never have seen this program again. On the other hand, if he did not have this kind of memory, he probably never would have attempted this approach to the problem. He might, for example, utilize his cleverness at creating critical test cases by solving the problem using the computer. For his inadequate memory, he would substitute an actual copy of the problem deck—which is nothing to be ashamed of.

Indeed, by attacking the problem on the machine, this programmer might have the solution to the problem before going home, leaving his sleep untroubled by bugs. Which method is superior? We really cannot give an answer in isolation. If, for example, machine access is poor, the second programmer will be at a disadvantage; but if, on the other hand, everyone is working overtime and barely has time for sleep, let alone quiet reflection, the first programmer will never get to show his brilliance. Naturally, it would be best to have both abilities to an equal extent and to apply each as is appropriate to the problem and the overall situation; short of that, we must make the best of what we have.

Just as different working conditions favor the application of different forms of intelligent behavior, so do different programming phases give different programmers a chance to shine. For example, when we are making the overall design of a program, what we most need is the ability to create new programming ideas and to screen them on the basis of broad principles. Examples of such screening ideas are symmetry of structure and generality of function—one leads to simple coding of difficult problems and the other leads to the solution of difficult problems with simple coding. Still, these critical abilities are useless if there is a paucity of ideas to which to apply them. Nothing cannot be criticized. Thus, a programmer lacking in either ability—creativity or selectivity—will be handicapped in attempting to design programs.

When coding, however, different abilities come to the fore. Instead of the broad, sweeping mind, the mind which is clever at small things now excels. Then, when testing, the programmer must switch to yet another group of gifts—particularly the eye for wholeness, or *gestalt*. Consider the following tale.

> I was eating breakfast and reading an article by Stephen Spender called "The Making of a Poem." On page 120, I reached the end of one section and set the book down to put some more sugar on my cereal. When I picked the book up again to start reading a section called "Memory," I immediately had a feeling that there was something wrong in the first sentence which started:
> *"If the art of concentrating in a particular way. . . ."*
> I felt, more or less simultaneously, that the trouble was in the word "particular" and that it involved a misprint. The misprint, however, was rather confusing for I sensed that it was a letter inversion but I also sensed—a little bit more weakly, though, I have a definite impression of that—that there was a letter missing. I examined the word "particular"—which, by the way, I often mistype as "particluar"—first for the inversion and, failing to find that, for the omitted letter. I spent a rather long time looking for the error—I could measure that because I ate five or six spoonfuls of cereal in the process, the amount I ordinarily eat between sips of water. But I could not find anything wrong, and when I reached for the water glass, I was rather confused.
> The water glass was empty, so I set down the book and went to the sink to fill it. Upon returning, I drank some water, picked up the book, and started to read. I finished the paragraph without further difficulty, but when I commenced reading the next, I immediately saw that the line:
> *"All poets have this highly devolped sensitive apparatus. . . ."*
> contained the misprint of the word "devolped," which stood in the same position in that sentence as "particular" had stood in the first sentence of the preceding paragraph. I had the right impression, but I had "focussed" wrongly.

Although this error was in printing, its discovery and location followed very closely the process by which many programming errors are found. First, there is only the *gestalt,* a general feeling that something is out of place without any particular localization. Then follows the ability to shake loose from an unyielding situation—the ability to change one's point of view, even by employing external devices such as going for a glass of water. Then, however, one must go from the general to the particular— "focussing," as it was called here. Although one does not find errors efficiently by a detailed search of each line, or word, or character, the ability to get down to details is essential in the end. Thus, for debugging, an almost complementary set of mental powers is needed. No wonder good debuggers are so rare!

Even more of a rarity is the good documenter. Documentation difficulties come from many sources. In the first place, if the program is not well written, there is not much that documentation can do to resuscitate it. Since programmers usually document their own productions, the good documenter has to be a good programmer to begin with—and then he must add the capacity to express himself verbally and graphically. Finally, he must have the patience to work out those last few ambiguities in his documentation—for the last 5 percent of the work makes the document 100 percent better.

APTITUDE TESTS

If intelligence is so important for programming success, what can be done to select those people who have what it takes to do the job? The possibility of administering tests to select programmers had long be-witched programming managers, but over the years nobody has ever been able to demonstrate that any of the various "programmer's aptitude" tests was worth the money it cost for printing. We should be remiss, how-ever, if we did not attempt to explore the reasons for this universal failure.

In the first place, of course, programming is a diverse activity, and any test that gives a single "grade" is hardly adequate to measure the aptitudes required. Some tests have been designed to give multiple scores, but even if these had individually valid measures, they would be difficult to apply sensibly, and the average personnel manager simply would not bother. Moreover, just *because* of the multidimensionality, someone who is sorely deficient in one area may turn out to be outstand-ing in another—provided that the opportunity to use his strong points exists. On the other hand, sometimes a person who scores high on every possible scale performs poorly because he is missing some "minor" ability, such as the ability to get along with the people he has to work with.

These are theoretical conjectures, however, because nobody has put together a test with any measurable validity. The closest thing we have to a validation of a programmer's aptitude test are studies which show that people who scored high on the test were better students in the ensuing programmers' training. When it got down to the nitty-gritty of actual programming, however, there was no correlation—or even a slight negative correlation—between test scores and rated performance.

This sorry picture is not unique to programming. Intelligence tests gen-erally—such as the famous IQ tests—are able to predict success in school-type situations—and in nothing else. In fact, as one wit put it, intelligence tests measure the ability to take tests. We have reason to believe that this appraisal is not far from the truth. For example, in IQ tests, speed is very much a factor, as it is in school situations generally. But, in the office, the difference between one hour and one hour and ten minutes is only ten minutes—not the difference between an A and a C. Slow and steady may not win the race, but programming is not a race.

Another typical distortion of intelligence tests is in the emphasis they place on short-term—rather than long-term—memory. They could hardly be expected to do otherwise, given the constraints under which they must be administered. In an IQ test, one is asked to memorize nonsense words or arbitrary lists. But in "real life," it is *selective* memory which pays— the ability to forget the unimportant and retain the important over long periods. Not so in school, however, and so we have the IQ test and the school grades going hand in hand—off in a different direction from anything we are interested in.

Finally, and this leads right into our next topic, IQ scores, and programmer's aptitude scores, are demonstrably correlated with certain forms of training. In big cities, an eager parent can take his child to a special tutor who guarantees to raise his IQ by so many points for so many dollars. The same techniques are used by certain programming schools to help their graduates get jobs with those companies that rely heavily on aptitude testing. So, no matter how much we would like to have a magic wand which would point out the best programmer prospects, we are just going to have to learn to do without.

APTITUDE TESTS FOR PROGRAMMING

All of this leads up to specific tests that have been used in a grand attempt to measure aptitude for programming. Probably the foremost among these is the so-called PAT, or Programmer's Aptitude Test. Actually, this is not a single test, but an unknown number of variants on an original test made up one afternoon by a group of programmers in IBM's New York Scientific Computing Center sometime before 1956, and administered there to all job applicants and interested visitors. One of the reasons for the profusion of variants is that the test has been so widely used and so unprotected that nobody knows how many people have taken it, or, in particular, which people have taken it.

Not that the variations give much protection, since there is considerable transfer of learning from one variant to another. Over a series of classes involving IBM and other programmers, I asked people to report the number of times they had taken a variant of the PAT and what their scores had been. Since this was a "safe" situation—with nobody's job at stake—there is reason to believe that the replies are not too inaccurate. Out of 27 people who had taken the PAT more than once, 23 received A's the last time they took the test—they were all employed programmers working for companies which regarded A's as an important hiring criterion. Of these, 12 had A's the first time they took it, 7 had B's, and 4 had C's. Nobody had done worse the last time than the first.

A typical case was a girl working for IBM as a programmer who had graduated from college with a Math major and applied to RCA for a programming job. They had given her the PAT, and she had scored a "low" B. She didn't get the job, so she interviewed with IBM, who administered a slightly different version of the test, on which she scored a clear A. She was asked whether she had ever taken the PAT before, and she said "no," whereupon she was hired.

This previous experience with the PAT may be one reason researchers have been unable to correlate PAT performance with job performance. A few correlations have been reported (see Reinstedt, 1964), but we must be careful as to what we regard as "significant" in these cases. For example, the best correlation found in these studies was 0.7 between the PAT and supervisor's ranking. What does 0.7 correlation mean?

For a single study, a 0.7 correlation between two variables means that $(0.7)^2 = 0.49$, or 49 percent of the variation in one variable can be accounted for by the other—although it doesn't say which is which. This still leaves more than half of the variation to be explained, even if the correlation coefficient were an "explanation." One of the reasons for the popularity of the correlation coefficient is the way it seems to overstate the case, since the number used is always larger than its square.

The second problem with such correlations is that the score—which is definite enough—is correlated with the supervisor's ranking, which is an uncertain measure of programmer performance, to say the least. There really is no instrument today for measuring programmer performance— or reducing it to a single number, in any case. Consequently, there is nothing *really* reliable with which to correlate the PAT. It may even be that the PAT is a marvelous predictor of programmer performance, but the supervisors are not themselves sufficiently trained to know it.

We must also be wary of one other thing in using such correlations. Nobody knows how many times people have tried to correlate the PAT with job performance. Those who did try and did not obtain "significant" results more often than not would not publish their trial. We know of similar trials because correlations have been found between test scores and school grades (Biamonte, 1964, Gotterer, 1964). But, you see, if given sufficient chances to correlate, we will eventually get some correlation coefficient above any level we desire, if the data are random. Thus, we could say that a correlation of 0.56 will arise, by chance, no more than one time in a hundred, but if we do not know how many trials have been made and not reported, we have no way of evaluating the significance of such a statement. We do know, however, that the PAT is used in hundreds of places.

Furthermore, even if the trials have only been made a few times, a correlation of 0.56 occurring one time in a hundred by chance assumes that the true correlation is zero. If there is a small positive correlation, say of 0.1, then a spurious measure of 0.56 will occur more frequently than one time in a hundred. But a correlation of 0.1 means that 1 percent of the variation is accounted for by the correlation, and this is hardly the type of information we can use to make personnel decisions.

Assuming that the correlations were reliable, we have, on the basis of the recorded literature, no instrument any better than the PAT. Admittedly, it does predict scores in programming classes fairly well, but that is not what we are buying when we hire a programmer. As Mayer (1968) puts it so well,

> Very probably if you would use all of the tests to select an individual, you can [sic.] obtain a person who has a high probability of successfully completing your training program. Whether this individual is going to like programming or will possess the motivation that will allow him to take the successful training onto the job site is a question that is not yet answered.

Even this condemnation implies that the tests may be all right as far as they go, but that other factors may be more important on the job than pure "aptitude." Although we can not quarrel with the conclusion, we think a possibility may have been overlooked—namely, that the tests are just not good ones for programmer aptitude. Given the history of the PAT, one wonders why so many hundreds of firms use it slavishly, year after year. A little examination into the structure of the test itself might give us some hints as to what is wrong with it, now that we know that much *is* wrong with it.

The original PAT had three sections: relationship rules for geometric figures (much like standard IQ series), arithmetic reasoning, and number series. The first two have been retained in almost all of the variants of the PAT, although the number series has often been replaced by letter series. Just to get an idea of what might be wrong, consider the letter or number series problems, a typical one of which might be

1 4 7 . . .

where the examinee is asked to supply the next number in the series. It is certainly plausible that a modicum of intelligence is required to answer "10", but is this really the ability we most need in a programmer?

Let me give an example of what a good programmer did with such a series. A FORTRAN program had been written with the statement

DO 15 I = 10000, 30000, 10000

The program went into a strange loop which finally ended but produced output that nobody could decipher. When it was brought to this programmer, he thought for a while and then asked himself under what circumstances this particular DO would *not* produce the series

10000 20000 30000 . . .

Suddenly he realized that if the numbers were being kept in a 15-bit register, the next number in the series would be 7232, and the series would look something like this:

10000 20000 30000 7232 17232 27232 . . .

which explained precisely what was wrong with the program.

In other words, the PAT tests for the ability to see the *conventional* pattern in a series of numbers or letters, but the programmer, especially when debugging, has to look precisely for the *unconventional* pattern—the deviations. Possibly a much better type of question for programmer aptitude would be something like this:

"Given the series

1 4 7 . . .

tell what might normally be expected as the next number, and then describe at least three other choices which might be correct, giving reasons for each choice."

Another section of the PAT is arithmetic reasoning, but I have never had anyone who has been able to explain to me why programmers have to be good at arithmetic. Perhaps before 1956 arithmetic was more important, when most programming was done much closer to machine language than it is today. If you are working in a relatively crude language, it is useful to be able to add two or three hexadecimal numbers so that you can find an address in a dump, but how many programmers do that today? Don't we have computers just so we don't have to do arithmetic? I myself have never been able to add 7 and 5 rapidly, but I don't think that is the thing that is holding me back as a programmer. In fact, knowing that I am not very good at arithmetic, I am more suspicious of my programs, and of my check calculations—which forces me to do more testing of them. It would be rather easy to make an argument that poor arithmetic ability is an asset to a programmer.

The third part of the PAT leaves me entirely befuddled. Even in 1956, geometric relationships never seemed to have much to do with programming aptitude, but perhaps I missed the point. The one thing that programming doesn't seem to be in today's world is geometric. I've never met a programmer who was asked to tell whether two programs were the same if one was rotated 90 degrees. (There was once an article about palindromic programs, which read the same forward and backward, but its contribution to the profession was minor.)

Perhaps it is time that some new thinking go into these aptitude tests, if people are going to persist in using them. And persist they will, since even if the promise of success is not great, the rewards are. So let me suggest a few things that might make more sense for identifying potentially successful programmers:

1. Give the examinee thirty or forty papers with random printing on

them and ask him to place them in ten boxes. One week later, ask him to find the paper with the word "COMMODITY" on it. Time his retrieval performance—giving high scores for fast work.

2. Give the series-exception type question suggested above.

3. Tell him you are thinking of a problem which he must solve. Don't give him any more information unless he specifically asks for it, but answer all his questions literally. Score him on how well he figures out what the problem is. I don't really have much hope for such tests—either that they will work or that they will be applied if they do work—but they certainly seem more promising than what we have been using so far.

Yet all is not quite so bleak. When we are selecting among experienced programmers, the situation is potentially different, although few authors or employees seem to realize it. For example, out of 282 organizations using the PAT in one survey, 138 of them still use it for selecting experienced programmers. Why? Because they feel they have nothing else. Lacking anything better, they try what is available in a vain search for the elusive magic test. Such companies are sitting ducks for anyone who comes along with a fancy package of promises—and with lots of sitting ducks, can the hunters be far behind?

Not very far—even closer than I thought. After writing the above package, I ran across the following ad in a trade magazine:

"TEST THE SKILLS OF YOUR PROGRAMMERS
A Program called _____ consists of procedures, software, instructions and problems designed to evaluate programmer skills. _____ measures the ability to write correct, compact, and efficient programs, and can be used to test experienced programmers or to evaluate the programming aptitude of non-programmers. The tests used are language independent, and are weighted in accordance with the difficulty of the problems and the time used to solve them. The _____ program will run on a ***** System. It is priced at $5,000. . . ."

An evaluation of this ad is left as an exercise for the reader, but aside from its claim to test experienced or inexperienced programmers alike, it does offer one clue as to the proper direction for testing when it speaks of the "ability to write correct, compact, and efficient programs." What does this phrase suggest?

As one author comments, if we were hiring an oboe player for an orchestra, we would be able to give an audition, which would determine in a matter of a few minutes what his qualifications were, at least insofar as rejecting an obvious misfit. After a longer performance, we would have a moderately good measure of the oboist's abilities. He then goes on to lament, "There is no equivalent of an audition" for programming. But why isn't there? Certainly there is not for a person without experience, but neither is there much for a child who is applying for a traineeship in oboe playing.

For a programmer who claims to have experience, why not just have him sit down and write a small program or read and interpret a set of specifications, sketching out his approach to implementing them? Why not, indeed? Perhaps it is because we so rarely read programs that this action never occurs to us, or perhaps it is because when we intend to hire an "experienced" programmer, we deem ourselves lucky if even a single applicant shows up. Testing a single applicant is like testing your wife—if she fails, what are you going to do about it?

SUMMARY

Everybody involved in hiring programmers has an opinion about what qualities are essential to a good programmer—even though we know that programming is no one single activity. Mayer, as cited previously, believes that his "X-factor" is related to aptitude." He speaks wisely, with the caution of one heavily involved in psychological testing. People more involved in programming are more confident of their impressionistic view. Not all of them, however, are as explicit about their X-factors as E. W. Dijkstra, who said:

> I am engaged in teaching, at graduate level, in producing one variety of "mathematical engineer." The most powerful test that I know of for an applicant to be one of my students is that he have an absolute mastery of his native tongue: you just need to listen to him.

Since Dijkstra is "engaged in teaching," we cannot be too swayed by his remarks, for he may indeed have isolated a factor in academic success, as have several other workers. "Verbal ability" is as good a measure as we have of *academic* success in programming, so Dijkstra's intuition is probably a good one. But for actual programming performance, on commercial programs rather than "toy" programs, we lack any aptitude measure at all, except perhaps for general intelligence. For myself, I believe that intelligence has less to do with the matter than personality, work habits, and training. These things, unlike intelligence, can be changed by experience later in life, which turns the problem from one of *selecting* programmers to *creating* them. In other words, good programmers are made, not born; therefore we should turn our attention to the manufacturing, or training process.

QUESTIONS

For Managers

1. Do you use any aptitude tests now in choosing programmers, or does your personnel department use them? If so, what do you know about their validity? Do you make any effort to validate them by evaluating programmers after a period of time on the job? What methods do you use for this evaluation? How convinced are you of their effectiveness?

2. What single important aptitude do you find most often lacking in your programmers? What kind of test do you think would discover that such an aptitude was missing?

3. Would you spend $5000 for the package in the ad? Or $100 per test? If not, why not? If so, have you been reading this book?

For Programmers

1. Were you tested for aptitude when you applied for your present job? If so, did you find the test relevant? Do you know if your organization still uses these tests? If they do, and if you feel they are not relevant, what are you doing about it?

2. Do you feel it is possible to test for at least certain crucial aspects of programming aptitude? Make a list of what you consider to be crucial aspects of programming aptitude, and a list of suggestions as to how they could be tested.

3. Has this chapter indicated to you any areas of problem-solving ability or habit in which you may be deficient? If so, what plan do you have for doing something about it?

BIBLIOGRAPHY

Mayer, David B., and A. W. Stalnaker, Use of Psychological Tests in the Selection of Computer Personnel, *SHARE/GUIDE Presentation,* October, 1968.

Reinstedt, R. N., *et al., Computer Personnel Research Group Programmer Performance Prediction Study,* The RAND Corporation (RM-4033-PR), Santa Monica, California, March 1964.

Biamonte, A. J., Predicting Success in Programmer Training, *Proceedings of the Second Annual Computer Personnel Research Conference,* Association for Computing Machinery, New York, 1964.

Gotterer, M., and A. W. Stalnaker, Predicting Programmer Performance Among Non-preselected Trainee Groups, *Proceedings of the Second Annual Computer Personnel Research Conference,* Association for Computing Machinery, New York, 1964.

Okimoto, G. H., The Effectiveness of Comments: A Pilot Study, *IBM SDD Technical Report TR 01.1347,* July 27, 1970.

Luria, A. R., *The Mind of a Mnemonist,* New York, Avon Books, 1968.
A fascinating example of how an individual can use his peculiar abilities or disabilities to achieve fantastic performance—in this case on tasks involving memory.

Hunt, J. M., *Intelligence and Experience,* New York, Ronald, 1961.
Hunt reviews the process by which the intellect develops, with an end to seeing what can be done to influence intelligence. Unfortunately, it seems that by the time one is old enough to become a programmer, most of the opportunity for modification has been lost. Perhaps we should start younger. Now that more and more programming fathers and mothers are taking terminals home with them, can it be long before we produce a programming Mozart?

Wertheimer, M., *Productive Thinking,* revised ed. New York, Harper, 1945.
Wertheimer is the main founder of the Gestalt school of psychology, and in this book gave his prescription—based upon his experiences and experiments with young children—for teaching people how to think more productively. It seems unlikely that many of the ideas can be applied directly to teaching programmers to program better, but the book certainly is rich in suggestions as to which things to try and which to avoid.

Polya, George, *How to Solve It,* Princeton, Princeton University Press, 1946.
Polya, one of the great mathematicians of our time, gives a popular version of his work on techniques of solving mathematical problems and puzzles. Again, the work is highly suggestive for programming, but nobody has put it to a direct test, though many programmers have read it.

Ghiselin, Brewster, *The Creative Process,* Berkeley, California, University of California Press, 1952.
People have been studying the "creative process" for a long time—since Plato and Aristotle, at least—and we are a long way from understanding it. We don't know, even, if programming really requires creativity, or creativity on the level of a Mozart or an Einstein, or even if there are different levels of cerativity, or just different levels of creations. But for those who suspect that there may be some element of creativity in programming, this collection of original works and excerpts will certainly add fuel to their flame. Even for those who don't believe in creativity in programming, who could miss a chance to read what Einstein, Mozart, van Gogh, Wordsworth, Coleridge, Yeats, Nietzsche, Jung, and Spencer—to name but a sample—have to say about the subject. Besides, this is the source of the Stephen Spender misprint (in the paper edition).

Sackman, Harold, *Man-Computer Problem Solving,* Princeton, Auerbach, 1970.
Sackman's studies are not concerned solely with programming, but with the more general category of problem-solving behavior. His book contains many useful insights into the effects and lack of effects that working with a computer has on problem-solving behavior, but in a certain way he misses the point on programming as problem solving. Sackman himself is not a programmer, but a psychologist, and the one thing he never seems to have done in his studies was to *read the programs* produced. Like most psychologists, he apparently assumes, that all completed solutions to the same problem are equivalent, and that only failures to complete a program and get the correct results need be considered carefully. But all programs that give the same output are not alike, as we

know, and until psychologists recognize this, most of programming/problem-solving behavior will remain a fog.

Weinberg, G. M., *Experiments in Problem Solving* (Doctoral Thesis), Ann Arbor, University Microfilms, 1965.

Recommended for the psychologist who does not understand the commentary in the previous citation. This study shows how sufficient resolution in the observation of the problem-solving task and the ability to characterize the task in terms of the individual subject's strong and weak characteristics lead to striking insights into problem solving. Such insights will never be available if the level of resolution remains too high, or if individuals are averaged together to get "statistically significant results."

10 MOTIVATION, TRAINING, AND EXPERIENCE

Psychologists know that human performance on a given task is a function of the task itself *and as understood* by the subject. They also know that performance will be influenced by individual differences in such areas as personality and intelligence. But even though personality can be changed, and intelligence can be raised somewhat, real improvement in performance has to come from training and experience.

However, psychology is not an exact science, nor can it ever be. Once the psychologist takes into account the task and the subject's understanding of the task, once he has taken into account all measurable individual differences, and once he has taken into account all the training and experience, he is still left with a residue of unexplained performance. For example, the same individual doing essentially the same task a day later may do a worse job than he had done previously. Since his intelligence and personality are presumed not to have changed in one day, and since his understanding of and experience with the task should only have improved, how can such a decrease be explained?

This residue, after all the other factors are taken into account, is called "motivation." Volumes have been written on the subject, even though there is still doubt in psychologists' minds whether or not such a thing really exists. We have already spoken about some aspects of motivation as they are seen through variations in group or team performance, and in a certain sense we would be better off not opening this Pandora's box again, since we can hardly give it adequate treatment here. But we must say something about motivation before we can say anything useful about education and training, for two reasons. In the first place, if there is a residue of performance attributable to motivation, then this residue is inaccessible to training and education and sets limits on how much we can hope to accomplish by these means. Secondly, the residue might be all there is to education and training. It could very well be that if someone is not motivated, there is no easy way to make him learn, and if someone is motivated, there may be no way to stop him from learning.

MOTIVATION

Probably the best illustration of what motivation is came to me when I was reading the following passage from the beginning of the section on Motivation from a standard psychology text:

> Even the most cursory examination of the behavior of man leads one to the assertion that man is not a passive victim of circumstances. Instead, we all easily assert that man seems to decide which stimuli to react to, which to ignore, and which information to learn, which to neglect. These observations form the basis for ascribing to man some sort of an inner "directing drive" or "inner spring." This inner directing force is what most of us mean by "motivation." (Krech, Krutchfield, and Livson, 1969)

Now the interesting lesson in this passage arose from the fact that this was not a new book, but had been bought used from the college bookstore. The previous owner of the book had, in this passage, meticulously circled in orange pencil certain letters in various words. Evidently, it was a form of doodling, either when he was supposed to be studying or when he was supposed to be listening to the lecture. When the letters were read off in sequence, they spelled

S-A-L-L-Y-S-A-L-L-Y

What better illustration could we give of the "inner directing force" which "most of us mean by motivation."

It is certainly unnecessary to point out that programmers, too, may be, at times, wondering what became of Sally when their managers would rather they were wondering what was wrong with some tally. One error that managers make, however, is to assume that a lack of performance means a lack of motivation. Consequently, they may attempt to supplement the lack of "inner driving force" with a little "outer driving force," just when the programmer is suffering from too much, rather than from too little.

One of the best known and accepted results of motivation research is that increasing "driving force" will first increase performance to a maximum, beyond which addition of further driving forces will quickly drive performance to zero. The rapid fall-off in performance is especially observable in complex tasks, which is why it is so important for programming. Trying too hard, say, to find a bug, is as bad, or worse, than not trying at all, and many bugs have been exterminated only after the programmer had given up and stopped pressing. Pressing a programmer for rapid elimination of a bug may turn out to be the worst possible strategy—but it is by far the most common.

From the point of view of a programming manager, or of the programmer himself, the first important question about motivation, then, is how motivated is the programmer already. The answer to this question tells whether to look for ways to increase or to decrease the driving force. Overall, it has been my experience that programmers as a group are overmotivated, which is a major reason why so many programming projects fall apart as the pressure grows.

But once we have established whether force has to be added or subtracted, what can we do about it? The problem facing an individual is probably insoluble, for how can he change his inner driving force unless he is motivated to do so? Actually, though, he has available the same kinds of strategies that a manager has—he must change something in his external environment in order to have a chance of changing something inside.

Of course, a particular external change will not produce the same internal change in each group of people. Parading a naked lady by the door will certainly affect men differently from women. And individual men or women will be differentially affected—as the Candid Camera movie, "What Do You Say to a Naked Lady?" showed so vividly. But perhaps programmers as a group have some commonalities in their reactions to external stimuli, just as men, no matter how different, generally share some reaction to a naked lady—the reaction of interest, at least.

We have made some preliminary studies to try for some insight into what external factors motivate programmers. We did not run experiments, in which we would have had to subject programmers to different stimuli and then observed their work patterns. Instead, we surveyed programmers and their managers about what they *thought* motivated programmers. We emphasize the word "thought" because there is no necessary relationship between what a person says he does or will or would do and what he actually does. With that reservation, we can report some of the more interesting findings.

Among software programmers at one large shop, we found that "a salary increase and/or bonus" would "make a large effect on the results my manager would see in getting me to work at a sustained fast pace or keeping me diligently at work." A very close second, as we already expected from social psychology, was "personal involvement in planning of our task." Then, tied for third place were the two items—"a promotion" and "more time to give my work a personal touch of quality."

These four topped the list of nineteen choices. At the very bottom of the list was "lessening the scope of my work," which is reasonable in that it seems to jibe with the favoring of more involvement in overall planning. Just above this choice were four other low-favored choices. The first was "assistance in documentation, copying, etc." which seems to contradict the folk-wisdom about the universal distaste for documentation work. But such a conclusion may be premature—it could be that these people had already reached a state where they were not doing documentation anyway and that factor wasn't important. Next of the four was "placement in a prestige position," which seems to contradict "promotion." Further investigation revealed that "promotion" was essentially associated with "more money," rather than the acquisition of a new title—which goes to show the difficulty of taking opinion surveys.

The last two of the four seemed to be contradictory: "relaxation of target dates" and "tightening of target dates." The contradiction is resolved if we observe that it is consistent with the view that target dates are not very important to this group at this time. At this time—an important qualifier. At the time of the survey, the project deadline was not within six months. We would have liked to check again in several months and see if "target dates" were still at the bottom of the list.

Which brings us to another major difficulty with motivation studies. Even if these responses truly reflect differential strengths of outside forces, they represent those strengths in a particular circumstance at a particular time. Toward the end of a project, people are motivated differently than at the beginning when the goal-setting is at hand and the target date is far off the horizon. Early in a career, one is motivated differently than later on—money, for example, may grow less important as savings grow, salary grows, and debts to oneself are progressively paid ʻff, Or, in certain circumstances that we have seen, additional money can actually drive a man off the job.

It would be tempting at this point to say that the money motivation is not as real as the concern with participation in goal setting and quality of the work, but there is no real justification for believing that programmers as a group are any less concerned with money than any other group at a comparable pay scale. Of course, programmers tend to be on a rather high scale compared with the general populace, so we might expect that money would be less motivating for them. And it may be, but we haven't proved it by our studies. Then again, money is an ambiguous motivator. Some people it motivates as a means of obtaining what they want or need, some it motivates as a symbol of the value that is placed on their work. But what difference does that make; money is money, isn't it? Not precisely, for if the money is valued more as a symbol, then programmers could be motivated with other rewards than money—such as extra time to give work a personal touch, or a piece of the planning responsibility. Not just to save the company money, mind you, but to motivate them more effectively, for an increase in salary only motivates for a short time—it is the *raise,* not the salary level which is a symbol of current value. A continuing series of raises is probably out of the question over any long interval, but continuing participation and continuing time for quality work are not out of the question at all.

Anyone who has ever seen a programmer at work—any wife or husband of a programmer who has ever tried to interrupt a terminal session or a conference over a bug—knows that programming itself, if the programmer is given a chance to do it his way, is the biggest motivation in programming. There is an old saying about chess that goes like this: "Chess, like women and music, has the power to make men happy." I think we could safely say that "programming, like chess, women, and music, has the power to make men happy." Someday, I suppose, I will pick up a used copy of this book and find that somebody has circled various letters to form

F-O-R-T-R-A-N-F-O-R-T-R-A-N.

TRAINING, SCHOOLING, AND EDUCATION

Certain people claim that they can take any person who walks in the door and train him to be a competent programmer. Although this is a slightly biased view—because not just anyone walks in the door of a computing center looking for a job—there is at least a grain of truth in it. Once, on a visit to a highly successful software firm, we had the opportunity to spend the afternoon with their systems programming team.

The five members of the team had the following backgrounds to qualify them for their positions of high responsibility:

1. A man of 33 who had been thrown out of an Ivy League school in his sophomore year because all he wanted to do was play bridge.
2. A woman of 28 who had majored in Spanish literature at a private girls' college in the South, then went on a binge from which she emerged three years later in a narcotics recovery program where she learned programming.
3. A former computer maintenance engineer, also 28, whose only formal education past grade school was at a Navy electronics school.
4. A 55-year-old mother of five grown children who had taken a Teachers' College degree thirty-three years ago, but had gotten married and never taught—and who decided to take up programming to occupy her time when her children had gone away.
5. A 30-year-old man had gone straight through college (with honors) to the M.A. in mathematics, whereupon he entered the programming business. He was considered the odd-ball of the group.

Although the heterogeneity of this group might seem to argue against training for computer programming, it is actually only an argument against the "normal" educational process as a training ground. What the members of this group had in common was four years of working together under one man—one of the founders of the software firm—who devoted that time to shaping them in his own image.

Such a situation is not as unusual as it may sound. Most people who have been around the programming scene for a while can describe similar groups they have encountered. The striking factor is always the same—several years of working together on real projects under a formidable leader. But those years represent training and experience—not, perhaps, the common or conventional kind, but all the same holding promise of what we might achieve could we but extract the essence of the process.

One of the confusions standing in the way of educational progress is the confusion between schooling and education. Another is the confusion between education and training. To illustrate these confusions and how they impede progress, I would like to present some results concerning the effectiveness of my own teaching. In the course of several years of trying to teach operating concepts, I found that without machine experience with operating systems, the concepts seemed to have no force. That is, I would visit my students on the job a year or so after they left school and find that they were not applying what they had "learned" in my classroom.

Since I attributed this loss of learning to lack of practical experience,

I decided to change the course into a workshop in OS/360. But in the workshop mode, I discovered that the students were having a terrible time seeing the concepts for the details. In particular, the details of the Job Control Language seemed to be standing in their way—an observation that corresponded well with reports coming in from the field. In more particular, the handling of "nonsignificant" blanks and continuation cards seemed to be the source of enormous trouble—if the amount of griping was any measure.

I therefore decided to emphasize these petty syntactic details in the lectures and to keep records of the student performance through some class problems. The problems involved creating, punching, and testing a series of job control cards through successively more difficult exercises. The results were rather discouraging, as shown under "Class #1" in Figure 10–1. Eighty-three percent of all JCL errors were "blanks" errors—that is, the types of errors I had specifically emphasized in class.

I then decided to compare this behavior with another class using the same exercises—but without spending any class time on the subject of "blanks" errors except to answer specific questions. The behavior of that class is shown as "Class #2" in Figure 10–1. It appears from this chart that the net effect of my arduous attempt to teach JCL syntax by lecturing was a reduction of relative error rate from 87 to 83 percent. This is assuredly *not* a statistically significant result. It *is* a significant result, however, for the psychology of programmer education, for it shows that schooling—or lecturing, in this case—need have little or nothing to do with education. It may be, of course, that some other

		PROBLEM 1		PROBLEM 2		PROBLEM 3		TOTAL FOR 3 PROBLEMS		
CLASS	SIZE	JCL ERRORS	BLANKS	TOTAL	BLANKS	TOTAL	BLANKS	JCL	BLANKS	%
#1	23	63	49	101	88	103	84	267	221	83
#2	17	51	42	86	78	105	88	241	208	87

Figure 10–1 Errors by JCL beginners.

instructor could have had an influence on this behavior—I don't claim to be the world's finest lecturer. But then, I can say in all modesty that I am not the world's worst, either, so a good many other lecturers would have had this problem getting across their "material."

Now, why is it so important to get across such trivial material, anyway? Unfortunately, although the intellectual content of the material is not great, failure to learn it absolutely impedes further progress in learning to use the operating system. Which brings us to our second distinction—education versus training. Roughly speaking, by "education" we mean acquisition of general principles and skills, and by "training" we mean acquisition of specific skills. Thus, we speak of "driver training," "military training," "adult education," and "liberal education." Not that the words necessarily tell what is going on in the school. Military training certainly teaches general principles that affect one's point of view for a lifetime, and adult education is more often than not merely training in some specific skill.

But more important, *education* may be impossible without certain *training* as a prerequisite. In our case, experience on the computer was necessary to impart operating systems concepts in a lasting way, and ability to manipulate JCL syntax was necessary to get operating system experience. Thus, *failure to train* in JCL syntax led to *failure to educate* in operating systems principles.

Perhaps we should say "failure to *school* in JCL syntax" led to failure to educate, because eventually Class #2 did become *trained* in JCL syntax, as shown in Figure 10–2. By the end of ten exercises, 13 of the 17 students had mastered the skill of creating JCL cards without "blanks" errors (although two of them regressed slightly on problem #11, which was a bit larger than the others). The other four students did not show any marked increase in this skill, however, and this failure was still standing in the way of their progress in operating systems concepts. No doubt they would have learned the skill eventually, but the class terminated at that point and they were sent back to their home locations. Quite likely, they remained aloof from the operating system, whereas the other 13 could now approach it with confidence for further learning.

In summary, then, the difficulty of acquiring skill—training—in JCL syntax creates a barrier that blocks further progress in operating system education (and incidentally creates an elite group of JCL "experts" upon whom other programmers remain slavishly dependent). This barrier cannot be removed by lecturing about it, but it can be removed by putting the learner in a situation where the machine keeps giving him the experience he needs. No doubt a system could be created which would do this job more efficiently and effectively than OS/360 itself—an on-line terminal with JCL syntax-checking facilities, for example. But bad

		CLASS #2	N-17	
PROBLEM	JCL CARDS	BLANKS ERRORS	ERRORS PER CARD	# WITH NO BLANK ERRORS
1	85	42	0.50	0
2	136	78	0.58	0
3	170	88	0.52	1
4	136	63	0.46	2
5	136	58	0.43	2
6	102	30	0.29	7
7	153	49	0.31	5
8	170	47	0.28	8
9	85	17	0.20	13
10	119	19	0.16	13
11	187	39	0.21	11

Figure 10–2 Errors by JCL beginners with training.

as OS/360 is, it is a kind of teaching machine if we can but get the students to use it. This is the service the "school" can provide in this situation—encouraging the student to keep trying in face of OS/360, or as one student termed it, "Obstacle System/360."

FORCES AGAINST LEARNING

To a surprising degree, the only time we fail to learn is when there are negative forces set up against it. We say "surprising" because so much emphasis in teaching is placed on motivating people to learn by using all sorts of clever devices or tricks. If we could observe children learning, however, we would see that any child really left to his own devices will learn vast numbers of things—not necessarily the things we want him to learn, but vast numbers all the same. In order to try to shape his learning into the form of the things we want him to learn, we build certain walls and open certain doors. When he learns, we congratulate ourselves, but he would have learned—possibly better—without us and our artificial barriers.

With adults, however, the barriers to learning have usually become internalized, and the average adult learns very little if left to his own devices. First and foremost, in order to learn we have to acknowledge that there is something we don't know that might be worth knowing. For a professional programmer, this acknowledgment represents a lowering of status—unless he is perceptive enough to see that a true professional, a person with true strength, loses nothing by admitting to weakness.

Some people, however, are only too willing to admit weakness. They, however, will not try to learn because they are convinced in advance that they will fail. Such fear of failure may be engendered by a general lack of confidence, or may spring from the experience of earlier failures in the same kind of endeavor. Most often, however, the fear is not so much of failure itself, but of having other people witness the failure.

For certain types of material, being in a group inhibits new learning but facilitates performance in using material already learned. To learn, we must be willing to make mistakes, and this is difficult to do when there is an audience present. Indeed, it is probably the presence of the others that gives the incentive *not* to make mistakes when the material being used *is* well known. To the extent that this observation applies to the learning of programming skills, we might expect that initial learning of, say, a new programming language would best be done when cloistered with a terminal—and when no record is kept of mistakes.

Our observations have tended to confirm this prediction in several ways. In one study, which was attempting to determine the most commonly made errors in using PL/I and to examine how well the compiler detected and corrected them, we attempted to collect *all* runs made by a group of fifty beginners. The difficulties in making this collection were astounding. Every sort of evasion was used in an attempt to cover up the very existence of errors. Although we had explicitly told the group that we were not studying them as individuals and that the *purpose* of the study was to measure all errors, we continually received the reply: ". . . but you're not interested in *this* run; I left off that silly semicolon. Wait for the next run; then I'll have something good to show you."

Another observation pointing in this direction is the enthusiasm that beginners often generate for terminal systems—enthusiasm that often dampens after they reach the point where trivial syntactic errors have all but disappeared through learning. More experienced programmers seem less enthusiastic about the terminal as other than a data entry device —perhaps with mild syntax-checking features to help eradicate keying errors. For beginners, or amateurs, the difficulties with syntax, keying, and such auxiliary operations as job control usually far outweigh any deeper difficulties that might arise from subtle semantic points or from the problem itself. Since most psychological tests involving comparisons between terminal systems and batch systems have involved beginners and/or fairly trivial problems, they have failed to give us definitive data on the different strengths of these two approaches. Careful observation of terminal use by programmers in different stages of development and working on different types of problems will be necessary if we are to design systems that are best for initial learning and best for later use.

Precious little of the controversy over diverse programming languages and systems ever touches on the distinction between ease of learning and ease of use. There is no particular reason why a feature that is easiest to learn will be easiest to use in the long run. The important concept here is that of *extensibility* of a technique—is it applicable to situations other than the one for which it was first learned? When we learn a general technique, we do not simply add to our repertoire of facts, we multiply our power of performance.

At the opposite extreme of general, extensible techniques are what we might term "dead-end" techniques. We may, for example, learn Cramer's rule for solving simultaneous linear equations by means of determinants in order that we can solve systems of three or four equations. Indeed, this is the normal course of teaching high school algebra. But Cramer's rule—though in theory perfectly general—is essentially impossible to apply to large systems of equations, for the computation of determinants grows too rapidly in complexity. Although no definite end point can be drawn beyond which it is impractical to employ Cramer's rule, it is without a doubt a dead-end technique.

In programming, we often encounter a programmer who has had much success working on problems of a certain size but has never been able to go beyond them. In fact, we sometimes encounter the converse situation—the programmer who was not notably successful until he began to work on bigger systems. In the first case, the techniques that worked so well on small programs just cannot be applied effectively to large ones; in the second, application of powerful and general techniques to simple problems may have resulted in excessive overhead.

Consider, for instance, the difference between a binary search and a sequential search. If we are writing a program which has to search through a table of ten items, it will probably slow down the programming and even the execution if we try to apply a binary search. The programmer who does not know of the binary search concept may, on this problem, outshine the programmer who does know it but doesn't quite have the sense to detect its limitations. All the same, the binary search will probably not be more than half the speed and twice the work—which cannot be said for the linear search when applied, say, to a list of 1000 items.

For the programmer who has mastered certain dead-end techniques (or dead-end programming languages), new learning requires that he give up, at least temporarily, some current satisfaction. His early success with the new techniques will probably not be great; and he is, in a sense, putting himself back on a par with the novices. This fear of loss can be especially great when faced with the learning of a new programming language. Anyone who has ever lived in a foreign country knows the feeling of helplessness the first time he really tries to get along with his meager knowledge of the language; and it is hardly different when one learns to program again. Just as the traveler is embarrassed by the way little children speak better French than he, the experienced FORTRAN programmer feels his power slipping away when he has to ask one of the trainees about some simple syntactic point in PL/I.

The fear of new things, the expectation of failure, and the reluctance to admit weakness all have a direct retarding effect on learning, whether in a formal classroom situation or on the job. Other problems arise indirectly, most often from an inadequate perception of what has to be learned or how to go about learning it. In one introductory programming course, the instructor noticed that most of the students were having trouble with their laboratory assignments, although they were of a simple nature. Each student was supposed to solve two or three simple problems using a terminal connected to an APL system, but after the fifth week, only about five out of fifty had turned in results.

The instructor decided to visit the laboratory, and what he found there were two different problems leading to the same end result—no significant learning. The first problem involved the students he found in the terminal room. Typically, they had signed onto the terminal the moment they knew how and started typing away. With more confidence than thought, they blundered about for hours and hours of terminal time and got nowhere. The second problem, however, involved the students he *didn't* find in the terminal room. In their case, because they were accustomed to working problems by hand, they were afraid to come to the terminal before having every last detail worked out. And, of course, they were unable to work out every last detail without the aid of the terminal itself.

When faced with a problem arising out of some unfamiliar situation, there are two general errors we can make—either we think the problem is harder than it really is or we think it is easier than it really is. A poor teacher is not usually poor for lack of mastery of the subject matter—subject matter is commonly in books or other sources, which the students can peruse for themselves. The poor teacher may give his students the impression that things are too easy, perhaps by being too smoothly prepared so that they do not see the difficulties underlying his examples. Or, he may choose intentionally simple examples to highlight certain points and, in so doing, give the impression that in real problems things always seem to fall into place.

In our APL class, the instructor had, to take one example, given a program which found the position of one character string in another—essentially the INDEX function of PL/I. The example presented in class took exactly one line, and was quite elegant. Unfortunately, this solution was inadequate in several ways. If either of the strings had only one character, or none, it failed entirely. If the sought-for string happened to be "wrapped around" the sought-in string, the routine incorrectly said that it was found—as in the case of 'XA' being found in "ABCX." Many other details had been left out of the problem; but when the students were given a similar problem to do on the terminal, they had to deal with such details even though they didn't expect them.

On the other hand, the same instructor had been guilty of making things seem too hard for other students. At the end of one lecture, finding himself with an extra ten minutes, he attempted to show them a problem he had been working on in his own research. The solution was completely beyond some of the students because they did not have the mathematical grounding even to understand the problem. These students were discouraged from even trying the homework.

When there is a teacher, we expect that he will be able to perceive such situations and intervene as necessary to get the students back on the track to learning. But much of programming learning takes place without a teacher, or at least without someone formally designated as one. Moreover, much of programming learning takes place without certain other essential elements—textbooks, reference material, software or hardware on which to run the software, released time to study new topics, authorization to try a new technique on a production problem, or other programmers who have some experience. Each such missing ingredient compounds the problem of learning and makes it more likely that the learner will give up at the first discouraging sign.

The school is a place where these essential elements are supposed to be supplied. We have no way of knowing how much of the success of a school depends on these factors rather than on its teachers, who form only the most conspicuous part of the teaching system. And yet, although nobody would argue that it is improper for a school to furnish these elements, the very existence of schools may tend to mean that they are not furnished elsewhere. A manager's reasoning may go something like this: "He's asking me for a job number to use in running some practice problems. What does he need that for? We just sent him to school for four weeks—what did they teach him there?"

This attitude—"school is where you learn; office is where you work"—is not, of course, confined to the programming business. Nevertheless, the programming business relies more than any other on unending learning, so we need not apologize for any attention we pay to factors that stand in its way.

HOW TO LEARN PROGRAMMING

The programmer who wants to advance himself cannot afford to rely on formal training and the grace of his manager to get the education he needs. Neither can he depend on pure "experience," for experience doesn't necessarily teach anything. If a programmer is going to make something of his experience, he must learn how to learn.

The first step in learning how to learn anything is to learn your own assets and liabilities—"know thyself." The person who is his own teacher has one major advantage over the classroom student—he can tailor the lessons precisely to the needs of his one and only student. In the previous section, we gave an example of a teacher whose students were failing to learn APL for two different reasons. Not only were the reasons different, they were complementary; for if the teacher tried making things seem harder to help one group, he would lose the group that already was having difficulty in following his examples. Moving in the other direction would be no better, so the teacher was caught in an essential paradox. The only way out of this dilemma would have been between its horns: he would have to deal with each student's situation individually.

This individual attention is precisely what the self-taught student gets automatically, if he but has the self-sensitivity to use it. For instance, every modern theory of education recognizes the existence of *favored modes of perception.* For example, some people retain (learn) information better when they hear it spoken, as in a lecture; others retain best when they see the information written. People of the first type may have more success in a class when the lecturer is a fine speaker, whereas people of a more visual bent will be at an advantage when the lecturer has well-prepared visual aids. Most people have an awareness of whether they favor auditory or visual presentations for learning, but few use this information in charting their own educational plans.

The person who favors auditory learning should try to find lectures, either live or taped, from which he can learn. If he can find taped lectures, he may have the additional advantage of being able to listen to the same lecture several times—something he cannot do very easily with live lectures. In fact, the tape recording—or even television tape recording—promises to give the auditory learner equal parity with the visual learner, who always had the advantage of being able to read a book or survey a diagram as many times as he thought necessary.

The individuality of the learner is not only reflected in his passive acceptance of information from a book or lecture, but also in the activity he performs while using these media. For instance, some people cannot learn effectively from a lecture unless they take notes, even if they never refer to the notes again. The very act of writing while listening enhances retention for some. For others, however, taking notes during a lecture is merely a distraction, and they retain best by concentrating on the lecture as it is given. Such learners are handicapped by being forced to take notes in a course, as when the instructor requires that each student turn in his notebook at the end of the term. When learning individually, however, no such outside pressure is present, yet many people continue to take notes because they were forced to, or taught to, when they were in a formal school situation.

Another important dichotomy is between people who learn best by doing—by working problems, writing programs, and so forth—and those who learn best by discussing problems with other people. Of course, the dichotomy is not a genetic one, and we can learn to profit from one form of interaction even if we favor the other. In fact, it may be that we learn different kinds of material best in different modes—we may learn a new programming language best by writing programs in it, but we may come to understand a problem best by discussing it thoroughly before plunging in.

One final area in which idiosyncratic learning methods should be studied is that of work habits. Some people learn best first thing in the morning, and some "night people" pass their early morning hours in an impenetrable fog. Some people learn best when seated in a hard straight-backed chair at a desk, whereas some hedonists in such a situation cannot take their mind off their discomfort long enough to learn that one plus one is two. Some people like to write with a hard pencil, some with a soft one. Others must have a fountain pen, a ball-point, or a felt-tip; still others must have a typewriter—and a particular model, to boot. Some people prefer unlined paper, some prefer wide-lined, some prefer narrow. Still others like to use graph-ruled paper, at least for some types of work. One programmer must code on a preprinted coding sheet, another must use plain paper, and yet a third might prefer composing his programs on a typewriter, or a terminal. Even in the case of terminals, some prefer a graphic terminal, and others must have a hard copy produced before their eyes. One of the reasons for preferring a graphic terminal is that some people cannot work well in a noisy environment, and yet we know that others actually *need* a substantial amount of noise in order to learn at all—even to the extent of having to play a radio while they study.

The debate over the optimum conditions for learning is probably endless, for it is essentially a debate over an unresolvable problem. When we are establishing a school, it may be necessary to accept one mode of operation as best compromise for the "typical" student, but why should an individual working alone have to make any compromise whatsoever with the conditions that will be optimal for him? Indeed, even in schools the quest for efficiency is often carried beyond any reasonable need. Why, for instance, must all students be forced to work on the same type of terminal, the same type of coding pad, or with the same type of pen or pencil? Making several reasonable alternatives available in the school situation should encourage students to think about their own learning habits—so that when they leave the school they will be better prepared to continue learning, rather than feeling that if they never study another thing it will be too soon.

No matter how well we establish the best physical environment for learning, they have little influence on our success if we do not use all the information available to help us learn. Just as we lose efficiency by ignoring our idiosyncratic needs, we lose when we ignore sources of information—or pieces of information lying available in sources we are already using. Probably the greatest cause of this type of loss is the concept that something that is not "right" is "wrong." This binary distinction—this Aristotelian fallacy which pervades our culture today—results in countless amounts of lost information, which, if recovered, could lead to a major increase in educational efficiency.

As a simple example of such loss of information, consider the case of two students trying to do the arithmetic problem, 25 - 16, on a test. If one student gets the answer "19" while the other gets "41," both are graded as being "wrong," yet the first is obviously suffering from a different problem than the second. In a large class, these two students are merely lumped together as "pupils who cannot subtract." If either were fortunate enough to have a tutor, the additional information in their answers would be turned to good teaching advantage.

When we undertake to tutor ourselves, we must learn to pay attention to all such information. When we write a program, for instance, and when that program does not run "correctly," there is usually a plethora of information lying about in the output. Rarely, if ever, do we just get back a program which says "incorrect," although many programmers operate as if this were all they had to work with, and all they care about. If, on the other hand, the output seems to be "correct," they lay it aside without a further thought.

Learning is an active pursuit. When learning to program, there are two times when one should actively pursue learning—when the program runs and when it doesn't run. When it runs is the time to step back three paces and take a broad look at what has been accomplished. Why was this program successful when we have had more trouble with seemingly similar programs? Why did we have as much trouble as we did? If we were starting from scratch, what would we do differently to make the programming job easier, or to make the program more efficient, or to make the documentation better? Can we do any of these things now? All too often the program that "works" is mistaken for the program that is finished, frequently because of management pressure to "produce." But the programmer who wants to learn must resist such pressures and take the time to review his success. It might be a good practice for management to give the programmer a day off when his project is "finished," not so much as a reward but as a chance to get a little perspective.

When our program does not run correctly, we have the opportunity to learn more specific lessons. Quite often, under the pressure of production, the programmer is tempted to bypass a trouble spot with a "fix" that he knows will work, since it does not use some new technique which he was trying to master. Suppose, for example, that he has just been studying array expressions in PL/I, but that he has some trouble with an array expression in his production program. If he decides that array expressions are too "complicated" and substitutes a DO loop such as he has been using since his FORTRAN days, he will have missed a golden opportunity for learning. No time will be more propitious for learning than that time at which the *need* for learning is felt most strongly—the very moment when we detect an error.

But be realistic: production work comes before learning in most environments, and managers will not tolerate substantial current delays even when promised ultimate rewards in the great beyond when the new technique is mastered. What is the programmer to do when faced with this conflict between his job and his learning? Actually, the resolution is simple. If, after a reasonable amount of time trying to understand the failure of the new technique, he has had no success, he should proceed with his "fix," if he has one. At the same time, he should construct a test case that will enable him to discover why his original approach failed.

In our example of PL/I array assignments, the programmer could write out the DO loop in the production program and initiate a job in which the array assignment is tested in isolation. By pursuing this test example to the point where he understands the problem, he will not only learn the one thing he did not know, but perhaps will learn others as well, for test programs such as this are often better learning instruments than are production programs.

As a matter of good practice, the test program should be constructed *before* the "fix" is made to the production program. In the first place, there will be an all too human tendency to forget about the problem once the production program is working correctly, so we must impose a little discipline on ourselves. Possibly more important, however, is the chance that by the mere act of constructing the test case we shall discover the problem. In one case we observed, the programmer had been having trouble with the PL/I array assignment statement

A = A/SUM(A);

He did not know where the trouble lay, so he created a test case in which the SUM function was applied separately, in order that he might see the sum printed. As he did this, however, he suddenly realized that SUM(A) would not be computed separately in the problem statement— that it would, indeed, be computed after each assignment of an element of A. He was able to check this idea against the erroneous output (using more of the information than he had originally when he just perceived the result as "wrong") and confirm his hypothesis. The production program was then corrected to read

B = SUM(A);   A = A/B;

He had not only learned something, but his production program reflected his new insight. Moreover, he had overcome a substantial proportion of his fear of array statements, having met the beast in mortal combat and emerged victorious.

In the construction of "learning cases," the programmer has to develop a feeling for the "critical case"—that is, the case that is just like the case at hand except for one critical difference. Through the contrast between these two cases, he learns precisely how much discrimination he must make—neither more nor less. For instance, if he is having some trouble with the expression

INDEX(X||'ABC', 'ABC');

and is unsure of the INDEX built-in function, he can construct several minimally contrasting cases in his test program, each differing from the original in one aspect. Thus, for instance, one case could use a variable instead of an expression as the first argument, a second could use a string of different length, a third could use a variable second argument. Each case gives him information somewhat different from the others, and by running several cases at once, he increases his chances of obtaining the information he wants in a single run.

To implement such an active program of learning, the programmer must already know quite a bit. If, for example, he does not have sufficient proficiency with his programming language to make the construction of a critical case a relatively simple and foolproof affair, he will quickly become embedded in a morass of detail, which he cannot possibly handle on his own. It should, therefore, be the goal of formal educational programs to train the programmer to the point where he can use his tools as tools to further his learning. Instead, we all too often find that the formal education has merely served to inculcate in the programmer a hatred for his tools. How many college graduates take their diplomas with the secret thought that now, at last, they are freed from such things as books and lectures? It is a poor workman who hates his tools—all the more because it is the tools themselves which can teach us to become good workmen.

SUMMARY

The two major influences we can exert on a programmer's performance are on the desire he feels for working and on what he knows that is needed to do the job. The first is called motivation and the second is called training, or, if it is sufficiently general, education. But little is known about why programmers program harder, or even whether they are already programming too hard for their own good. Possibly even less is known about educating programmers, even though vast sums have been spent on training schemes. Indeed, more articles and books have been written on programming education than on all other aspects of programming psychology put together, yet few of them have any lasting importance.

Perhaps we expect too much from formal training—from schools. The education business is still essentially medieval in its practices, so why should schools for programmers be different? Typically, where there is a carefully worked-out educational program, it is to train future professionals with amateur habits, so perhaps it is better that they don't do much of a job. At least there's less to unlearn once you get into a real programming environment.

The one factor that saves us in the computing education business is the computer itself—ever silent, ever patient, ever teaching the programmer who has but the skill to learn. Perhaps we should set as a goal for our schools merely to leave the students alone, so that they do not turn off to learning before they get on the other end of that log with the real teacher of us all. It may be expensive, it may be inelegant, it may be old-fashioned, but for programmers, computer assisted instruction (but not CAI!) is still the best.

QUESTIONS

For Managers

1. What is your impression of what motivates your programmers? Is it the same thing for all of them—for men and women, for old and young? Do you assume that they are motivated by the same things that motivate you?

2. Do you take steps to keep your programmers from overworking, from getting too involved in their job? Do you ever envy their involvement, their dedication to their work?

3. What are your attitudes toward providing resources for programmer education (not necessarily programmer schools)? What do you do to encourage your programmers to educate themselves as they work? Do you do this just as an excuse not to spend money on schools?

4. Do you encourage programmers to work in their own preferred modes? Do you, for instance, permit programmers to have different sorts of equipment in their offices, to take work home, or to shift their working hours from the normal working hours of the shop?

For Programmers

1. What things could your manager do for you to make your work faster or better? Have you ever discussed these things with your manager? If not, do you think he understands which things they are?

2. Write a personal history of your training in computer programming. Make notes of which experiences taught you which things, and which were most beneficial to you. On the basis of this list, what are you going to do about your future education? Or do you already know everything there is to know about programming?

3. What are your favored modes of perception? What do you do to try to take advantage of them in your educational effort?

4. Do you have any "peculiar" work habits which you think enhance your performance? Does your manager permit or prevent you from working in these ways? Does your manager know of your preferences?

BIBLIOGRAPHY

Sackman, Harold, *Man-Computer Problem Solving: Experimental Evaluation of Time-Sharing and Batch Processing,* Princeton, N.J., Auerbach, 1970.
Again, Sackman has a number of important things to say about programmer training, and his largest and most recent studies were carried out on trainees at the Air Force Academy. One of his observations, which bears out the point of view of this chapter, is that by far the most desired improvement to help cadets in solving programming problems was "improved instruction." Part of the problem, I suspect, is the restriction to individual work, which is particularly emphasized at the Academy. Thus, group cooperation in learning, which is essential in any real programming effort, is set aside by the school as "cheating."
See also the last chapter, which Sackman relates some of his findings to the general psychological literature. He seems to feel that in the end, for programming, experience and training come to dominate all other variables in programming success.

Cofer, C. H., and M. H. Appley, *Motivation: Theory and Research,* New York, Wiley, 1964.

Covers the multifaceted motivation theories in a professional way. A good place to start into the classical work in the field of motivation, as seen by psychologists.

Hilgard, E. R., and G. Bower, *Theories of Learning,* 3rd ed. New York, Appleton-Century-Crofts, 1966.

This book does for psychological learning theories what Cofer and Appley do for motivation. Again, a good place to start on an endless topic.

Proceedings of the Computer Personnel Research Conferences, Association for Computing Machinery, New York, published annually.

Articles on training schemes and systems for programmers are scattered throughout the computing literature like plums in a pudding. The articles on training in these procedings should give the reader enough of a sample to make up his own mind.

Hall, Douglas T., and Edward E. Lawler III, Job Pressures and Research Performance, *American Scientist,* Vol. 59 (Jan.–Feb. 1971).

Although we still do not have a study of the effect of job pressures on programming performance, the programming manager might profit from reading this article, just so long as he keeps a slight reservation in the back of his head that programming is not, so far as we know, the same activity as "research." At least this article shows that for complex intellectual activities, the relationship between various job pressures and productivity is not a simple one, and is oversimplified only at a manager's peril.

PART 4

PROGRAMMING TOOLS

. . . a word of advice to such of my hearers as may happen to be professors. I am allowed to use plain English because everybody knows that I could use mathematical logic if I chose. Take the statement: "Some people marry their deceased wives' sisters." I can express this in language which only becomes intelligible after years of study, and this gives me freedom. I suggest to young professors that their first work should be written in a jargon only to be understood by the erudite few. With that behind them, they can ever after say what they have to say in a language "understanded by the people." In these days, when our very lives are at the mercy of professors, I cannot but think that they would deserve our gratitude if they adopted my advice.

Bertrand Russell*

If the poor workman hates his tools, the good workman hates poor tools. The work of the workingman is, in a sense, *defined* by his tools—witness the way in which the tool is so often taken to symbolize the worker: the tri-square for the carpenter, the trowel for the mason, the transit for the surveyor, the camera for the photog-

* Taken from *Portraits from Memory,* Copyright 1951, 1952, 1953 and 1956, by Bertrand Russell. Reprinted by permission of Simon and Schuster and George Allen and Unwin, Ltd.

rapher, the hammer for the laborer, and the sickle for the farmer. Working with defective or poorly designed tools, even the finest craftsman is reduced to producing inferior work, and thereby reduced to being an inferior craftsman. No craftsman, if he aspires to the highest work in his profession, will accept such tools; and no employer, if he appreciates the quality of work, will ask a craftsman to accept them.

Is the situation any different in programming? At first glance it may seem to be, but this misunderstanding can be traced to the relative immaturity of programming as compared to other crafts. The tools of any trade evolve, but the tools of programming have had but a decade or two to arrive at their present forms. Thus, there is no common standard for programming tools, and no common experience in the use of the best tools that do exist.

The programmer who is working in machine language—and many more of these still exist than is commonly supposed—may not even be aware of the advantages that the crudest assembly language can provide. In our course on the psychology of computer programming, one of the students undertook an analysis of more than 2000 programming errors encountered in his shop—where all programmers were coding in machine language for a small special-purpose machine. Of these errors, 65 percent were attributable to such housekeeping matters as inserting the wrong number of no-ops for delay cycles, incorrect operation codes, errors in placing a bit for such features as indirect addressing, using the wrong absolute address, or incorrectly calculating a displacement. By using an assembly language of the most primitive design, these programmers could have eliminated two-thirds of their coding errors—but they did not even know that such a thing was possible.

As we move up the levels of possible programming aids, we find the situation repeating itself, for although the assembly-language programmer may scoff at the machine-language programmer, he may be in turn the object of amusement for the user of a language with macro facilities. Not all of this titillation, however, is attributable to the superiority of one system over another. Much of it, indeed, is a way of concealing an insecure feeling that one's own programming system might not be, after all, the pinnacle of man's technological achievements.

In this section of the book, we shall attempt to examine the major tools used by the programmer from the perspective of psychology, in order to see if we cannot put questions of system design and selection out of the reach of ignorant squabbling and squalling. No doubt we shall be unable to achieve this high aim, but we hope to make at least a start in a direction which promises more than some heretofore explored.

11 PROGRAMMING LANGUAGES

Countless papers have been devoted to the subject of programming languages, but the topic of psychology is not easily found in any of them. The most typical attitude about programming languages was expressed by one author who pleaded for an effort "to *really* attempt to understand what programming and programming languages are all about." Although we all could agree with this laudable sentiment, we might not agree with his explication of what *he* thought they were "all about," namely, "how they related to our mathematical foundations on the one hand and to current as well as imagined computing equipment on the other." In that analysis, there is no mention of *people,* the poor critters who have to use programming languages, except perhaps for the type of people who spend their time imagining computing equipment—hardly the typical language user!

In this chapter, we also shall attempt to understand what programming languages are all about, but our point of view will consider people first and machines and mathematics second—and then only as they impinge on the psychological discussion. As we have already, in this book, spent considerable time discussing what "programming" is, it will be appropriate to begin our study of programming languages by considering what a "language" is, and to what extent programming languages are languages in other senses of the term. With that understanding as a basis, we will attempt to throw some small light on the subject of programming language design. Since most programmers do not have much to say about the design of a language, we shall attempt to satisfy a more universal need by providing principles for *selection* of a programming language from among those already designed for us.

PROGRAMMING LANGUAGE AND NATURAL LANGUAGES

If there is one area in which every man is an expert, it is language. We all speak a language, and some of us can even read and write the language we speak. If a foreigner says "I would like of dinner," any of us can correct his erroneous use of the preposition—even those of us who do not know a preposition from a proposition or a prepossession. The typical person's understanding of the language he uses, however, is not so profound as to prevent him from labeling something as a language that might resemble one only superficially. Thus, it is not surprising that the systems of notation which we use to communicate with our computers came to be known as "programming languages." In fact, the very first programmer, Lady Lovelace, seems to have had the idea of a programming language as a language as early as 1846. Although she was the niece of Lord Byron, it was not her knowledge of poetry but, rather, of mathematics which led her to think of a symbolic system as a language—for the idea of mathematics as a language seems to go back into the misty ages of the past. Thus, the idea of "programming language" was really born with the idea of programming itself.

In view of the venerable past of the programming language concept, it would be pedantic to attempt to demonstrate that programming languages are not "real" languages. Languages are what they say they are, and we are perfectly entitled to include systems of communications between man and computer under the same rubric as systems of communication between man and man or beast and beast. What might be possible, however, is to inquire about possible differences between computer languages and the other kinds.

One possible point of departure for comparing the two types of language is the list of "design features" which Hockett has given for the natural language of human beings (speech). The first of thirteen features which he lists is the use of a "vocal-auditory channel"—that is, I speak and you listen. The use of this channel has several advantages, particularly the freeing of the hands and other organs for separate activities. Programming is generally a manual operation—we laugh when someone asks us to "say something in FORTRAN." It is a written language, and in spite of its resemblance to other written languages, it differs from them in not having a speech system behind it. Not that written languages are simple transcriptions of speech, not at all; but a written language such as English is strongly influenced by its relationship to a spoken language. This influence is not so strong in other written languages, such as those using the Chinese writing system, but the influence—the mutual influence —always exists.

One effect of not having a spoken form of a programming language is a possible slowing down of language innovations, for the spoken form of the natural language is most often the source of new language forms. Another effect is the difficulty with which we can talk about a programming language without a blackboard or pencil and paper. Every programming office should have a blackboard, chalk, and many erasers.

The second of Hockett's features is "rapid fading." We need many erasers because what we "say" about a program on the blackboard does not erase itself the way an utterance does. Sometimes it is a convenience to have rapid fading in a programming language. Once, when installing a computer in Bermuda, we fell into the habit of sketching our rough programming ideas in that portion of the coral sand between the apogee and perigee of the wash of waves. The ocean saw to it that each idea lasted only about as long as it was worth; but in ordinary programming work, we usually have to make explicit provision for getting rid of our obsolete listings, unless we have a graphic terminal.

The third feature is "broadcast transmission and directional reception," which means that we speak more or less in all directions at once, but we can detect, when listening, from what direction the speech is coming. Programming, of course, is quite the opposite. Programming shares with prayer the feature of directional transmission and broadcast reception. Heaven receives prayers, and the computer receives programs, from all over at once. We might imagine, then, that what variation is permitted in programming languages would be on the way out of the computer, but just the opposite is true. In spite of the diversity of its listeners, the "system" simply broadcasts identical messages to all of them. Certain possibilities for change lie here.

Probably the really important difference between programming languages (of today) and natural languages lies in Hockett's fourth design feature—interchangeability. Although we often listen to people whom we cannot understand, or often speak to people who cannot understand us, the normal image of human speech communication is that each participant can reproduce any linguistic communication he can understand. In short, we "talk the same language." When we talk to our computers, unhappily, we are usually speaking in different tongues. Here, at least, for all their other faults, the machine languages have the upper hand, for at least a dump looks a little like the stuff we put into the blasted machine. Not so—not nearly so—when what we put in was FORTRAN or COBOL. How truly sad it is that just at the very moment when the computer has something important to tell us, it starts speaking gibberish.

There is, fortunately, a trend today to try to introduce interchangeability into the dialogue between man and machine through a programming language, and this step is bound to have important psychological effects on programming effectiveness, even though it may decrease machine "efficiency." But there is another kind of noninterchangeability which is perhaps even more severe and yet less subject to mechanical remedies. Programs are used not only for man-machine communication, but for man-man communication as well. Yet communication in programming languages does not seem to have the interchangeability we take for granted in natural language communication, even between the same two people. At the extreme of this problem is the case of the man who can read COBOL programs but cannot write them. Probably, he cannot discuss them, either, which makes for most difficult communication problems if he is, say, a programming manager.

In Hockett's remaining design features, programming languages do seem to measure up to natural languages—actually going beyond them in the exhibition of such features as productivity, the ability to express something that has never been expressed before. In a way, the design of programming languages reflects different patterns of use than are commonly found in natural language. To be sure, it is important that a natural language be productive, in the above sense, but for a programming language, productivity is the *sine qua non.*

When we consider function of a language, rather than the design features which realize function, the deepest differences between programming languages and natural languages emerge. Bruner gives six general functions of natural language—emotive, connotative, referential, metalingual, poetic, and phatic. Although we can identify each of these in programming languages, their relative importance and frequency of use is quite different.

Emotive language consists of utterances such as "How do you do?" and "Fiddlesticks!," which are ritualized expressions of the emotional state of the speaker. Generally speaking, the computer is not interested in the emotional state of the programmer, although evidences of it may creep into his program. Phatic language consists of utterances such as "Uh hu . . . but . . . and . . .," which serve the function of keeping the channel of communication open or testing its state of operation. An exact counterpart of the phatic "and" is found in some terminal systems where the user can keep his program from being pushed down in the priority stack by fiddling with the shift key while he is thinking. Without the shifting, the computer would fail to get a communication for a long period and assume that the user's program could safely be put in a more passive state. Of course, jiggling the shift key defeats the purpose of the scheduling algorithm, but more important than that is the interference it probably causes with the programmer's thought processes. Hopefully, such phatic communication can be removed from the already cluttered field of programming language phenomena.

At first blush, poetic language would seem to have no place in programming, yet it plays a role which should be increasingly recognized. In poetic language, the patterning of the language itself—for esthetic reasons—is uppermost. But what, in programming, is there to correspond to Keats' lines such as these?

O Attic shape! Fair attitude! with brede
  Of marble men and maidens overwrought,
With forest branches and the trodden weed;
  Thou, silent form, dost tease us out of thought . . .

If we mean to read aloud, the answer is nothing, for we have already seen that programming language is not speech, let alone song. But is there not, indeed, something in form for form's sake which "dost tease us out of thought"?

A programmer would not really be a programmer who did not at some time consider his program as an esthetic object. This part is not quite symmetrical; that part is clumsy and doesn't flow in an appropriate manner; the whole thing does not look proper on the page. To be sure, it is fashionable among programmers to be rough and tough and pragmatic, but deep down each programmer knows that it is not enough for a program just to work—it has to be "right" in other ways. Later, when we discuss language design and program testing, we shall see that the correlation between the esthetic and the pragmatic value of a program is not accidental—the more pleasing to the eye and mind, the more likely to be correct. Or, put more poetically, "Beauty is truth, truth beauty."

The prose of programming consists largely of referential and connotative parts. Referential statements are statements or questions of fact—"That is Heidi," "This is a fixed-point binary number with 13 bits and a sign." Connotative statements give instructions—"Stop pulling my leg,"

"Find the inverse of this matrix." Of these types, we shall say more later. But here we should note that, although both are common in natural and programming languages, the universe of discourse is much, much smaller in programming. Thus, even though there is essentially no limit to the number of assignment statements or declarations in PL/I, the number of possible utterances in English is enormously greater. We are aware of the importance of the size of the universe of discourse in programming languages, but it is probably most important for their psychology, as we hope to show.

Metalingual utterances—talking about language—are of primary importance in programming, especially in the learning process, when programming such things as compilers, and when designing and defining programming languages. Until recently, programming languages differed from natural languages in that they relied exclusively on natural language as a metalanguage—with the possible use of a little mathematics. This chapter, for example, is one long metalingual statement about programming languages, completely couched in English. Now, however, increasing attention is being turned to special formal or informal languages designed to facilitate metalingual expression and reasoning. Moreover, certain programming languages are beginning to incorporate metalingual features of great power—giving us the ability not only to manipulate programming languages but to manipulate assertions about programming languages. Although the future of these efforts is not clear, and empirical evidence is almost entirely lacking, we hope to be able to give some hints of the role which metalingual features can play in the psychology of programming languages.

PROGRAMMING LANGUAGE DESIGN

It is impossible to begin a discussion of psychological principles of programming language design without recalling the story of "Levine the Genius Tailor." It seems that a man had gone to Levine to have a suit made cheaply, but when the suit was finished and he went to try it on, it didn't fit him at all. "Look," he said, "the jacket is much too big in back."

"No problem," replied Levine, showing him how to hunch over his back to take up the slack in the jacket.

"But then what about the right arm? It's three inches too long."

"No problem," Levine repeated, demonstrating how, by leaning to one side and stretching out his right arm, the sleeve could be made to fit.

"And what about these pants? The left leg is too short."

"No problem," said Levine for the third time, and proceeded to teach him how to pull up his leg at the hip so that, though he limped badly, the suit appeared to fit.

Having no more complaints, the man set off hobbling down the street, feeling slightly duped by Levine. Before he went two blocks, he was stopped by a stranger who said, "I beg your pardon, but is that a new suit you're wearing?"

The man was a little pleased that someone had noticed his suit, so he took no offense. "Yes it is," he replied. "Why do you ask?"

"Well, I'm in the market for a new suit myself. Who's your tailor?"

"It's Levine—right down the street."

"Well, thanks very much," said the stranger, hurrying off. "I do believe I'll go to Levine for *my* suit. Why, he must be a genius to fit a cripple like you!"

Would it be inappropriate to concoct a version of this story called "Levine the Genius Language Designer"? The first problem in discussing language design is that we do not know the answer to that question. We do not know whether the language designers are geniuses, or we ordinary programmers are cripples. Generally speaking, we only know how bad our present programming language is when we finally overcome the psychological barriers and learn a new one. Our standards, in other words, are shifting ones—a fact that has to be taken into full consideration in programming language design.

Why are our standards so flexible in this matter when they are all too often rigid in others? The problem lies in the rigidity of our machines and, through them, in the rigidity of our programming languages. Whenever a man is confronted with a new machine, he is forced to choose between making some adjustments himself or adjusting the machine to narrow the gap between what is desired and what exists. Although machines, and especially computers, are adjustable, the time scale for them to be changed is generally much longer than for a person. Programming languages are attempts to adjust the raw computer to better fit human propensities and limitations, but they too suffer from a long update cycle. Thus, the user is faced with the choice of waiting for months or years while he develops his own programming language—a primrose path which many a man has trod—or gritting his teeth and learning to live with what he has.

Humanists often contend that machines tend to dehumanize people by forcing them to have rigid personalities, but really, the contrary is true. Because the machines are rigid, the people who use them must— if they are to be successful—supply more than their share of flexibility. Perhaps this is the effect that the humanists are describing as "dehumanization," for in ordinary human intercourse, each party gives and takes his share. Relationships in which one party does all the giving or all the taking are not fully human, and tend to produce personality distortions in one or the other.

In making our adjustments to our particular programming language, we can easily become attached to it simply because we now have so much invested in it. We often listen to a man complaining about his nagging, slovenly, and prodigal wife, only to find that when asked why he doesn't leave her, he replies that he cannot live without her. Most people would prefer almost any amount of pain to giving up the familiarity of some constant companion for an unknown quantity. We see this effect when we try to teach a programmer his *second* language. Teaching the first is no great problem, for he has no investment in any other. By the time he has learned two or more, he is aware that more things exist in this world than he has dreamed of. But letting go of the first is, to him, just a promise of pain with no promise of compensating pleasure.

Perhaps this situation could be improved if we could enunciate and teach certain principles that are not tied to particular languages, so that even the beginner would have some less relative measure to hold up against the language he is learning. But teaching practice today in our universities and programming schools seems to be pointing in exactly the opposite direction. Instead of trying to teach principles, or at least trying to teach two contrasting programming languages simultaneously, or at the very least trying to teach one programming language which rather broadly represents the major possibilities, the schools seem devoted to teaching how to program in a single simple and artificial language. The objective seems to be to get the student writing some kind of program as soon as possible—a not unworthy aim—but at the expense of limiting the future growth of the programmer.

To be fair, we should recall our distinction between the professional and amateur. The schools, it seems, are devoting themselves primarily to turning out vast quantities of amateurs—perhaps under the assumption that the professionals can and should take care of themselves. But when the language designers begin to believe that the principles underlying the design of an amateur's language are the same as those upon which a professional's are based, then we have trouble.

In order to get at the principles underlying the design of programming languages to fit psychological realities, we shall have to get down to fundamental empirical data. Reading programs will be a help, but reading is not enough. When we read a program, we can seldom tell with certainty why a particular piece of coding is present. To understand the psychology of programming languages, we shall have to do more than read programs—we shall have to observe programs being made. Even this process—even interviewing programmers—will not tell us all we want to know, and we shall have to resort to many sources and devices to get even a slightly better picture than we have by intuition. One reason for these complexities is that the programmer himself seldom knows why he does what he does—which is a general problem in the study of any human behavior.

Consider, for example, the following situation. A programmer writing in FORTRAN wants to use a subscript expression such as (J-21). He knows that there are rules—perfectly explicit and unambiguous—about which subscript expressions are permitted and which are not. But he is not quite sure of the rule as it applies to this case, so what does he do? Well, he might look up the rule in his manual, but if he is a clever fellow, he will probably just make a preliminary calculation by such a statement as

$K = J\text{-}21$

He is *sure* that K is an acceptable subscript, and this is much faster than looking up the rule. It may—to be sure—be slower in the program, but that is not the question uppermost in his mind at this moment.

Now, why did the programmer do this? Because of a limitation in the FORTRAN language? But, you might argue, J-21 is not prohibited by FORTRAN, so it must be a limitation of the programmer—of his *understanding* of FORTRAN. Although this argument places the blame, it misleads us in designing or evaluating a programming language, for would it not be also correct to say that in PL/I, the programmer would have been much less likely to make this error? Why? Because he would be more likely to know that there were no restrictions on subscripts in PL/I, so it would not even occur to him to worry about whether a particular expression was permitted or not.

When we assess a programming language, or a machine, from a psychological point of view, we cannot grant ourselves the luxury of putting all the burden of poor programming on the poor programmer. If the same programmers get consistently better results using language A than using language B, what good are arguments that they would have done better in language B, if only they had been smart enough to master it. Of course, there is a time dimension to this argument, for one must *learn* to use a programming language or a machine. Thus, the evaluation of these things depends on the entire system comprising the courses, teaching materials, language, compiler hints, programming assistance and anything else, which may lead to one language being better used than another. Perhaps the messages coming from the terminal when an error is made are more motivating in one system than another. Perhaps the programmer feels he is more important if he is chosen to program in machine language instead of FORTRAN. If we are to be effective in improving the quality of languages, we shall not be able to dismiss any such factor out of hand.

In a way, the reason it is so hard to attribute the source of programming inefficiency to either programmer or programming language is that if we had ideal programmers, programming languages would not be necessary. It is a *psychological* difficulty which prevents us from writing our problem specifications directly in machine language. Let's face up to it: people don't think the same way that computers do—that's why we use computers. Programming is at best a communication between two alien species, and programming languages with all their systems paraphernalia are an attempt to make the communication simpler for one of those species. Which one? Not the computer, certainly, for nobody ever heard a complaint from a computer that it couldn't do the work.

SUMMARY

The use of the term "language" in the phrase "programming language" is in many ways damaging to progress in communication between man and machine. Just calling it a language doesn't make it one, and may instead lead to false analogies which, in turn, lead to misguided research efforts. To make progress in programming languages, we must first give up the holy grail of trying to program in a "real" language, for programming languages can never be the same as human speech. We may then transfer our quest to making programming languages more "natural," not in the sense of being identical to English or some other culture's contribution to the Tower of Babel, but in the sense of a consonance between the mode of expression and the mind of the expressor. But in the end, to get a good "fit," perhaps the customer will have to scrunch over a little—perhaps we are ultimately going to have to change our ways of thinking to fit our computers. Why not? Hasn't every other human invention changed man?

QUESTIONS

For Managers

1. Are chalkboards standard equipment in your programming offices? Have you ever turned down a request for a chalkboard?

2. How were the programming languages used in your shop chosen?

3. Relate any experiences you have had with a change in programming languages in your shop.

For Programmers

1. Is the person who designed your language a genius? Give some examples of his genius, from your own experience.

2. Relate your experiences in learning your first and second and third programming languages, trying to point out psychological differences in the experiences based not so much on the languages themselves but on the order you learned them.

3. If you are an experienced FORTRAN programmer, can you give the precise rules for subscript expressions? Are you *sure?* How does it influence your programming when you are not sure of a rule? Do you look it up?

4. Has being a programmer changed the way you think when you are not programming? If so, give some examples.

BIBLIOGRAPHY

Morrison, Phillip, and Emily, eds., *Charles Babbage and His Calculating Engines,* New York, Dover Publications, 1961.
Along with Babbage's writings on his machines, we find Lady Lovelace's comments, which show a clear understanding of many of the fundamental principles of programming languages. Those who believe that the progress of knowledge is monotonic and increasing should read this book carefully. What happened, they should ask, to this understanding between the years 1860 and 1940? Perhaps because Babbage was unable to separate clearly the principles of his machine from their mechanical embodiment, his works lay scattered and forgotten in libraries all over the world, only to be rediscovered after his inventions had been reinvented in an electric and electronic embodiment. Is there a lesson here, too, about programming languages?

Zemanek, H., Semiotics and Programming Languages, *Communications of the ACM,* **9,** No. 3 (March 1966), pp. 139–43.
Zemanek was the head of the IBM Vienna Laboratory while it was developing the Universal Language Document for PL/I, probably the most ambitious metaprogramming document ever attempted—and probably the most successful. This article gives some of the structure of his thought, which clearly influenced the course of the ULD development.

Greenberg, Joseph H., *Universals of Language,* 2nd ed., Cambridge, Mass., M.I.T. Press, 1966.
Based on, but not a verbatim account of, a 1961 conference, this book gives a good introduction to the search for universal features of languages. In addition to Hockett's paper, it contains at least six other papers that should be of interest to programming language designers, although, of course, programming languages are not considered languages by these linguists.

Bruner, Jerome, *Toward a Theory of Instruction,* Cambridge, Mass., Belknap Press of Harvard University, 1966.
Bruner gives his six general functions of language, along with many other thoughts.

Bruner is one of the most important modern thinkers and researchers in the areas of language, learning, and thought, and this book is a good introduction to his ideas.

Miller, George A., *Language and Communication,* revised ed., New York, McGraw-Hill, 1963.

No programming language designer should be permitted to design another language until he has read this book. As Miller says in his introduction: "A scientific study of language, as opposed to a speculative discussion, begins with direct observations of communicating individuals and searches for the relation of these observations to the existing body of scientific knowledge."

Vygotsky, Lev Semenovich, *Thought and Language,* Cambridge, Mass., M.I.T. Press, 1962.

The translation of the work by the great but short-lived Russian psychologist remains today probably the most stimulating and readable work on the relationship between thought and language. No programmer could fail to profit from reading this book.

Steel, T. B., Jr., ed., *Formal Language Description Languages for Computer Programming,* Amsterdam, North-Holland Publishing Co., 1966.

These papers are the proceedings of an IFIP working conference on formal language description languages—that is, on formal metalanguages for programming languages. Although uneven, it is a rich mine of conceptual nuggets for those interested in the language of language, or the language of language of language, or . . . .

Symposium on Extendible Languages, *Sigplan Notices,* **4,** No. 8, Association for Computing Machinery, New York, 1969.

Extendible, or extensible, programming languages are languages in which the language itself can be manipulated by the programmer, This symposium fairly well represents the state-of-the-art at the time it was published.

Sammett, J. E., The Use of English as a Programming Language, *Communications of the ACM,* **9,** 3 (March 1966), pp. 228-30.

Higman, Bryan, *A Comparative Study of Programming Languages,* Section 15.3: Subsets of English, New York, American Elsevier, 1967.

Two essays to discourage those who think that the answer to all our problems is to program in a "real" language.

12

SOME PRINCIPLES FOR PROGRAMMING LANGUAGE DESIGN

Having said that the elucidation of programming language design principles is an empirical matter, we shall now proceed to give a largely speculative survey of some ideas that have been put forth as general principles of good design. The presentation must be largely speculative simply because most of the empirical data do not exist. Yet such data are not necessarily difficult to obtain—most of the studies which we *can* cite were done by students working with limited time and low budgets. The real problem is that psychological factors are not recognized as part of the programming language design problem—or, if they are recognized, they are thought to be solvable by introspection on the part of the language designer and his pals.

UNIFORMITY

In some cases, we can draw experimental data from the mainstream of psychology, at least for suggestions as to areas of potential programming difficulty. One such case is the principle of *uniformity*. The difficulty of remembering a set of items has been shown in numerous experiments to be related to the "information content" of the set. The "information content," however, is difficult to measure, for it depends not only upon what is in the set, but on what is *not* in it—what is in the rememberer's mind. If, for instance, we ask a subject to memorize the set

000 001 010 011 100 101 110 111

he will have little difficulty if he knows the binary number system.

But suppose the subject knows the binary number system and is asked to memorize the set:

000 001 010 100 101 111

Now, although there are only six cases to remember, the job is more difficult. Why should that be? Because the complexity of remembering —for the person who knows the "system"—is not related to the number of cases, but to the number of *exceptions from the system*. Once one knows the binary number system, it is just as easy to "memorize" the first 1024 numbers as it is to memorize the first eight. In our first example, the subject only had to remember "the first eight binary numbers," but in the second example, he might have remembered in the form, "the first eight binary numbers—*excluding* 011 and 110." We do not have to be expert psychologists to see that the second case is at least no easier than the first, and should be somewhat harder.

Now, the preceding argument would be invalid if the subject was naive with respect to the binary number system, for then the two lists might appear more or less "random" to him. In that case, six items should be somewhat less difficult to memorize than eight—exactly the opposite result obtained by the more sophisticated subject.

In programming languages, precisely the same situation prevails. In the last chapter, we mentioned the case of FORTRAN subscripts. If programmers were perfectly naive on the subject of arithmetic expressions, we could argue that the FORTRAN subscript rules were easier to remember than, say, the PL/I or APL subscript rules, for the set of possible subscripts is obviously smaller in FORTRAN. But programmers are not perfectly naive, and they can learn most possible PL/I or APL subscripts by remembering only one simple rule: "any scalar expression can be a subscript." In FORTRAN, however, they must learn the following set of seven forms:

a

v

v + a

v − a

a*v

a*v + b

a*v − b

where v represents an unsigned, nonsubscripted, integer variable, and a and b represent unsigned integer numbers which must be greater than zero.

In order to test the difficulty of remembering these rules, a survey was taken of 117 experienced FORTRAN programmers. First we asked them to say whether the expression

21 − K

was a valid FORTRAN subscript, an invalid FORTRAN subscript, or they didn't know for sure. 31 said it was valid, 9 said it was not valid, and 77 said they were not sure. (As a control, we asked 53 experienced PL/I programmers the same question about PL/I, and all but 4 said it was a valid subscript; these 4 were former FORTRAN programmers.)

Following this test, we asked the 9 correct FORTRAN programmers to write down the exact rules for permissible FORTRAN subscripts. None of the 9 were able to give the rules exactly. Of the 49 correct PL/I programmers, all were able to give the answer roughly equivalent to "anything." Although this is not an exact rule—it encompasses, for example, array expressions, which are not valid—it is a rule which at least does not prevent the programmer from trying something that *is* valid, such as K-21 in FORTRAN. If the PL/I programmer does, indeed, happen to write an array expression as a subscript, he will be caught in the act by the compiler; but a FORTRAN compiler is not likely to tell the K-21 programmer that he is not using the full power of the language.

What we mean, then, by *uniformity* should be reasonably clear from this example, although no precise statement of the principle can be given, since it is a psychological principle rather than a mathematical one. Roughly speaking, the principle of uniformity in programming language design might be stated thusly: "The same things should be done in the same way wherever they occur." To the extent that the language contains deviations from this rule, it violates the principle of uniformity and will thus be more difficult to learn, more difficult to use without error, and more difficult to use for producing "new" techniques.

We explored the question further by comparing two languages, one of which was a "subset" of the other, used on the same problem. The two languages were the OS/360 and the DOS/360 versions of PL/I. The DOS version is not a perfect subset of the OS version, but to a large extent it can be characterized as such—as the OS version with certain restrictions and omissions (which are a special case of restrictions). With 14 relatively new PL/I programmers working in each language on the same problem, we found that the OS group had detectably less difficulty in getting working versions and that the code was shorter. In analyzing the different programs produced, we found that the DOS programmers often failed to use a feature that was, in fact, in their subset. When asked about this, they invariably replied, "I wasn't sure I could write that." (See Figure 12–1.)

What seems to happen, then, is that the more "covert categories" —things that you cannot do or say—there are, the more one expects other such covert categories in the language. Even if the restrictions are in another part of the language, they may affect the actual usage of a part without such restrictions. Another way of putting the rule of uniformity, then might be this: "If a programmer asks, 'Can I write . . . ?' the answer should be 'yes.' " Just like the child who is told "no" too often, the programmer working in a nonuniform language will tend to be discouraged from trying new things.

Another important aspect of uniformity is that the same syntactic construction should not mean different things in different contexts. For example, we are told in PL/I that "redundant parentheses are never required, but may always be used if desired." This is a good rule, but one which, unfortunately, has a few fairly critical exceptions. For instance, the two statements

    CALL X(A);
    CALL X((A));

	INDEX PROBLEM		
	MEAN # OF RUNS	MEAN RUN TIME	MEAN # OF STATEMENTS
FULL-LANGUAGE	32	1	243
SUBSET-LANGUAGE	41	1.2	319

Figure 12–1 Comparison of a programming language with its subset.

do not usually mean the same thing at all, for the second always causes a dummy argument to be passed to X (roughly, a call-by-value instead of a possible call-by-reference). On the other side of this coin, the two statements

   GET LIST(A(I) DO I = 1 TO N);
   GET LIST((A(I) DO I = 1 TO N));

do not mean the same thing because the first is syntactically incorrect—"redundant" parentheses being needed for the data list and for the iteration specification.

Such syntactic nonuniformity definitely discourages semantic exploration, for it renders the programmer uncertain about his power with the language. For instance, having encountered these two exceptions to the parentheses rules, the programmer may be reluctant to put parentheses in a complex expression to clarify its meaning, or he may feel impelled to put in extra parentheses because he has to "make sure." In general, he is going to be confused, and programmers should not be confused about their programming language.

As an interesting sidelight on the uniformity question, we might note that this trouble over parentheses in PL/I stems from the overuse of parentheses required because of the limited character set. This effect of limiting the character set is quite general, because any time the same character is used in two different contexts, you have nonuniformity. APL probably goes the furthest of any current language in the exploitation of a large character set, even to the extent of using a different symbol for the operator "minus" and the "minus sign" of a number, and supporters of APL claim that it is a most powerful language because of this uniformity.

Such statements, of course, should be subjectable to experimental test. As an example of how such a test can be made, recall the long parenthesized statement of Figure 3–1, which in PL/I had six levels of parentheses. This statement can be recoded in APL, as shown in Figure 12–2. To the casual eye, this statement does not appear as complex as the one in Figure 3–1, partly because of the two types of brackets, and partly because two pairs of parentheses can be eliminated because of APL's function form and right-to-left rule. Is this casual observation verifiable? We studied the question by making several variations of the two statements which were ill-formed and testing the ability of pro-

LES[I]←2×ATAND SQRT (S-A[IND[I;1]])×(S-A[IND[I;2]])÷S×(S-A[IND[I;3]])

Figure 12–2 An APL version of Figure 3–1.

grammers experienced in PL/I and APL to identify the ill-formed versions. There was a definite edge in both speed and accuracy to the APL statement, which seems to indicate that APL's claim to uniformity is at least partially well founded.

The limitation of the character set is but one case of machine limitations leading to failure of uniformity. The restriction of FORTRAN subscripts to another example, or at least an example of failure of nerve on the part of the implementers, who thought they could not give efficient code if subscripts were unlimited. Another source of nonuniformity is the quest for certain other design principles, not all of them well founded. The deepest of these principles go unchallenged, particularly the assumption of unambiguity. Even so sophisticated a writer as Bryan Higman says: "Because every language must have a character set and an unambiguous, decidable grammar . . . ," but he leaves the assumption of unambiguity unchallenged. Any assumption that deep should be challenged once in a while, just to keep it healthy.

A nice example of the obsession with unambiguity is the syntax of the WHILE clause in PL/I. Following the keyword, WHILE, is a logical condition, as is found following the keyword IF in an IF-statement. However, in the case of the WHILE but not in the case of the IF, parentheses must surround the condition—a nonuniformity which leads to a number of errors in syntax. The reason for the seemingly extra parentheses is that a syntactic ambiguity can arise if the programmer has declared an array named WHILE and writes a statement such as

DO WHILE(I) = 1;

For this one case, every programmer using a WHILE must use an extra pair of parentheses.

Actually, even with the morbid dread that programming language designers have of ambigiuity, it creeps into all languages. But the ambiguity that creeps in is, in most cases, *psychological* ambiguity—which seems to be beneath their consideration. A classic case is intermixed multiplication and division, as in

A = B/C*D

Although the language designer and the compiler do not regard such a statement as ambiguous, programmers certainly do—as evidenced by the number of bugs we find related to this type of situation.

What needs to be done about ambiguity is to recognize that there are two types—physical and psychological. Compilers, of course, are never ambiguous—one may interpret the above statement as

A − B/(C*D)

while another may interpret it as

A = (B/C)*D

but each will be consistent in its interpretation. Because of possible different interpretations by compiler writers (which is really psychological ambiguity in the end), it is important to eliminate this kind of ambiguity from a language so that all implementations will be no farther apart than necessary. But eliminating physical ambiguity does not solve the psychological problem.

Ken Iverson, the inventor—the developer—of APL, once told me that APL's "right-to-left" rule for resolving ambiguity was "more natural" than the rules used, say, in PL/I. Certainly the strict right-to-left rule is simpler to state than the PL/I rules (which in a formal sense often leave the order of execution undefined anyway), but its "naturalness" is an open psychological question certainly worth exploring as a way of resolving ambiguity. From an introspective point of view, I can say that I have never entirely come over to a right-to-left way of thinking, after writing perhaps 400 APL programs. Certainly my students have not come over after writing a few dozen, and the psychological ambiguity remaining from their early habits with left-to-right and other rules remains one of the greatest, if not *the* greatest, single sources of APL errors I see. For myself, I have come to the adaptive reaction of overparenthesizing (even in PL/I) to avoid possible psychological ambiguity.

There is some ray of hope on the horizon that programming language inventors realize the difference between these two kinds of ambiguity. Klerer and May have taken the interesting approach of permitting the user to write in a way which is natural to him, and then to give him a message which says:

THIS IS THE WAY WE INTERPRET YOUR STATEMENTS.
IF ANY ARE INCORRECT PLEASE RETYPE THE STATEMENT
   CORRECTLY.

Such an approach becomes particularly appealing in a terminal situation, where we at last get something approaching the dialogue of a natural language. It requires that we revise our static notion of what is a "language."

This approach would be especially useful for such rare ambiguities as the PL/I WHILE. If complete unambiguity is desired, why not simply make a secret rule in the language that is applied only when the programmer uses an array named WHILE. In that circumstance, the compiler can tell him to change such a WHILE-clause should it appear, and the rest of us need not bother. In practice, of course, compilers recognize this situation and warn us that they have inserted the parentheses for us. Why not dispense with the warning, and only punish the programmer who is stupid enough to use keywords as variable names?

Which leads us to our final point about uniformity. Not all of the blame lies with the language designers—individual programmers can be far more guilty of this sin. For example, choosing keywords as variable names means that the name is used in a nonuniform way in the program, which certainly confuses the task for anyone trying to read the program. (I have been particularly guilty of this in some of my examples in earlier books.) Other sources of nonuniformity are declaration of variables with different sizes for no particular reason, use of abbreviations sometimes and full names at other times, arbitrary indenting and spacing of the source program, and commenting densely in some places and not at all in others that seem more difficult.

But the major source of programmer nonuniformity remains the choice of mnemonic names. Abraham Lincoln used to ask this riddle: "If we call tail a leg, how many legs does a dog have?" When the respondent could answer "five," Lincoln would admonish, "No, four. *Calling* it a leg doesn't *make* it a leg." How many times—how many thousands of times—have we seen a program in which OLDX has not been assigned the old value of X, SUMAB has not been assigned the sum of A and B, or BIGGEST has not actually been given the biggest value? *Calling* it OLDX doesn't *make* it the old X; but no matter how often we deliver this admonition, the fallacy seems to perpetuate itself. Just as with nonuniformity in the language itself, this practice hurts us just because it leads us to believe something that is not true.

From a debugging standpoint, a slight amount of nonuniformity is really worse than a great deal, for the general uniformity lulls us to sleep. If most of the time, OLDX *is* the old value of X, we are more likely to miss the one time that it isn't; and if most of the time (A) means the same as A, we may never find the bug in our program.

COMPACTNESS

We have already mentioned the principle that the human mind has certain inherent limitations in capacity. Although these limitations vary from person to person and from one sort of material to another, we can safely say that for a given person, a short program will have a tendency to be more easily comprehended than a long one. Our studies of comments seemed to indicate, for instance, that even the addition of nonexecutable text tended to increase the difficulty in reading a program—even when that text was added explicitly to make the program *more* readable.

The compactness of a program, however, is not measured merely by counting the number of characters needed to express it. Although the number of characters *is* important when we are trying to account for such factors as keying errors, the critical unit may generally be somewhat larger than one character. For instance, the expression, A + B, is not one-third as difficult to understand as the expression, BIG + SMALL. The reason it is not is that we rarely use single letters as our fundamental units of thought processes: we are in the habit of using "words." Many experiments have shown that a word such as BIG can be handled just as readily as the word A.

In psychology, this information processing ability of human beings that combines several small units into one large unit, which is just as easy to handle as its individual parts, is called *chunking.* Chunking is a recoding process, one which we usually do without conscious effort. Nevertheless, even though the process of chunking is something we do quite naturally, each individual chunk has to be learned by experience. When we first begin to encounter such binary strings as 110010111100, we have to remember them as twelve separate characters. After a while, however, we begin to learn octal or hexadecimal, both of which are more or less formal systems of chunking. Soon, we begin to "see" this string immediately as 6274 or CBC, so that the length of any program containing it becomes "shorter."

Some program chunking is a natural ourgrowth of chunking learned elsewhere, as in the recognition of such "words" as DO, READ, and ALLOCATE. Other chunking we begin to learn the moment we first set pencil to a coding pad, so that at different stages in a programmer's experience with a language the same program will have different lengths. To an experienced PL/I programmer, the statement

DO I = 1 TO N;

can probably be taken in at a single glance. The novice, however, might have to break it into six or seven smaller chunks.

Although chunking tends to make commonly used character sequences seem shorter, the programming language designers are limited to taking advantage of the chunking which they can assume the programmer brings to the language, or to that which he just happens to learn as he uses the language. By providing the user with alternative ways of expressing the same thing, however, the language designer gives the programmer a chance to do another kind of compression. The simplest example of this type is the provision of abbreviations for keywords, such as PROC for PROCEDURE in PL/I. In natural languages, there is an empirical observation known as Zipf's law, which says that the most frequently used words tend to be the shortest words—words such as "is," "the," "a," "I," "he," and "it" in English. We also see the operation of Zipf's law in the creation of contractions, such as "don't" or "there's," but the most common operation is probably concealed in the long dead past.

In programming, however, we can often see the tendency to this type of compression in action, as when a programmer begins to write PROC all the time instead of PROCEDURE. He may never learn the abbreviation for seldom used words such as STRINGRANGE, even though it may be much longer than some word he does abbreviate. Other abbreviation occurs through the substitution of more powerful functions for less powerful ones, as when the programmer learns to write SUM(X) instead of a DO-group, or a DO-group for a list of cases written out sequentially. Iteration, of course, is the most basic of the compression steps possible in programming—it was known to Lady Lovelace, and without it modern computers would essentially not be possible. Functions —such as SUM—were also a concept known to our first programmer and, although they are not conceptually as important as iteration, they are probably more important from a psychological and practical point of view.

The language designer, of course, can provide either built-in functions such as SUM and SQRT or facilities for the programmer to make his own functions. Probably no modern programming language lacks both of these general features, but there exist great differences in the details of what is actually provided. One particular limitation on the use of programmer-defined functions is that the programmer is seldom given the facilities to duplicate what the language designers can build into their functions. For instance, PL/I has many powerful subroutine-defining features, but the programmer cannot yet provide such things as full generic capability for his routines, even though that ability exists in the built-in functions.

Another source of compactness—newer in use, but perhaps ultimately more powerful than iteration or subroutine definition—is data structuring. In APL, for instance, most operations apply in uniform ways to arrays of all sorts as well as scalars. In PL/I, many array operations are possible, and there are also structure operations. As an illustration of the power of these operations to permit many actions to be specified as one, consider the OLDX problem we raised earlier. If, instead of declaring an OLDX, OLDY, and so forth, we had declared a structure such as

1 OLD, 2 (X, Y, Z, . . .)

we would have been able to execute a single statement

OLD = NEW;

which assured that *all* the old values were replaced by all the new ones.

Many special-purpose programming languages draw their power from the higher-level data structures they provide, structures not yet found in multipurpose languages. Where these structures are in consonance with the user's needs, the resulting compression can be manifold. Where they are not—as when we try to do simple arithmetic operations in LISP or SNOBOL—the data structures have just the opposite effect. The most promising escape from this dilemma is through embedding special data structures in a multipurpose language such as PL/I. PL/I does provide a number of features which assist the programmer in creating data-structure-processing systems not built into the language, although the inability to replicate the general abilities of the language itself is once again an impediment.

Another way in which appropriate data structures lead to compression is by causing lower-level operations to have higher-level results. For instance, if we are processing a sorted file in sequence, the assumption that the records are in order permits us to make inferences about missing records which would otherwise require elaborate programming. Overlaying of one structure on another is a further case of promotion of operations—as when we set all bits in a string by setting the whole string, rather than processing them one at a time. The difference between this sort of operation and the operation of implied repetition through array and structure expressions is really in the relationship between what the language specifies and what the computer on which the language is implemented can do. Given the appropriate machine, array processing can be done directly, too, just as we now do the assignment of strings.

Before leaving the subject of compression, we must scrutinize the other side of the coin for a moment. Perhaps the ultimate form of compression is the elision of certain cases entirely—usually the most frequent ones. In PL/I, we write SKIP instead of SKIP(1), since that is by far the most frequent case. When declaring a variable, we get many attributes by default, so that when we write

DECLARE X;

we get the equivalent of something like

DECLARE X FLOAT DECIMAL(6) REAL AUTOMATIC INTERNAL;

Indeed, in many cases the declaration can be left out altogether, causing X to be declared implicitly or contextually. The difference between these extremes is much like the difference between Chinese and English grammar. English has many redundancies, as when we say

He went two time(s).

The plural ending is redundant, in that plurality is clearly specified by the "two," and in Chinese, there would be nothing to correspond to this extra letter. Such redundancies are quite useful in normal speech transmission, for they help in catching the precise meaning of the utterance even though there have been distortions in parts of it. In writing, however, they seem more of a burden than they are worth, so it seems worthwhile to have a sensible default system in any programming language.

The ability to use such a default system, however, depends on the existence of a limited universe of discourse, or a least a universe of discourse which is statistically limited. That is, the default case does not help us much if it is used only a small fraction of the time. As there are more and more possible cases, the burden of remembering which is the default can become greater than simply writing the complete specification. If the cases occur with more or less equal frequency, the default system then loses its value because it cannot be used often enough to make it worthwhile. On the other hand, if, the defaults are used often, we may not remember the nondefault cases when we have to use them. Although we have not studied this situation empirically, we might conjecture that defaults are most useful when they are used fairly frequently, but not too frequently.

Of course, the above principle applies to the psychology of a particular programmer using the language. Defaults may be very useful when several different types of programmers use the language. For instance, the default of REAL is needed only in contrast to COMPLEX, a feature which perhaps nine-tenths of PL/I programmers will not even know about, let alone use. Defaults such as these serve to produce different languages from a single language, for, in effect, the nine-tenths who do not know about COMPLEX are programming in a language that cannot handle complex arithmetic.

This type of automatic subsetting through defaults, however, will not work unless many details are accounted for. For instance, in PL/I, the built-in functions are generic, in that they adjust their operation according to the type of data passed to them. If we perform SQRT(X), the operation is different for X REAL than for X COMPLEX. For REAL X, $X = -1$ will cause an error condition to be raised; and for COMPLEX X, the result will be 1I. But why not yield 1I when X is REAL? Consider what would happen to the unsuspecting programmer who writes

A = SQRT(X);

without knowing about COMPLEX at all. If 1I were the result on the right-hand side, A would be given the value zero, for $1I = 0 + 1I$, so that only the real part would be assigned. Such a trouble would be most dificult for the programmer to find if he had no knowledge of complex arithmetic, so he must be protected if the default is to help him work in a true subset.

By eliminating redundancy in an appropriate way, then, we can reduce tedium and error. In the limit—in a programming language from which all possible redundancy were eliminated—it would not be possible to have any syntax checking of the program, for every possible string would be a syntactically correct program. An example of such a language is the machine code for certain systems, where all op codes are permitted and all address specifications are legal. We know that machine language programming can be extremely difficult—is it possible that this difficulty is due to lack of redundancy being carried too far?

To answer such a question, we must make a clear distinction between psychologically useful and psychologically useless redundancy. As a case in point, consider the FORTRAN expression, A(1 + I). If our FORTRAN prohibits this string, the compiler will signal an error. Not all strings are permitted, so error checking can be done by detecting illegal strings. But what is the compiler really checking here? The rule prohibiting A(1 + I) was not set down for the psychological comfort of the programmer, but, rather, to make it easier to compile "optimum" code. Although it is true that this expression is in error, the error has nothing to do with our problem, but only with FORTRAN's restrictions. In a sense, it is not the programmer, but the language, which is in error.

LOCALITY AND LINEARiTY

In an earlier discussion, we gave an example of how memory helps a programmer by enabling him to keep the relevant information in his head even when he does not have the program in front of him. A properly designed programming language can help the programmer in the same way that a good memory can—by keeping the relevant information close at hand.

Two types of human memory that interest us in this regard are the so-called "synesthetic" and "sequential" memories. Synesthetic memory is the faculty that enables us to recognize a face, a neighborhood, or the layout of a page in a book—without recourse to specific details. The word itself is derived from the Greek—"syn" meaning "together," and "esthetic" meaning "feeling" or "sensing." Our synesthetic memory, then, is that part of our memory that enables us to remember things as a whole, all taken in one glance.

Sequential memory may be more related to auditory things, as when we can whistle the tenth bar of a tune after hearing the first nine bars, but not if it is asked for alone. The sequential memories we have seem to be constructed like unidirectional chains—like speech, if you like—chains in which each link's appearance triggers the memory of the next. We exhibit sequential memory when we recite a poem, remember the route to a certain place as we traverse it, and sometimes when we memorize a list.

In a program, the concept of "locality" corresponds to synesthetic memory, and the concept of "linearity" corresponds to sequential memory. By locality, we mean that property that obtains when all relevant parts of a program are found in the same place—on the same page, perhaps. Without good locality, a programmer working with the listing of a program has to be turning pages constantly—unless his synesthetic memory is sufficiently good to remember the material on the other pages that is relevant to the current page. One way that a programming language encourages locality is through compression, that is, if the entire program fits onto one page, all relevant parts are obviously on that page.

Locality is also encouraged or discouraged in other ways. The ability to use literals is a big help, because all that we need to know about a literal is contained within its name. The use of well-chosen mnemonic names can have the same effect, if it helps the reader to remember what he needs to know about the variable without referring to the place it is declared. Of course, if a variable is only used locally, it is helpful if the language permits us to declare it right at that location. In some languages, however, usually to enable the compiler to make one less pass, all declarations must come before all other parts of the program. In such cases, reading a long program involves constant flipping back and forth to the first page.

Yet even when the language requires all declarations to be given in one place, a certain locality is obtained, for we can always tear off the first page and keep it alongside whichever page we are currently using. Indeed, some people complain about languages such as PL/I, which give great freedom in the choice of where declarations are made. This freedom, like any other, is often abused by programmers who do not understand why it is given. Ideally, a program written in PL/I should have all global variables declared together on one page—at the beginning or end—and all local variables declared within the section of coding that uses them.

As an example of the type of trouble that nonlocality causes, consider the typical situation arising from such a loop as

```
DO I = 1 TO 10;
PUT LIST(I,F(I)); END;
```
where F is a programmer-defined subroutine, such as

```
F: PROCEDURE(J) RETURNS(FLOAT);
    S = 0
    DO I = 1 TO J;
        S = S + I;
        END;
    RETURN(S);
    END F;
```

Because the variable I is not made local to the subroutine, we will find that the main loop only puts out five pairs of output values:

```
1  1      3  6      5  15      7  28      9  45
```
instead of the ten the programmer probably expected. He expected ten values because he thought that I was local to his DO-loop—that nothing he could not see right in front of him would affect I. But, as it happens, I is used inside of F and not declared inside of F, so I changes each time F is entered. (Recall that when the DO-loop

DO I = 1 TO J;
is finished normally, I has the value J + 1.)

Typically, this sort of bug causes great difficulty, for when we are not able to find a bug, it is usually because we are looking in the wrong place. In this case, we are looking in the wrong place because we assume —as is quite natural to do—that only what we see at the moment in front of our nose is what affects the value of I. In whichever programming language we use, we must learn, when debugging, in what ways nonlocal effects can manifest themselves. For example, in PL/I, subroutine calls (through global variables or through arguments passed "by address"), ON-units (which are similar to parameterless subroutine calls but can be invoked without any local mention of the ON-unit at all), and defining of one variable on another can lead to effects that are not to be found by looking at the place in the program where they seem to be arising.

Features of a language that can lead to nonlocality are not usually there just because of poor language design; otherwise they could be eliminated and nobody would mourn their passing. Defining one variable on another, for example, is provided so that compression can be achieved— which in itself can help locality. Therefore, there is a limit to how far the language can go in preventing nonlocality from arising from poor programming practices or mistakes. In the example given above, however, it might have been a better decision on the part of the PL/I language designers to have variables, such as I or S within F, be automatically local to F unless the programmer made explicit declaration to the contrary. Of course, if he makes any kind of explicit declaration of I or S, as in

DECLARE I FIXED BINARY, S FLOAT;
the declaration will restrict their scope to F, as long as it is within F. Thus, the programmer can overcome this difficulty by always declaring all variables, even if he only writes

DECLARE I, S;
The ON-unit of PL/I represents a particularly interesting case of nonlocality, because the basic function of ON-units is to permit us to obtain linearity. In fact, in the sense that the ON-unit is ordinarily used to handle an exceptional case—one that may never arise in some programs—it can be thought of as a way of achieving additional locality. In the first place, by not forcing us to mention the condition by name, PL/I permits us to achieve greater compression in the main body of code. Secondly, a statistical compression occurs because the exceptional case is taken out of our sight when we are considering ordinary cases. Thus, the ON-unit permits us to forget about exceptional cases, which simplifies coding —but which exacts a price when we need to remember the ON-unit.

But the ON-unit helps us to achieve linearity, which aids our sequential memory. Experiments with problem solving in programming-like situations indicate that a series of decisions arranged in a strictly linear sequence is typically easier to handle than a branching or looping sequence. Experience with programming languages seems to bear this out, for programs with numerous GO TO statements or other branches are notoriously difficult to understand or debug. Part of this difficulty comes because of simple nonlocality, for the branch address may be on a different page—and in a 50-page program, this type of branching can cause a lot of page turning.

Confusion can arise, however, even when the branch address is on the same page as the branch. For one thing, it may be that some unnoticed branch also leads to the same point, so we cannot easily figure out how we got where we got in execution. For another, each branch breaks our normal sequential mode of scanning the program or thinking about it. Even though we don't turn a page, our natural progression has been interrupted, making error more likely.

Many higher-level language features can help us mask the nonlinearity of the typical stored-program machine. The IF statement, which allows the statement to be executed to be attached to the IF; the DO or BEGIN, which allows us to group several statements as one under the THEN or ELSE clause; the logical connectives, which enable us to group decisions under one IF statement; the iterative DO, which permits us to eliminate explicit branching; the array operations, which enable us to eliminate explicit iterative DO loops; the ON-unit, which permits us to handle the exception condition without even mentioning it, or even thinking about it—all these and other features help to banish the nonlinearity from a program. Indeed, in PL/I and other languages, many programmers regard the presence of a statement label for branching to be a mark of poorly constructed code. Although we might not want to go that far, it does seem true that the GO TO is the one "major" statement that could be eliminated from PL/I with the least loss to the programmer.

TRADITION AND INNOVATION

One of the most important ways that a programming language can achieve ease of expression with a minimum of error is by being "natural." One way of achieving naturalness, as we saw, was through uniformity, but uniformity only applies to those programmers who have some experience with the language. When we begin to use a language, we are not able to notice the uniformities—instead we notice those things in the language that do not seem to correspond to our preexisting sense of "rightness." Where do we get this sense? Probably, it comes from two sources—the natural languages—English, French, Chinese—and the programming languages—FORTRAN, ALGOL, COBOL—which we know before we start to learn the new language. By making a programming language in some sense consonant with the other languages the user is likely to know, we may simplify his entry into its strange new world.

As an example of the natural language concepts we bring to a programming language, consider the case of the significant blank. In the orthographic forms of the European families of languages, at least, the concept of the significant blank is quite natural. In FORTRAN, however, there is no such thing as a significant blank—except within a literal string.

Moreover, the concept of "multiple blanks equal one blank" is natural, up to a point, as is the concept of a delimiter *or* a blank. The word "orate" is not the same as the two words, "or ate." Elision of the blank, however, would usually be correctible, since some grammatical or semantic violation would occur, due to redundancy, but not necessarily, as in,

"He gave it to you, or ate it."

"He gave it to you, orate it."

When the elided blank changes the sentence to a meaningless one, the reader will usually be able to correct it, but almost always with the conscious insertion of a blank:

"He lost it or ate it."

"He lost it orate it."

The blank next to a delimiter, however, can be left out without usually being noticed, as in

"Leave it alone,will you!"

When the programming language is not in consonance with these natural language rules for blanks, it may be more difficult to learn, or at least more difficult to debug. In FORTRAN, for instance, there is the classical type of bug which is typified by the statement

DO 33 I = 1 . 20

Here, the comma has been changed to a period—perhaps by keypunching—with the result that the entire statement is interpreted as

DO33I=1.20

The blanks here fool us into thinking that DO,33, and I are three separate entities, but they actually form only a single variable, DO33I, under FORTRAN rules for blanks.

A much more costly mishandling of blanks arises in the syntax of the job control language for OS/360. Here, the operand field—as in assembly language—is terminated by the first blank. This strange convention was used to permit comments to follow the operand field, as is done in the System/360 assembly language. But simply carrying this idea over from the assembly language—though consonant as far as the OS/360 designers were concerned—proved to be a poor choice for other users. First of all, FORTRAN, COBOL, and PL/I users were not familiar with the convention. Secondly, nobody really wanted to use comments on job control the way they did in assembly language. Finally, the frequency of continuation cards in job control usage was much greater than in assembly language, where continuation only arises frequently in the use of macros.

A typical mistake caused by this unthinking design carry-over might be the following:

```
//XX     DD     DSNAME=ABC,  DISP=(NEW,KEEP),                    C
```

The programmer, in punching, unconsciously leaves a blank after the comma following 'ABC.' He does not realize this blank because in English, or FORTRAN, it has no significance. The computer notices it, however, and thus takes it to be the beginning of the comment field. Consequently, the DISP parameter is ignored entirely, and the programmer finds that his data set is not saved, since DISP=(NEW,DELETE) is assumed. Much worse cases can be constructed, and it is difficult to estimate how many millions of dollars of machine time and programmer time have been wasted because of this design error. In effect, of course, it is not a design error, for the job control language was not really designed, in the sense that PL/I, FORTRAN, or COBOL were designed. Being part of the operating system, it was not thought of as a "programming" language at all, so somebody just carried over a technique which was fairly satisfactory from the nearest available source—with disastrous results. (See also Figures 10-1 and 10-2.)

Another area in which programming languages could be more consonant with natural languages is spelling. When we read natural language text, we often pass over misspellings without notice, even when they make nonsense words. In speaking, even greater flexibility is allowed, for we can understand the Atlantan when he says "pie," the Omahan when he says "milk," and the Bostonian when he says "yard." Programming languages, however, are often pedantic to the extreme when it comes to spelling, even in cases where what was meant could have been perfectly clear. Abbreviations, of course, are alternate spellings; but the concept could be carried much further—even to the point of making guesses—as many commercial systems now do—as to a correct spelling.

Spelling, of course, is only one example of a more general concept of "looseness" found in natural language. We can say either

> "Bring it here, will you?"

or   "Will you bring it here?"

and nobody will notice the difference. Programming languages, however, rarely are as flexible as natural languages, although we do have some leeway. Noise words in COBOL are one example of flexibility which permits the programmer to achieve some additional feeling of consonance with English. In PL/I, there are a number of places where reordering of part of a statement is permitted, as in

DO I = 1 TO N BY K;   DO I = 1 BY K TO N;

or   DECLARE A FIXED BINARY;   DECLARE A BINARY FIXED;

or   PUT SKIP LIST(A);   PUT LIST(A) SKIP;

By permitting two possibilities where only one might have existed, the language should be easier to learn, for each user can choose the form easiest or most natural *for him*. He may not, however, be conscious that he has made a choice. He might never have had the alternative form presented to him, possibly because his teacher prefers the other one. Or, he may get the impression that there is some *semantic* difference between the forms, and so be afraid to use one once he feels he knows the other.

And, indeed, there might be semantic differences, although these might be as slight as to be unnoticed in the ordinary programmer's lifetime. The two statements

DO I = 1 TO N BY K;   DO I = 1 BY K TO N;

are not quite precisely the same in PL/I, nor are the expressions

(A=2)&(B=3)   (B=3)&(A=2)

Aside from the psychological differences—from one person to another, or between reading and writing—there are possible performance differences which, by always lurking in the background, may discourage the programmer from taking advantage of the looseness available to him.

In the same way that some differences within a language are significant and some are not, so too are some differences between languages insignificant—or at least of so little significance as to not be worth the bother of trying to preserve. For instance, it may make some difference initially whether our language requires

DO I = 1 TO N BY 3;

or   FOR I: = 1 STEP 3 UNTIL N;

but any capable programmer should be able to move from one to the other with an absolute minimum of difficulty. Indeed, the difference between them is so insignificant that both could easily be permitted to exist in the same programming language. In arguments about the relative merits of programming languages, however, we often find the most heat about those points where there is the least significant difference, for it is only at those points that the two languages can be directly compared. Perhaps someone will someday perform an experiment to see whether DO or FOR is the "best" keyword for this situation—but there is little chance that mere facts would disturb such an argument.

When we design a new programming language to be similar to another commonly used one, we can definitely speed up early learning by remaining within the earlier tradition wherever possible. We pay for this early learning in an interesting way, however, for no two programming languages are exactly alike—otherwise they would be the same language.

If the languages are *slightly* different, then the psychological phenomenon of *inhibition* will occur. Inhibition comes in two forms—retroactive and proactive. Proactive inhibition occurs when the similarity of earlier learned material interferes with the learning of later material. Thus, for instance, FORTRAN programmers have an inordinate amount of difficulty learning to use format items such as F or E in PL/I, because, although they are similar, PL/I uses a comma where FORTRAN uses a period. When we look at the PL/I programs of a FORTRAN programmer, we often find such format items as F(10.2)—the results of which never fail to confound the FORTRAN programmer.

It is the *similarity* between the languages which causes the inhibition, as can be seen by examining the use of picture formats by the FORTRAN programmer. Such PL/I beginners have little or no difficulty learning to write P'SSSSSSSV.99', because there is no comparable structure in FORTRAN. (But, of course, COBOL programmers do have trouble.) The retroactive inhibition also depends on the similarity, but it works on the previously learned language. Thus, typically, the FORTRAN programmer who has learned PL/I finds it difficult to go back to writing FORTRAN programs—and not just because some time has elapsed.

Inhibition, therefore, is the price we pay for making two languages similar but not identical in some feature. It might be better, when identity is not possible, to make the two more clearly dissimilar, so that inhibition will have less force. But the cost of inhibition is not the only price we pay for trying to make one programming language match an earlier one. The old structures simply may not fit in with the new things we are trying to do, in which case the overall unity of the language will suffer. In this case, early learning slows down later learning—learning of new and powerful techniques. Alternatively, we may not be able to fit the new techniques to the old language, so that trying to achieve consonance may wind up achieving only sterility.

Because individual programmers are so different from one another, there is a definite limit to how far we can make our language consonant with the ideas and structures the programmer already knows. To be sure, we can pretty well count on all programmers recognizing such forms as numeric literals and simple arithmetic expressions, but we soon run into areas where different people prefer different ways of doing things. Looseness is one way a programming language allows for individual differences—by permitting a selection among two or more built-in things. Thus, in a sense, a loose language can adapt to preferences of individual programmers.

But there are other ways a language can be adaptable. These ways are characterized by the creation of new things, some for a single program and some to be used across a whole class of programs. One familiar example of such adaptability is the ability to define functions and other subroutines. Another is the ability to define new data types—structures and lists, for example. Some languages permit the definition or redefinition of operators, but these are, after all, just another type of function. Finally, there are languages with more elaborate metalanguages—compile-time facilities, for instance, or dynamic generation of code at execution—which can permit changing the entire face of the language.

When we use these facilities for adaptation, we may be able to gain a degree of consonance with our idiosyncracies which cannot be approached by the language designer directly. But in getting closer to our own specific modes of thought and expression, we may easily get further and further from the modes of other people. Programming is not just communication between one man and a machine. Other people will probably have to read and understand the program; but if the use of adaptive devices is too extensive, the program may be as closed to them as is the private language of a schizophrenic.

Within an installation, a certain amount of adaptation may be advantageous to adjust the language to the precise needs of the local type of work. Of course, at some point this type of redefinition becomes the design of a new language—a job not to be undertaken lightly by amateurs. If the language being used is really so far from the needs of the installation, it might be better to search for a language that is closer to the needs *before* modifications are made. There certainly are enough languages to choose from.

SPECIAL-PURPOSE, MULTIPURPOSE, AND TOY LANGUAGES

To some extent, our discussion of languages has been biased toward the languages of the professional programmer, with comments on the needs of the amateur. But the principles involved are deep ones, and they apply to amateur languages as well, although with modified emphasis. If we design a special language for a particular application area, we start immediately reaping psychological rewards by limiting the universe of discourse. Thus, a statistics language does not have to have facilities for complex arithmetic, a string processing language does not have to have much arithmetic at all, and a machine-tool control language might have more of a geometry than an arithmetic. Sometimes, however, these limitations are imposed simply by limiting the capacity, under the assumption that problems in that field never get any larger than a certain size. Thus, a simulation language might have no facilities for using auxiliary storage, which means that many language features can be dropped entirely—but it also means that certain problems cannot be simulated.

Limitation of the universe of discourse is so important for the design of special-purpose languages that it should be the first and most carefully considered step. Much of the success of APL, for example, had to do with the careful limitation of the universe with which it could deal, although most APL programmers think of it as a "multipurpose" language. But simply by limiting the language to terminal situations, to relatively small workspaces, and to no auxiliary files, the designers were able to provide a problem-solving tool *par excellence*—for problems within its scope. The success of the language can be attributed to the existence of large numbers of people whose problems fall within that limited scope— or at least fall within it while they are learning APL. Programmers who progress to, say, data-processing problems, in which large quantities of data are processed, soon find they have "outgrown" APL. Much of the enthusiasm for the system, however, doesn't take cognizance of the limitations that are built into it and account for a good deal of its success.

One reason why the limitations are not as obvious to users as they are to nonusers is that the programming language does indeed shape thought processes. We are not speaking here of simple inhibition effects, but of larger effects on the organization of programs and data. I became aware of this effect most clearly when teaching a beginning PL/I class composed of COBOL, FORTRAN, and Basic Assembler Language programmers, and people with no programming language at all. As I was reading the programs handed in for the first assignment, it struck me that I could conjecture the background of the programmer, and I recorded my guess for each one. I did not have any background sheets on the programmers, so there was no external way in which I could know their experience. The next day I checked my guesses with the class and obtained the results shown in Figure 12-3.

To be sure, a number of guesses were made simple by specific feature clues, such as the use of a decimal point instead of a comma in an F-format item. But these specific clues also led me to make several wrong guesses: I guessed "FORTRAN" for a BAL programmer because he used such decimal points, and "COBOL" for an inexperienced programmer because of the way he used symbols such as PART_COST, with the underscore standing for the COBOL hyphen. (It turned out that he had seen one of the COBOL programmers doing this and copied the style.)

As a consequence of the influence of language on thought, the problem that one will attempt to solve is limited by the programming language one knows and how much of it he knows. Therefore, there tends to be a self-fulfilling satisfaction with a special-purpose programming language, as

GUESSED / ACTUAL	COBOL	FORTRAN	BAL	NO EXPERIENCE	CORRECT GUESSES
COBOL	6	0	0	2	6/8
FORTRAN	0	5	0	0	5/5
BAL	0	1	6	1	6/8
NO EXPERIENCE	1	0	0	5	5/6

Figure 12-3   Guessing programming background.

well as with one's current level of knowledge. To the extent that special-purpose languages act as limits to thought in this manner, they are harmful to the user who potentially has larger problems to solve. The situation with COBOL is particularly instructive.

People have lost sight of the original intention of COBOL's designers. To quote one of them, Jean Sammet:

> The users for whom COBOL was designed were actually two subclasses of those people concerned with business data processing problems. One is the relatively inexperienced programmer for whom the naturalness of COBOL would be an asset, while the other type of user would be essentially anybody who had not written the program initially. In other words, the readability of COBOL programs would provide documentation to all who might wish to examine the programs, including the supervisory or management personnel. Little attempt was made to cater to professional programmers. . . .

The COBOL designers went to considerable trouble to see that these objectives were actually met. One result of their efforts for instance, is that programming managers in COBOL shops do seem to read programs somewhat more than do managers in other types of groups. Outside of the programming managers, however, it is doubtful whether many managers do read COBOL programs, or read them with any good effect.

However, the fact that COBOL was successful in getting nonprofessionals to writing programs in the sixties is proving to be an impediment to progress for the seventies. A crew of COBOL programmers is not, in general, an asset upon which an installation can build, say, on-line, fast response systems. Even the transition to effective use of random access files has been impeded by the sorting mentality that COBOL imposes. Seventy-five percent of the COBOL installations with which I have consulted on operating systems problems were essentially using their random access files as sequential devices, at best to get faster sorts, and at worst to get slower sequential processing than with tapes. Whether COBOL and COBOL users can grow with the expanding facilities available to them is an open question at the moment.

There seems to be no way out of this paradox—the better job a programming language does for the special purpose for which it was designed, the more limiting it is on the minds of those who use it, if they are faced with potentially new areas of application. In fact, this is another example of Fisher's Fundamental Theorem of Natural Selection. The professional programmer cannot afford to get into the trap of being so adapted that he is not adaptable, but we don't necessarily know in advance who is destined to become a professional. Only by studying the ways in which special-purpose languages adapt to their special circumstances do we have any hope of understanding what will be involved in reshaping thought processes if it is necessary to create a professional from an amateur or semiprofessional.

Special-purpose languages are also successful in exploiting special data structures which correspond to the user's needs in his special area, simultaneously achieving compactness and correspondence with previous learning. We would expect, for example, that a language to be used in social science research would provide for arrays of data such as questionnaire results, or that a language for doing algebraic manipulations would have standard data forms for polynomials or other symbolic expressions. And, indeed, they do, which accounts for a large part of their success—or failure, if they fail to be the right structures.

Along with special data structures, we find special routines for doing familiar processes on those structures. Thus, our social science research language would undoubtedly have various tabulation and data reduction primitives, and the algebraic language would have such primitives as analytical multiplication, differentiation, and simplification of expressions. Of course, the names of these functions and structures will be chosen to give the user the feeling that he is working in familiar territory, so as to take advantage of pre-existing learning.

In a special-purpose language where the main users will be nonprogrammers, the use of pre-existing learning is a major design objective, lest the user turn away from the system before he really has a chance to use it. Unfortunately, many of the special-purpose languages that have been invented—I cannot really bring myself to say "developed"—have *only* a correspondence with pre-existing learning to offer. A person is able to use them quickly enough, but soon finds that he cannot solve his real problems, but only "toy" problems resembling his real problems. Even when the language is theoretically able to describe his problem, the system may be so out of correspondence with the internal realities of computing that the capacity to do the real problem does not exist—either in time or in space. Once he reaches this situation, the casual user is likely to become an involved critic. And with good reason.

The casual way in which special-purpose programming languages are often thrown into the world—perhaps to get another publication on one's list, a publication which the specialists will not be able to read and the programmers will not want to—is a disgrace to the programming language design business. Not that the business is such a sparkling example in its own backyard—multipurpose languages—but when we move outside of the inner circle of computer professionals, we have an additional social responsibility toward those who cannot be expected to know how to protect themselves against a bad programming language. And here comes the pitch yet one more time: let's stop churning these languages out of our foreheads like full-blown goddesses and *develop* them in an environment where sound behavioral principles can be used in their design and testing. Let's become professional designers as well as professional programmers.

SUMMARY

On the cover of Jean Sammet's book, *Programming Languages: History and Fundamentals,* there is a picture reminiscent of Brueghel's *Tower of Babel.* The original painting is in Vienna, in the Kunsthistoriches Museum, but a wall-sized reproduction graces the conference room, across the ring, of the IBM Vienna Laboratory, where the PL/I Universal Language Document was born. All around the world, where programmers gather, one is likely to see some literary or pictorial reference to the Tower of Babel. Looking at the cover of Sammet's book, the reason is not hard to find—decorating the tower are the names of 117 programming languages. Actually, there are 118, for, although it is not listed in the index of this comprehensive book, there was once a programming language named BABEL—the name which tops the tower.

Indeed, to my knowledge, there are a number of languages (not even including "assembler" languages, which Sammet doesn't even attempt to cover in her list) that are not listed—and mercifully so. The 117 represented languages cover a period of about fifteen years, from 1952 (Short Code) to 1967, the latest language reference given. This average of eight new languages a year (worth mentioning) is misleading, since for the first ten years of the period the average was no more than two or three a year. The average for the last five years of the period is closer to twenty languages per year, and increasing toward the end. It seems likely that Sammet's 785 page tome will be the last work of its kind—at least the last to fit in one volume. If my extrapolations are correct, in 1972 programming languages will be invented at the rate of one a week—or more, if we consider the ones which never even make the literature, and enormously more if we consider dialects.

Is this bloom of languages bad, like the bloom of algae in a swimming hole? Or is it a healthy outpouring of a much needed original effort? We have passed the time when a language can simply be "invented" and then cast upon the literature, or upon the broad backs of all the programmers in a particular installation or working with a particular machine. We must now raise our sights and ask more of the would-be language inventor—we must ask him to show some indication of psychological usefulness of his language. But the inventors are not the only ones to bear the blame—the programming language theoreticians have too long ignored the psychological side of their trade. Programming is not a branch of mathematics, it is a unique form of communication in which human beings take an active role and machines often a passive one. Perhaps our troubles with programming languages stem from the unidirectionality of the communication. Only when the theoreticians turn to the "dialogue" aspects of programming "language" will they finally be forced to recognize that they are not students of symbol manipulation, but of human behavior.

QUESTIONS

For Managers

1. What programming languages are used in your shop? How frequently do you have occasion to look at a program? Do you see the programming language as an aid to your managerial task, or do you see it as a secret language in which programmers can communicate behind your back?

2. What psychological factors do you consider when deciding to introduce a new programming language into your shop? What kinds of experiments do you do?

For Programmers

1. Using your best-known programming language, give and discuss several uses of:
   a. uniformity
   b. nonuniformity
   c. covert categories

2. Of all the languages you know, which is the most compact? What makes it compact? Does its compactness depend upon the limited range of problems for which you use it?

3. List all the ways in which your best-known programming language can yield nonlocal effects. What influence do these effect have on debugging? Give examples of bugs due to nonlocality, and how you eventually found them.

4. Take some programs written by others and classify them by the ease with which they can be understood, for a given length of program. Count the statement labels and the branch instructions or statements, and see if there is any correlation between clarity and lack of branching. Also, compute the average length of a branch, and see what correlation that has with clarity.

5. Give some examples of the way in which the programming languages you previously knew affect the way in which you now program in your most recent language. Give some examples of ways in which the programming languages you know affect your thought processes in areas other than programming.

6. If you know a special-purpose programming language, describe the ways in which it takes advantage of:
   a. limitation of the universe of discourse
   b. consonant data structures
   c. consonant processing functions
   d. consonant terminology

BIBLIOGRAPHY

Rubey, Raymond J., *et al., Guide to PL/I, Vol. 1: Comparative evaluation* Detroit: American Data Processing, 1969

Brooks, F. P., *et. al. Guide to PL/I. Vol. 2: Experiences with PL/I* Detroit: American Data Processing, 1969
These two documents represent two approaches to assessing the value of a new programming language, in this case PL/I. The second is a rather conventional seminar-discussion approach, in which participants state their opinions of the value of PL/I in its various parts and as a whole. The first, however, is one of the few attempts to study a program language behaviorally. The method was to eliminate individual variation by having the same programmer program the same problem in

two different languages—COBOL-PL/I, FORTRAN-PL/I, or JOVIAL-PL/I. The authors of the study are evidently programmers, not behavioral scientists, but they are not without sophistication. Would-be experimenters would do well to compare this study with Sackman's work, perhaps leading them to something in between.

Sammet, Jean E., *Programming Languages: History and Fundamentals,* Englewood Cliffs, N.J., Prentice-Hall, 1969.

Along with its other qualities, this book is a gold mine of information on special-purpose languages, and, by induction, their design.

Wirth, N., PL 360, A Programming Language for the 360 Computers, *Communications of the ACM,* **15,** No. 1 (Jan. 1968), pp. 37-74.

Some people feel quite strongly that the only truly general-purpose language can be some sort of assembly language. But the difficulty of assembly language—particularly the lack of linearity—makes this a most discouraging prognostication. One bright ray of hope, however, is the approach taken by Wirth, to impose the advantages of block structure on an assembly language while still keeping, at least conceptually, full control of the code generated at the machine level. Certainly this is one of the most important papers for the future of systems programming to come out in the last decade.

Weinberg, G. M., *PL/I Programming: A Manual of Style,* New York, McGraw-Hill, 1970.

For detailed discussions of principles of language design in the context of PL/I, see especially Chapter 2.

Klerer, M., and J. May, A User-Oriented Programming Language, *Computer Journal,* **8,** No. 2 (July 1965), pp. 103-109.

From a language design point of view, the most intriguing feature of the Klerer and May system is the acceptance—indeed, the welcoming—of ambiguity. The second most intriguing feature is the lack of a name for the language—either the height of modesty or of egoism. For more complete references, see Sammet.

Shaw, C. J., *Decision Tables—An Annotated Bibliography,* Santa Monica, System Development Corp. (April 1965), TM-2288/000/000 (14 pp.).

Dixon, Paul, Decision Tables and Their Application, *Computers and Automation,* **13,** (April 1964), pp. 14-19.

The Decision Table Movement flourished in the early sixties, then seemed to go underground, and now is reviving. Unfortunately, the revival seems to be concentrated on formal problems on the one hand, and ill-conceived textbooks on the other. We have yet to see any empirical data on the value of decision tables in any psychological sense, which is particularly unfortunate in view of the claim that they represent a more natural way of programming than procedure-oriented languages. For those researchers who would like to throw some light on this murky field, we offer the bibliography and review article above, which should bring things up to date circa 1965. At the time of this writing, there really seems nothing better.

Weinberg, G. M., *Experiments in Problem Solving* (Doctoral Thesis), Ann Arbor, University Microfilms, 1965.

A study into the mental forms that subjects choose when given the freedom to choose, with implications for the types of structures most desirable in programming languages.

Whorf, Benjamin Lee, *Language, Thought, and Reality,* Cambridge, Mass., M.I.T. Press, 1956.

Whorf was an anthropologist or anthropological linguist who, through his study of non-"Standard-American-European" languages, gained great insights into the influence of language on thought—such insights as the significance of covert categories. Some of these selected writings are highly technical accounts of American Indian languages, and the others are accessible to the non-linguist. They are not always easy to read because of the unfamiliarity of the modes of thought described. And who knows, maybe even the technical articles would be useful. Can we possibly be so ethnocentric as to believe that only European languages contain useful models for computer programming? Perhaps we can, but not after reading Whorf.

Zipf, G. K., *Human Behavior and the Principle of Least Effort,* Cambridge, Mass., Addison-Wesley, 1949.

Zipf, like Whorf, was outside the intellectual fads of his time, and was a long time in gaining recognition. His work on the principles of language change should be read by anyone who has any interest, for example, in "dialects" of programming language, and particularly in "nonredundant" programming.

Shannon, C. E., Prediction and Entropy in Printed English, *Bell System Technical Journal,* Vol. 30 (1951), pp. 50-64.

See next reference for discussion.

Burton, N. G., and J. C. R. Licklider, Long-Range Constraints in the Statistical Structure of Printed English, *American Journal of Psychology,* Vol. 68 (1955), pp. 650-653.

These two articles attempt to measure the redundancy in English printed text, and they suggest an approach to measuring the redundancy of a program or a programming language. There are many difficulties in conducting such an experiment, such as selection of appropriate programs and texts, but our early results indicate that consistent differences exist among programming languages.

Miller, George A., The Magical Number Seven, Plus-or-minus Two: Some Limits on Our Capacity for Processing Information, *Psychological Review,* **63,** No. 2 (March 1956), pp. 81-97.

In this appealing little article, Miller describes how the human mind is limited in its information capacity, more or less, and what kinds of strategies it uses to overcome these limitations, such as chunking. These strategies seem to follow the kinds of strategies programmers use.

Smith, B., *Memory,* London, Allen and Unwin, Ltd., 1966.

Yates, F. A., *The Art of Memory,* Chicago, The University of Chicago Press, 1966.

Minsky, M., *Semantic Information Processing,* Cambridge, Mass., M.I.T. Press, 1968.

Three very different views of memory and the sorts of mental processes toward which programming languages are designed, or should be designed. One problem, of course, with designing programming languages according to psychological principles, is that there is so much controversy over mental processes, especially the "higher" processes such as memory, which are so important (or are they?) to programming.

13 OTHER PROGRAMMING TOOLS

Although programming languages get the lion's share of the attention in print, the working programmer has other tools of the trade. He spends much of his time reading and writing documents, wrestling with the operating system, and wringing the bugs out of his programs. In these tasks, too, he could use whatever crumbs the social sciences might throw him. Yet these tasks are even more neglected from the psychological point of view than are programming languages. In the following sections we shall try to suggest how certain insights could be used to better the design of tools for debugging, for management of operations above the program level, and for documentation. There are very few programming sources to call upon, but perhaps this effort will open up the subject to an era of new design efforts. We certainly could use them!

PROGRAM TESTING TOOLS

In September of 1962, a news item was released stating that an $18 million rocket had been destroyed in early flight because "a single hyphen was left out of an instruction tape." The article did not say how large the "instruction tape" was, but we can imagine that it might have contained 100,000 or so instructions. In any other business, one error in 100,000 would be considered a phenomenal reliability record, but in programming, it cost $18 million. The cost may be exceptional, but the story is repeated daily. Indeed, the job of programming can be fruitfully looked at from the point of view of testing alone—considering that the only real problem in programming is getting the program to work correctly and proving it.

It has been said that "the expert is a person who avoids the small errors as he sweeps on to the grand fallacy." In programming, however, avoiding even the small errors is no mean task. In reality, there are no "small" errors, since even a "single hyphen" can result in disaster. The nature of programming being what it is, there is no relationship between the "size" of the error and the problems it causes. Thus, it is difficult to formulate any objective for program testing, short of "the elimination of *all* errors"—an impossible job.

Obviously, we need all the help we can get in testing programs, but the problem of program testing has received less than its share of attention from designers of programming tools. Moreover, when testing tools are designed, the question of the psychology of testing is rarely evident. Yet testing is first and foremost a psychological problem. Consider, for instance, the question of *confidence.* The ideal testing tool should give us confidence in our program exactly proportional to the confidence it deserves, so that we neither pass on a program containing errors nor continue probing a program which is error-free. What program testing system today gives us even the minimum information in this regard?

For example, to have confidence in the testing of a program, we should want to know to what extent our tests actually covered the coding. By this we mean, as a start, that the testing system should keep and present to us a record of those areas of coding that have and have not been executed in the course of running tests. It is in the nature of people in our society to believe that things are as they want them to be, so a program testing tool must struggle to show us things as they are. Certainly, we could expect that the testing tools we use would continue to pester us until all pieces of code had been executed at least once.

Since people tend to be optimistic about the state of their code, a good testing tool might be designed on the principle of destroying confidence— a confidence that can be restored when necessary. In the case of one program—which calculated the prices of more than 30,000 manufactured objects—the customer for the program accidentally came across four cases in which the prices were wrong. His confidence in the program was destroyed, and even when the programmer was able to show him that the error occurred only when a certain dimension exceeded a certain size, he remained skeptical. As it happened, there was only one additional case in which this error existed, but having found four by himself rather quickly, the customer was not about to believe the programmer.

Overconfidence by the programmer could be attacked by a system that introduced random errors into the program under test. The location and nature of these errors would be recorded inside the system but concealed from the programmer. The rate at which he found and removed these known errors could be used to estimate—in some sense—the rate at which he is getting out unknown errors. A similar technique is used routinely by surveillance systems in which an operator is expected to spend eight hours at a stretch looking at a radar screen for very rare events—such as the passing of an unidentified aircraft. Tests of performance showed that it was necessary to introduce some nonzero rate of occurrence of artificial events in order to keep the operator in a satisfactory state of arousal. Moreover, since these events were under control of the system, it was able to estimate the current and overall performance of each operator.

Although we cannot introduce program bugs which simulate real bugs as well as we can simulate real aircraft on a radar screen, such a technique could certainly be employed both to train and evaluate programmers in program testing. Even if the errors had to be introduced manually by someone else in the project, it would seem worthwhile trying out such a "bebugging" system. It would give the programmer greatly increased motivation, because he now would *know* that there were errors in his program, that he did not put them there, and that if he didn't find them, other people would know about it. We have only to contrast this state of affairs with the currently prevalent one: he is not really convinced that there are errors there; he knows that if there are, they are "his"; and, if he doesn't find them, he is pretty sure that nobody will know about it.

The amount of confidence we ultimately have in the testing of a particular program, however, does not depend on the testing procedure alone. The *a priori* probability of a program being correct has a great influence on the amount of testing that has to be done to reach a given level of confidence. To take the simplest possible case, consider the two code fragments:

IF N = 1 THEN A = A + 1.5;

```
IF N = 2 THEN A = A + 2.9;
IF N = 3 THEN A = A + 0.1;
        . . .
IF N = 20 THEN A = A − 3.2;
```
and
```
A = A + B(N);
```
Clearly, the second case is less subject to errors although we certainly cannot rule out errors in constructing the array, B. For example, suppose one card in the first case were mispunched, so that in the middle of the sequence somewhere we found

```
IF N = 11 THEN A = A + 4.7;
IF N = 11 THEN A = A + 2.6;
```

The cases for N = 11 and N = 12 would both be completely wrong, but these cases might not arise in the testing. In the second method, however, each case is independent, that is, if we get that element of B correct, nothing else in B can influence it. Moreover, the second program handles the case of N less than zero or greater than 20 by raising the SUBSCRIPTRANGE condition, whereas the first program simply ignores those cases, which could be a disaster.

The psychological point of these examples is that we will have far more confidence in the second program than in the first, after an equal amount of testing. Why? Because the second program displays a *uniformity* that the first does not. A single test on this program does the work of many tests on the other. Whether we get this uniformity from our programming language or from our particular conception of the program structure, the effect is the same: For a given amount of testing, we receive a greater amount of confidence in the program. Thus, the best possible testing tool must be based both on a language and a program structure with a high degree of uniformity.

In a similar way, we can argue that lack of locality and lack of compactness make a program more difficult to test. But is there some way a testing system could measure the uniformity, locality, and compactness of a program? If there were, a scraggly, scattered, prodigal program could be sent back to the programmer or his supervisor for inspection after compilation and before testing is allowed to begin.

We have no experimental evidence that such a testing aid could be built, but we can make several suggestions about directions for research on the problem. For one thing, locality could be measured by counting the number of labels, GO TO statements, and references to variables declared on a different page. More sophisticated measures of locality could be obtained by calculating some sort of "mean distance of reference," either for the whole program or for sections of it. Potential trouble spots, such as partially open subroutines or ON-units which change variables, could be counted and warned about, in addition to the usual compiler warnings we get today.

Uniformity and compactness might be a little more difficult to measure, but an aid in judging compactness would be some idea before we started coding how long a program would be reasonable for a particular job. One measure of uniformity and compactness could be the number of references per variable. A small number of references to a variable could indicate that it has been introduced unnecessarily and could be eliminated; and a large number of such references could mean that scattered operations could be consolidated through a different program structure. We could supply a tally of the number of times each array was referenced without using array expressions as a passable indicator of lack of uniformity, for an array is, in a sense, a collection of homogeneous data items, and therefore a candidate for homogeneous treatment.

Another approach to detecting lack of uniformity and compactness would be for the compiler to detect certain *patterns* in the code. As a simple example, consider the use of similar names such as N1, N2, N3, N4, and N5 in the same program. In the first place, as we know, such a collection of names is an invitation to error, for one name may be easily written or read for the other. But, if the use of such names really represents some uniformity of meaning, perhaps the variables they represent could be collected into an array and treated in a more uniform manner. A more subtle example of pattern detection would be the repeated use of similar code sequences. Such repetition might indicate that more compression could be achieved by making a loop, a subroutine, or a macro definition, or it might indicate nothing at all. In any case, the field is wide open for the investigator with a few ideas and a knowledge of programming psychology.

Another well-known psychological bias in observation is the overdependence on "early" data returns. In program testing, the programmer who gets early "success" with his program is likely to stop testing too soon. One way to guard against this mistake is to prepare the tests in advance of testing and, if possible in advance of coding. We refer here to tests concerned with *detecting* the presence of errors—not to all tests. Obviously, we cannot construct tests in advance for *locating* the source of an error; nor can we construct the procedures for *correcting* the error once it has been found. But all testing begins with detection, so advance work on test cases is never wasted—unless we yield to the temptation to bypass the remaining tests in view of the "excellent" results we have so far.

The debugging system could help us to resist this temptation by forcing us to specify in advance the amount of testing we plan to do. Failure to complete this number of tests could result in a management report, or some other form of prodding to the programmer. In general, of course, anything in the testing system that simplifies the preparation and execution of test cases will help the programmer to overcome the temptation to quit too soon. One such system in use today is particularly designed to counteract the temptation to skip retesting when a "small" change has been made to the program. If the test cases are stored in the system and can be rerun automatically on demand, the programmer is less likely to skip the retest. The typical system of this sort, however, produces vast amounts of output. It is hardly useful to rerun test cases if nobody looks at the results of the rerun. A great improvement could be wrought in these systems by providing automatic comparison between old results and new ones, thus calling the programmer's attention only to those cases that differ from one run to the next.

One final observation must be made about the possibilities for improvement of the psychological behavior involved in program testing. Typically, as we discussed under the concept of "locality," when a programmer has a difficult time finding a bug, it is because he is looking in the wrong place. As simple as this sounds, that is how difficult it is to get the programmer to look in a different place, once he has "locked in" on the wrong one. In general, the best advice for human debugging consultants is to make the client look somewhere else, or at least do something different with the same place. Possibly an automated debugging system could force the programmer's attention to new areas of coding after he had been looking at the same area for a certain length of time. All sorts of algorithms could be devised for choosing the place to show him next, but the most important thing is just to get him unstuck. In fact, a good system is simply to turn off his terminal for a while, giving him a chance to look at some trees or grass or mini-skirts—anything but that wrong section of code.

OPERATING SYSTEMS

One of the persistent controversies in programming language design is this: What is the proper place for debugging tools—in the language or in the operating system? By raising the question in this section, we may seem to be taking sides in the argument, but no such conclusion should be drawn. Both sides have much going for them. On the one hand, the programmer should not be required to learn an entirely new language just to debug his programs—the horror of dumps makes that point clear. On the other hand, the language level conceals from the programmer many of the practical realities of an actual operating environment, and it is just these realities which may lead to the greatest problems in program testing.

The proper compromise—at least on psychological grounds—seems to be a certain amount of extension to the basic programming language which faces up to the realities of the operating environment. This extension, however, should not be added willy-nilly, as most operating system features seem to be, but should have a high degree of uniformity with the rest of the language. The requirement for uniformity, however, places a great burden on the operating system implementation, because the typical operating system supports not just one, but several, programming languages. Thus, it seems easier for the operating system people to supply a single, separate language of their own, a language which programmers in each of the supported languages must then master.

In the case of OS/360, for example, this language was based on the assembly language for System/360—with some consequences we have already noted. To the operating system designers and implementers, this choice must have seemed entirely natural, for didn't everyone know assembly language? But even for those people who did know assembly language, its format was probably not the most suitable for a job control language—at least as chosen by the designers. For example, the OS/360 job control language relies heavily on the use of so-called "positional parameters" and much less heavily on the "keyword parameters." But positional parameters would seem to be most helpful when the user was very familiar with coding in the language and wanted the greatest possible compression. In the typical use of job control, however, the user never gains much experience with the different options and is more likely to create his job control with the open manual at his side. In that case, the safe and sure identification of keyword parameters—no order to remember, no commas to indicate omitted items, mnemonic names with each keyword—would seem to have favored their use.

Two of our students tested these intuitive feelings about the superiority of keyword parameters for coding in relatively unfamiliar situations. They used groups of experienced and inexperienced programmers, coding some nonprogramming material first in one form and then in the other. They found that positional coding was somewhat faster, even for new material and inexperienced people. But the rate of making errors was from two to four times as high. Considering the situation in job control —where little time is spent in the actual *coding* of the parameters and little assistance is given to help find bugs in them—three times as many errors seems too high a price to pay for a 30 percent increase in coding speed.

Such matters were probably never considered in the choice of a job control format, for that seems such a small part of the problem of implementing an operating system. Another problem, which probably seems quite small to operating system designers, is the matter of accounting, or, in a generalized sense, performance evaluation. For many programmers, debugging is not the end of the line. The program may run, but it may cost too much to run. Operating system designers seem to be reluctant to ask for information on how long a program will run, how much core it occupied, how many records were processed on which files, how much CPU time was used, and so forth. Some cynics have even suggested that manufacturers do not want their customers to have such information, lest they see how little actual production is being done by the "giant brain."

Regardless of how the manufacturers feel, performance evaluation information is an essential part of the operating system's task. For one thing, performance figures often give independent clues to program bugs. A program that runs too fast may be bypassing certain segments of code; and one that runs too slow may be looping in a place where no looping was expected. But more than this side benefit for debugging, there is the direct need of such performance information if programmers are ever going to learn to turn out programs that perform well. Without the simple and automatic feedback of such information, those programmers who need it most will never see it. Moreover, good accounting information, sorted by programmer, aids the installation management in determining which programmers are in need of help and which programmers are prepared to give it. It seems astonishing that we can have progressed as far as we have in computing without every computer user demanding that the manufacturer furnish him with some sort of minimal accounting scheme.

Computer manufacturers sometimes argue that the customers have unique needs and would be offended if the manufacturer tried to tell them the kind of accounting information required. A more blatant rationalization would be hard to imagine, and it makes one think that the cynics might be right, after all. We could certainly identify a common set of requirements to serve as a starter for most installations and provide them in a standard accounting routine for the operating system. Any customer who was dissatisfied with this routine could replace it with his own— certainly no more confusing than what he has now. In fact, with one manufacturer at least, since there was never any standard accounting routine supplied with the system, the interface for the "user-supplied" accounting routine had a way of changing with each new release of the system. After five or six releases, most customers had learned their lesson and had stopped trying to keep up with the changes. Of all the people in the business, the manufacturers seem to have the most pragmatic grasp of psychological principles—at least when the principles can be used to avoid doing something they don't wish to do.

If we were to make a list of the information desired from an accounting routine, a measure of typical turnaround time in batch systems would be near the top. Of course, the operating system is not in a position to record the complete turnaround unless there is remote entry and exit of information under its supervision, but lacking the complete picture, the time between machine entry and exit would answer many questions. Yet, even if we had a complete grasp of the factors affecting turnaround, we would still have to face the problem—largely psychological—of what constitutes ideal turnaround.

One of our students undertook to investigate the question of ideal turnaround. He polled both programmers and their managers, using a technique in which individual identities were concealed but group membership could be known. His first important finding was that different groups tended to have different perceived needs for turnaround, but that within a group the opinion was relatively stable. Presumably, different kinds of work require different kinds of service. A second finding was that in several groups, the manager and the group members had diametrically opposed ideas about the group's needs. In one group a manager was pushing for remote access equipment "to improve turnaround" when the group members felt that what they needed—because they were debugging the input-output section of an operating system—was more opportunity to be in the machine room when their runs were made.

Sometimes, managers are inclined to think that the programmers want "zero turnaround"—instant acceptance and return of their jobs. This survey and other observations give evidence to contradict this impression, for the programmers' demands seem quite modest. In another study—one designed to compare the efficacy of two different programming languages—several of the participants complained that the turnaround was too good! They had been given special priority in order to facilitate the study, with the result that the measured average turnaround was 31 minutes from the time the job was passed through the window until the time the output was placed on the output table. The complaint was that if turnaround had been a little poorer, they would have spent a bit more time in making corrections and in perusing their output for additional errors.

In a way, then, if the programmer has invested very little waiting time in a run, he may tend to value that run less—an observation which seems to hold for certain terminal systems as well. At the other extreme, very poor turnaround puts the programmer in an almost neurotic state when he submits a run. The cost of making the smallest error is so great—

he might lose a week while waiting—that he may find himself making errors out of sheer nervousness. Moreover, he will try to put everything he can think of into the run, thus increasing his chance of making an error and also increasing the run time. It is common for a shop to drift into a poor turnaround situation with everyone making extra-long runs out of self-defense, and with these very extra-long runs causing the turnaround situation to deteriorate.

Because the type of work differs from run to run, it is really impossible to state a single optimal figure for turnaround time. Usually, more than four, or possibly five, runs per day of the same job cannot be utilized fully, and fewer than two begins to induce anxiety and unsound practices. For initial work, however, when the programmer is just getting syntax and keying errors out of his code, terminal access would seem to be desirable. However, people in shops where four runs per day are assured are apparently not as troubled about these "trivial" errors as are programmers in less well-run shops.

As we have noted before in other contexts, the *mean* time is not the only important psychological factor. If the turnaround is very uncertain —six runs one day and none the next—the programmer is not able to plan his work effectively. In a short time, programmers will react to uncertainty by setting up their test runs to defend themselves against the worst situation, with resultant waste and bad feeling.

Another source of bad feeling with respect to turnaround is the doling out of priority. Programmers in one of our studies complained that certain (other) people seemingly got favored machine access for no apparent reason. No particular rancor was evident when priority was given out in a uniform way with respect to some particular job characteristic, such as expected running time; but when no reason was given, or when the reason was inconsistent, enmity seemed to be directed against both the grantor (the manager) and the grantee (the programmer). Inasmuch as neither form of enmity would appear to be terribly healthy for a programming group, it might be best to dispense with such special favors altogether.

When a priority system is established to favor certain types of jobs over others, there may be some initial resistance, or at least anxiety, but this usually diminishes as the effects of the new system become evident. The existence and publication of good operating statistics apparently help in gaining acceptance, for then each programmer can judge for himself the consequences of certain actions and adjust his runs accordingly. A typical situation is one in which lower priority is given to longer jobs, jobs that take more than a certain amount of core storage, or jobs that require special setups. At first, everyone seems to feel that his jobs should be made an exception to these rules; but if the effect is actually better turnaround for those who fall within the limits, the nature of the jobs being submitted soon begins to change. Estimates of running time and core storage become better, and special setups that were once fervently defended as "essential" now seem to disappear.

Such a situation is just one more example of the "law of effect" as applied to the operating environment. Whatever the operating environment—be it good or bad—the programmers will eventually adapt to it in ways to do the best they can for themselves. Thus, if a programmer is rewarded for behavior that is detrimental to the operation as a whole—or even if he is simply not penalized for it—all programmers will eventually be adopting that behavior if it suits them. For example, some installations require that the programmers make time estimates of their jobs so that the operators can schedule the work better. If, to take one actual case, all jobs of fifteen minutes or less estimated time are treated in the same way, all programmers will eventually discover that it is best —for them—to put down an estimate of fifteen minutes even if they think they will need only one minute.

In fact, there is no sense bothering to ask the programmer to make finer judgments than the operating system is prepared to act upon. The installation might simply ask the programmer to classify his job as "under two minutes," "two to fifteen minutes," or "over fifteen minutes," possibly indicating at the same time the priority consequences of each choice. Similarly, if the system is multiprogramming and there are only two sizes of job partitions, the programmer should be asked to select one or the other—not give a space estimate down to the nearest byte. Setting rules that are not enforced, or setting limits that are not used, can only result in contempt for the system by those who must work under those rules and limits.

The action of the law of effect can be blatantly obvious or surpassingly subtle. Moreover, it is not just the usual "system" that is involved. Programmers adapt to any aspect of the environment that affects the performance of their jobs, regardless of whether or not the system manager considers it part of their system. Sackman, for instance, observed in one of his studies that waiting time for jobs or terminals dropped substantially for subjects with more than four problems, which he interprets in the following way: "It seems as if the cadets became more efficient in their timing tactics for requesting computer service as they gained more experience."

Although Sackman calls this result "unexpected," his surprise can probably be attributed to his being a psychologist and not a programmer. Any professional programmer has observed himself and others making such adaptations to the peculiarities of the system whose operation determines in large measure his success or failure. G. H. Stange, in a study for our psychology of programming class, studied the introduction of two remote entry systems which were intended to replace a dispatcher system. He observed many adaptations to the dispatcher's schedule and peculiarities, but the most unusual of these was the observation that the turnaround time of a job depended on the way the cards were packaged! A deck wrapped with a rubberband was the best (50 percent of the jobs were back in less than three hours), a cardboard card box was next (32 percent were back), and a metal card box was worst (only 12 percent back in the same interval). Stange checked on a possible correlation between container and time or core requirements and found none. Evidently, the smaller *looking* jobs got preferential treatment by the operators—and some of the programmers had begun to be aware of the difference. To compensate, they made every effort to make their decks look as small as possible; placing a small deck in a metal box would be a disaster.

When a remote job entry system was introduced into this shop, such preferential treatment of decks was theoretically removed, but Stange goes on to show how other factors led to differential treatment to which the programmers could adapt. The first factor was knowledge of the new system, which led to a certain incentive to learn how to use it and to keep others from knowing. But then it began to be clear that untrained people using the system led to card jams and other malfunctions that only interfered with other people's work. At this point the more knowledgeable people began to hang around and act as operators, so as to be sure that their own jobs would not be delayed. Because of this protective waiting, much of the apparent savings of the system was lost, because the programmers did nothing while waiting except make sure that nobody messed up the system.

Ultimately the congregation of programmers around the terminal led to other effects—in particular, to exposure of programs to other people. The printer was extremely slow, so the assembled throng could watch programs coming off and make comments. Also, people conversed about the RJE system itself and about other aspects of programming. What this increased social contact would have done eventually is not known, because it was cut short by the emergence of one individual as unofficial "operator." He took the job to protect his own interests when the system would break down often—he reentered all jobs, but always managed to get his in first. This improved service for his jobs was apparently his only reward for operating the system, but others accepted this price in return for not having to wait in the entry room. And so, after a short perturbation, the system settled back to a pattern that looked very much like the old expediter pattern, with another human being interposed between the programmers and the "system." The job of getting one's work done became once again the job of manipulating a human being rather than the operating system itself. Moreover, the old expediter system was not removed, since the expediter served other programmers in the area as well. His service was used as a backup when the RJE system was behaving badly, as a way of running jobs with many cards or large printout without tying up RJE, and as a way of getting overnight service on jobs without the attention needed for RJE. The second RJE system was used by some programmers. It had a CRT device, and was found to be useful in initial preparation of decks, but particularly for monitoring the progress of jobs submitted by the other two methods.

Overall, the installation of these two systems eventually had the desired effect—an increase in the number of jobs per programmer per day and a reduction in turnaround time. This improvement was not achieved simply by overpowering the problem with equipment, but by providing an enriched environment—an increased set of choices to which the programmers could adapt their strategy of submitting jobs. We do not know, of course, whether the increased flexibility available to this group was at the expense of some other users. Eventually, some rules and limits have to be established to maintain a balance among the various competing users.

If sensible rules and limits are to be established, however, the operating system must have sufficient flexibility to accept them and act upon them. Flexibility in the operating system is also desirable when setting up the procedures by which it is to be used. The best way to ensure that the system is used efficiently and effectively is to make the efficient and effective ways the *easiest* to use. In a well-designed operating system, the entire face of the system can be changed by making "catalogued procedures" of job control language that is, or should be, frequently used. In this way, the programmer can be guided into better ways of using the machine by the reward of making the job easier.

In view of the arguments about the specialized needs for accounting routines in each installation, it is interesting to observe how certain manufacturers tend—by deed if not always by word—to encourage customers to use their "standard" job control procedures, rather than custom building their own. The standard procedures, of course, must be sufficiently general to fit any configuration and any mix of words, so they are not usually optimal for any particular work or installation. Perhaps what we have here is an example of the law of effect operating on a grander scale. After all, computer manufacturers get paid more if more machine time is used. It is only natural, therefore that they should discourage the use of things (such as accounting routines), which might lead to greater efficiency, and encourage the use of things (overgeneralized job control procedures), which might lead to lessened efficiency. *Caveat emptor!*

TIME SHARING VERSUS BATCH

Suspicion of computer manufacturers is nowhere greater than in the reaction to the introduction of time-sharing systems. Old-timers are often heard muttering that time sharing is merely another scheme to introduce even more inefficiency into computing, so as to further line the pockets of the capitalists. Certainly time sharing, like other computer innovations, was undertaken on a large scale with no psychological investigation whatsoever. People thought it would work, or wanted to think it would work, so it was pushed onto the market and the battle began.

By and large, the fight between the time sharers and the batchards has been conducted on the level of name-calling. Then, suddenly, we had a breath of experimental fresh air rushing through the argument, as Sackman published his book, *Man-Computer Problem Solving: Experimental Evaluation of Time-Sharing and Batch Processing.* Those readers who still doubt the ability of psychological methods to clear up computing problems should read Sackman's book from cover to cover, as should all advocates of either side in the time sharing versus batch controversy.

We cannot hope here to survey the problem in the depth that Sackman has obtained, but we cannot leave without some comments on the kinds of lessons which the time sharing versus batch controversy has given us, since this is the one area in which we have the most empirical information.

One good starting place is the types of assumptions which creep into a field and may be taken for granted by even the most thorough investigator. In Sackman's case, the idea of the individual as the proper unit of study is never questioned at all, which is hardly unexpected since that assumption is built into the very hardware and software of all time-sharing systems! We do not, for example, have terminals that are suitable for two or more people working together at them and, lacking the terminals, we completely lack the software or even software ideas to support them. Moreover, Sackman's assumption is reinforced by the school environment in which most of his tests were conducted. Certainly at the Air Force Academy any cooperative work on a program would be regarded as cheating—heaven forbid!

Another lesson from Sackman's work is that even the most thorough investigator can occasionally make a wrong interpretation of his results. In one of his studies, Sackman plots mean number of syntax errors versus session number in the batch mode and finds "the classic error-extinction curve." Although it is true that errors are "extinguished," this is not at all the extinction which psychologists observe, for instance as a subject reduces the number of errors made on successive attempts to memorize a list. If our studies have any relevance to Sackman's group, the typical programmer working in batch goes through two phases. First he works toward his first error-free compilation, which might take 0–5 runs. Once he has that, he proceeds to change a single statement at a time, in the usual case, as he converges toward a semantically correct program. He may make an error in this single statement—especially if he is the "assertive" type we postulated earlier—but the bulk of his statements are never touched and thus remain error-free through no effort of the programmer himself. It is the punched card which "extinguishes" errors, not the programmer's memory.

Well, so what does it matter who does the extinguishing, as long as the errors do get extinguished? To the systems designer, it should matter a great deal. Let me give an example. A few years ago, I walked into a programming shop at the time they were firming up specifications for a syntax checker for a remote entry environment. The checker for PL/I interested me, and I took a look at the specifications. Whoever had written them had asked that the checker be able to detect "any error that the batch compiler could detect" within the context of a single statement. The image here was of a programmer attempting to get a perfect compilation on his first try, which would be unlikely anyway because of global errors not detectable by a line-at-a-time syntax checker. To determine how valuable such a checker could be, one has to have an accurate model of the error patterns to be fed on it.

Our model gives the following picture for PL/I programmers. Before the first successful compilation, the major cause of multiple compilations to eradicate syntax errors is the failure to close comments or strings, which causes large segments of code to escape syntax checking at all. But these are precisely the two errors not detectable by the batch compiler, and they were going to be left out of the syntax checker! By simply checking those two things and nothing else, the average number of compilations to reach an error-free state could probably be reduced by one, and the variance reduced even more.

Once the first successful compilation has been made, syntax errors are largely the most crude errors, such as those are caused by hasty punching. These errors are often global, in the sense that a name is mispunched, and are otherwise rather trivial, such as unmatched parentheses and misspelled keywords. The most useful checker here would be one that finds crude errors and then makes a check for compatibility against the symbols saved from a previous compilation. If, of course, each new session results in major changes in the program, saving the symbol table will not be worthwhile, and only an explicit model of programmer behavior tells us how to design our system. If we believe, with Sackman, that each new batch run is essentially a fresh start in which syntax errors have been "extinguished" by learning by the programmer, we will choose to make a syntax check that makes no reference to the previous compilation. But, if we believe that the programmer's knowledge of syntax remains largely unchanged (although obviously not completely so) over the course of one problem, and that he "extinguishes" errors simply by eliminating them one statement at a time, then we will choose a rather different system design—one that will give greater programmer satisfaction and even more efficient system performance.

The question of system performance pervades Sackman's work, and although he tries, as every good scientist should, to isolate the component that can account for a behavior, he consistently runs up against interaction effects, which make such separation impossible. For example, "language" is confused with "system" by the programmers, and differences in performance might be attributable to the use of ALGOL in the batch system and BASIC on-line. But even if the "same" language is used in both systems, they are not the same, since each system has its special control statements, which must differ from batch to on-line, as well as certain features that are essential in one environment and useless in the other.

Another problem in making batch and on-line systems "comparable" is the question of terminal availability versus turnaround time. Is a six-hour turnaround with a variance of plus or minus three hours comparable to an on-line system in which terminal users are limited to fifteen-minute shots on terminals that are available 90 percent of the time? Sackman is constantly running up against unsolvable questions such as this, and eventually he concludes that a bad terminal system is worse than a good batch system, whereas a good terminal system is better than a bad batch. Some may think this to be a trivial conclusion, but it represents a major step in the direction away from such vacuous statements as "on-line is better than batch," or "batch is better than on-line." Now we must continue Sackman's work to identify those factors that make a batch system good, and those that make a terminal system good. Unfortunately, we probably won't be able to separate "factors" as neatly as we would like, since our systems really are systems.

Finally, it may not be worth the effort anyway, in view of the individual variations found at every turn. Perhaps we should let Sackman summarize the entire case in his own words, and show us where the batch-versus-on-line controversy should now turn:

Perhaps the central result from these studies is that no really substantive case can be made for the overwhelming general-purpose advantage of one mode over the other. As in all studies, without exception, individual differences in performance overshadow computer system differences. The key to major breakthrough in improved man-computer effectiveness seems to lie in the nature and structure of individual differences and in human problem-solving styles. Whether the object of an institution is to teach computer science effectively or to produce cost-effective computer programs, the path to effective achievement of system and institutional goals is fundamental knowledge of human problem-solving in man-computer communication. (p. 223)

DOCUMENTATION

Documentation is the castor oil of programming—managers think it is good for programmers, and programmers hate it! In fact, the managers know it must be good because programmers hate it so much, just the way we used to know that iodine was good for that abrasion on our knee because we could feel the sting. Well, folk medicine dies hard, in programming as at home, so it is going to be difficult to sell the idea that documentation, as such, has no intrinsic value. The value of documentation is only to be realized if the documentation is well done. If it is poorly done, it will be worse than no documentation at all.

As far as can be determined, there is no way to *force* programmers to produce *good* documentation. Some programmers can be forced to produce documentation, just as some children can be forced to take castor oil; but there are so many ways to sabotage the usefulness of documentation that forcing only results in documents that are not worth the paper used to print them on. The only hope, then, for producing good documentation is to convince the programmer that it will benefit him to do so. If the act of producing the document has no value to the programmer, the job will always be done in the minimum possible way; but if producing the document has demonstrable good effects, there will be no way of *preventing* reasonably good documentation.

What do we mean by reasonably good documentation? Our emphasis is really on the word "reasonably," for we usually err in expecting just too much from documentation. In the first place, different people have different needs when they look at the documentation for a program, so that no system of documentation is going to satisfy them all equally well. We should set a goal that is reasonable and try to achieve good documentation which meets *that* goal. If it happens to meet some other goal reasonably well, that is a bonus; but if not, then we shall have to produce some different documents for the different goal, or do without. Secondly, there are certain things that no documentation will *ever* do. Primary among these things is making it possible for an untrained person to understand all there is to know about a program in twenty-five words or less.

Using the documentation for a program will always require some work and some minimum prerequisite knowledge. If the reader does not understand English, he is not going to understand a program document written in English, and nobody would blame the documenter for that. But it is equally unreasonable to expect that someone who does not understand FORTRAN can understand fully a program written in FOR-TRAN. He may be expected to understand how to *use* a program, if it is designed to be used by people, rather than to fit as one small cog in a larger system—if he understands the use for which the program was intended. We must not, however, expect that the use of a program for solving differential equations can be made understandable to a person who has not passed high-school algebra. What we can expect, as a minimum, is that if the reader has a high school education, he should be able to see from the first page of the documentation that he will not be able to understand it if he should get in any deeper.

"Depth" is one of the most important documentation concepts, especially for large systems. If a system is of any size at all, different users of the documentation will need different levels of detail in the information they extract. The highest level should be just sufficiently detailed to tell the user whether or not he will be able to read the documents. At each level—because we can never be sure which document will fall into the user's hands—the first and most conspicuous thing in the document should be a reference to the documents above and below it in depth, along with an indication of the depth to which this document goes and the knowledge the reader must have to use it.

Without this minimum of self-describing structure, no system of documentation can be expected to succeed, but the user must also take the time to understand this structural information and to use it. We cannot expect that any random document we pick up will be the proper entry point to the path of understanding a system, any more than we can expect to understand the role of Aloysha if we start reading *The Brothers Karamazov* on page 353. In novels, of course, there is a standard structure which the reader is assumed to know, and it simplifies the author's task no end to know that most serious readers are going to start at the beginning and read toward the end. In documenting a large system, however, the writers—in addition to suffering the deficiency of not being a Dostoevski or a James—have to contend with readers who don't know where to begin. Thus, each physical document must contain some guiding information.

Of course, it is a bit shortsighted of us to confine our thinking to physical documentation such as books. Most likely, the problems of programming documentation will not really be solved until we start using our data-processing machines to document their own program in a creative way. To be sure, we have started in this direction now—as we usually start toward automation—by mechanizing the same functions we used to do before mechanization. Thus, typesetting and composition are done with "administrative terminal systems," with all the benefits of automatic assistance of updating—that oh-so-frequent problem in programming. But, we are still by and large limited in what we can communicate to the user of the document because we are still working through the medium of books.

Now, it would not be smart for an author to decry too violently the continued use of books, but there are limits to the proper functioning of this medium. In the first place, books are not the most flexible medium for accepting and disseminating updated material. From the time these words are impressed on the typing paper until they are seen in print by the first reader's eyes, sufficient time will have elapsed in which to make a baby, starting with the basic ingredients. In some cases, at somewhat increased cost in money or accuracy or both, the time span can be reduced a bit, but the medium is not inherently fast enough for material which changes as fast as program documentation for a large system.

In the second place, no matter how nice it is to cuddle up before the fire with a cozy book in your hand, few people use programming documentation in that environment. For a general overview document—for teaching and learning general concepts of a system—a book might be the suitable medium. But for answers to specific technical questions, something else is needed. We cannot trust the user to find his way about in the maze of documentation which must of necessity exist for a complex system, so we must provide a system that guides him in an active manner. What could be better at this kind of active guidance than a computer, viewed through the window of a suitable terminal?

Well, of course, there is the cost of it all. Who shall pay? Psychologically, the question of cost of documentation always strikes a hard blow, for we are always unprepared. Why? Because we have not accustomed ourselves to thinking of the cost of documentation as a part of the programming cost. At bottom, then, when you talk in terms of what managers talk in terms of—money—you find that they, too, think of documentation as a separate, or separable, part of programming. It's a wonderful thing to have good documentation, but not if it has to be paid for.

From time to time, schemes are brought forth for some form of "automatic documentation" of programs—schemes which are supposed to be painless or costless or both. One example of this type is the many flow charting programs which exist. If you feed one of these programs your program input, it spews out a flow diagram as output. Certainly the process is—or can be—painless, and, in fact, turns out not to be very expensive. But is it documentation? Probably not. What it may be—and this is nothing to sneeze at—is one more weapon for the debugging arsenal.

The programmer, if he has been working without flow diagrams of his own, may find it difficult to follow just what his program is doing, particularly if its locality is not very good. A flow diagram, properly constructed, can help to gather many nonlocal points of flow into a two-dimensional form so that they may be seen on one page. This new view of the program may be extremely helpful to the programmer, not only revealing such solid errors as endless loops or unconnected branches, but showing whether or not his code has realized his intentions.

If the programmer has been working with a flow diagram all along, the machine-drawn chart can be used for comparison, which will certainly reveal any errors in transcription from the diagram to the code. In more linear languages, such as PL/I, the two-dimensional advantages of the flow diagram lose their strength. When a PL/I program without any labels was put into one of these flow charting programs, what came out was the original program, in the original order, with nice little boxes drawn around different pieces of code. What the flow diagrammers cannot do is add anything new *inside* the boxes, although seeing the code with boxes around it may help the programmer see certain things he had failed to notice.

However, if the contents of the boxes are obscure to all but the original programmer, the flow diagram drawn automatically from them—in any language—is not going to be much help to the person who needs documentation. If the comments were misleading, they will still be misleading —unless they mislead about the destination of a branch. If symbols were poorly chosen, they will remain the same symbols on the flow diagram. We have made a few pilot studies to test the documentation value of such automatically drawn flow diagrams, and we find no evidence that the original coding plus flow diagram is any easier to understand than the original coding itself—except by the original coder. Perhaps some of the companies that sell such flow charting programs would sponsor more carefully controlled studies into this problem.

A flow diagram, of course, is but one alternative way of representing the information that is in the actual code. Even if its total value turns out to be quite small, there are several reasons not to give up on it as a documentation technique. First of all, since it is an automatic procedure carried out by computer, we can expect that the cost of doing it will decrease, rather than increase, as computers get more powerful. Secondly, it has the absolutely outstanding advantage of being drawn directly from the code itself, so that maintaining the documentation is precisely the same act as maintaining the code. Therefore, there is no possibility of slippage—the death rattle of all documentations systems.

One extreme example of the view that the documentation should spring from the code itself is expressed by Klerer and May about their system. Not only can the written documentation for their system be placed on two sides of a sheet of paper, but they expressly state that they do not expect the programmer to learn how to use their system from the documentation but, rather, from experiments with the system itself. Instead of loading up the documentation with thousands of words to explain an obscure point that nine-tenths of the programmers will never use, Klerer and May leave the work of clearing up obscurities to the machine itself. This is, after all, only a return to the normal practice which we have been using for years. The machine is, and always will be, the court of last resort on documentation disputes.

In the past, however, the machine has been a rather uncommunicative documenter. In order to rely more on the machine itself, we must use more imagination in getting the machine to tell its story in as many alternative ways as possible. Each particular way, such as flow diagramming, may give but a small addition to the clarity of a program, but many small changes in viewpoint may add up to a sum much greater than its parts. If, as we believe, the main impediment to program debugging and program understanding is psychological set, any technique for getting the mind unstuck should be explored as a possible tool of debugging and documentation.

We have been conducting a series of studies on the usefulness of various alternative ways of looking at a program. We have tried to draw on any source of inspiration in coming up with alternative views. For instance, think of the painter, who finds that familiarity with objects may cause him to distort his perception of their actual color. To overcome his set, he bends over and views the scene upside down through his legs. In a similar manner, we are experimenting with printing programs backwards—either by character or by symbol—just to see what will happen.

Some of the other methods we are trying are more familiar, but a list of them may help inspire the reader to think of others:
1. Set off keywords in boldface or underline.
2. Set off nonkeywords in boldface or underline.
3. Set off keywords or nonkeywords in lower case.
4. Change multi-use symbols, such as the ambiguous equals sign, and parentheses at different levels of nesting.
5. Mark potential trouble spots—such as dummies created where references might be desired or references used where dummies might be wanted.
6. Strip comments from a listing and present the "naked" listing on one page and the comments on another.
7. Strip literals in a similar way.

8. Rename all variables.
9. Expand all abbreviations, or abbreviate all expansions.
10. Permute options to a standard order, or simply to a different order than the programmer used.
11. List symbols in alphabetical order, together with references to where used, set, or passed as references.
12. List symbols in groups according to specific attributes, such as all EXTERNAL variables or all FLOAT variables together, with multiple listing according to multiple attributes.
13. List the scope of symbols.
14. List potential ambiguities.
15. Extract and print separately groups at successive levels of nesting of DOs, BEGINs, and PROCEDUREs.
16. Decompose conditional statements into some canonical form, perhaps including decision tables.
17. Strip out expressions and list them with their values calculated under several sets of values of their contained variables.
18. Execute sample flow paths.

None of these viewpoints are intended to change the physical meaning of a program, but all are intended to change its psychological meaning. What we are hoping to do is present the programmer's eyes (and perhaps other sense organs) and mind with a richness of views on which he can apply his native talents as an adaptive system. In other words, we are not trying to make the machine solve the debugging problem and the documentation problem; we are trying to make the machine help people take advantage of the immense psychological resources they have in overcoming their immense psychological shortcomings.

It would be nice, of course, if these programs *did* solve, or partially solve, the documentation problem. Another worthy effort in this direction involves a bit more work by the programmer, but also promises to be useful. In this system, when the programmer has finished the program, he sits down at a terminal and is interrogated by the computer about the function of each of the various program and data elements in the coding. The replies he makes are stored away and presumably shipped to anybody who requests a copy of the program. The users, in turn, can go to a terminal and ask questions about the program and data elements that interest them—the computer keeping from them the job of sorting through the mass of documentation material. There is no chance of their going to the wrong place for the information, for they always go to the same place—the terminal.

This type of system really seems to get at the problem of the user who does not understand the structure of the documentation, but it still leaves the problem of entering the documentation data originally. The intercourse with the computer will certainly be a motivating factor for some programmers; but even the most motivated programmer, if he cannot write an English sentence, will not be transformed into an able communicator by this system. One possible modification would be to use the computer merely as a referee in a dialogue between the programmer and a number of "typical" users. The users would ask questions through their terminals, and the programmer would attempt to answer them through his. The computer might even help the users by prompting them to ask certain questions, but would not record the programmer's answers until they had been accepted by the users as giving them the information they desire. The entire set of answers could then be classified and shipped with the program for other users to interrogate.

Even better, of course, though conceptually further in the future, would be a single central pool of answers to such questions. Any user, or potential user, of the system could interrogate the central pool. If he obtained the information he needed under the computer's guidance, that would be that—although statistics could be kept on frequent requests so that they might be answered more directly in the future. When, however, the user could not satisfy his information needs from the answers already in the pool, the computer would issue a request to someone at the programming facility to get on the line with the user. In the ensuing dialogue, the question would eventually be answered, but it might take a few days in the worst cases. Once the answer had been obtained, however, it would be added to the records and thus made available for future users.

What such a system does—with suitable provision for updating as changes are introduced—is to take us back closer to the time when the documentation was the programmer himself. In a small shop, on a small program, little attention was paid to explicit documentation, for it was always easier to go to the originator to get the answer. After all, you probably had to ask him in order to *find* the documentation. In fact, in such a situation today, this is probably the best method. Any programmer knows a lot more about his program than he will ever be able to put in his documentation, or than anyone would be able to find as needed even if it had been put in. The major problem with this method is when a programmer leaves the shop, but if egoless programming is practiced— and if the management is not so bad that all the programmers leave at once—this problem is minimized.

There are, of course, limits to this personalized method. One particularly strange situation occurred in 1961 concerning a network analysis program I had written in 1956 while working in San Francisco. The program had been distributed informally and used widely during those years, but I had in the meantime wandered from place to place, finally resting for the moment in New York. Then, one day, I got a long-distance call from Stockholm. At the other end of the line was a desperate programmer who had been tracking me down for three days. He explained that he was trying to modify the program to handle a certain case which was not in the original conception of the problem, and then asked, "If I change the sign of location 1003 to minus, will that do the job?"

Over five years, and across the continent, I had hardly retained the memory of having written the program, let alone a memory of what was in location 1003. Quickly calculating the cost of a transtlantic telephone call and comparing it with the cost of computer time, I told the caller, "Yes, that should do it. Why don't you put it on the machine and try it out. If it doesn't work, call me back." Fortunately, I never heard from Sweden again.

Even when programmers remain fixed, their memories fade. Very few programmers can recall what was in any location—symbolic or absolute —of any program they wrote five years ago and have not looked at since. But then, very few programs of one-man type can be expected to remain in use over such a long time span. It reaches a point, even with the best documentation, that it pays to throw a program away and start over.

What we must consider, then, when deciding how to document a program, is who will use it, how it will be used, where the users will be, and for how long it will stay in use. If it will only be used locally, for the type of work it was designed to handle, by people who know the programmers, and for a year or two or three, then perhaps the money that might have been spent on elaborate documentation could be put to better use on some other project. If many people in remote locations are going to use it, the cost of elaborate documentation must be reckoned with from the first, and the programmer will have to be involved from the beginning in making documentation a possibility.

Notice that we did not say "in making documentation" but, rather, "in making documentation a possibility." When a program is going to be used as a marketable commodity—whether or not it is actually sold— the users have a right to expect that the documentation be done as professionally as the programming. And, considering the matter coolly, there is no reason to believe that a professional programmer will be qualified as a professional documenter. Thus, if professional documentation is to be done, it should be done with the *assistance* of the programmer, but not *by* the programmer. If documentation is elevated to a professional status all its own, so that the documenter can work side by side with the programmer without being made to feel inferior, we have the right to hope that documentation will improve.

We have come through a strange cycle in programming, starting with the creation of programming itself as a human activity. Executives with the tiniest smattering of knowledge assume that anyone can write a program, and only now are programmers beginning to win their battle for recognition as true professionals. Not just anyone, with any background, or any training, can do a fine job of programming. Programmers know this, but then why is it that they think that anyone picked off the street can do documentation? One has only to spend an hour looking at papers written by graduate students to realize the extent to which the ability to communicate is not universally held. And so, when we speak about computer program documentation, we are not speaking about the psychology of computer programming at all—except insofar as programmers have the illusion that anyone can do a good job of documentation, provided he is not smart enough to be a programmer.

SUMMARY

The main lesson of this chapter is simple: Systems are complex. A computer system is not just hardware, not just software, not even just people plus hardware plus software. The procedures, formal and informal, that have evolved with the system are part of the system; so is the current load on various components, and so is the attitude and experience of the users. Even among the commonly accepted "parts" of a system, clear lines of separation do not exist. Hardware merges with operating system, operating system merges with programming language, programming language merges with debugging tools, debugging tools merge with documentation, and documentation merges with training, and all of them mingle with the social climate in which the system is used.

This complexity means, on the one hand, that experimental evidence is doubly essential, but, on the other hand, that it is doubly difficult to obtain and intepret. The time has come to sweep the myths out of our closet and replace them, if possible, with hard experimental evidence. Not that any of these problems will ever be "solved"—the complexity is too great for that. But what worthwhile problems are ever solved? It's not so much the solutions we need, anyway, but the experience in trying to get them.

QUESTIONS

For Managers

1. Have you ever been offered a "debugging compiler" or other debugging aid? How did you decide whether or not to purchase it?

2. Do you ask your programmers to estimate their level of confidence in

their "debugged" programs? Do you try to make your own estimate of confidence? What factors do you use in making this judgment?

3. Describe the systems of performance evaluation in use in your shop. How do you use them in being a manager? What additional information would you like to have them supply? What information do they now supply that is useless to you?

4. What do you consider to be ideal turnaround in your batch system? What do you consider to be ideal access to terminals in your on-line system? What do your programmers think about these issues?

5. Do you give certain programmers priority in using the batch system? The on-line system? Have you ever observed adverse effects of your favoritism? What do you think you could do in the future to give priorities without creating bad feeling? It is possible that the bad feelings created do more harm than the priorities are supposed to do good?

6. Which is better for programming, on-line or batch?

7. How are the documenters chosen in your shop? Are your documentation rules sufficiently flexible to permit different kinds of documentation for different types of programs? Is there resentment against documentation work? If so, what do you think is the source, and what can be done about it?

For Programmers

1. Recall from your experience a "tiny" error that had a big ultimate cost. What debugging tools or techniques could have prevented that error? Would their cost have been greater than the cost of that one error?

2. Give examples of when you have been biased in your program testing by "early returns," both good and bad. Give examples of other factors that have biased your debugging strategy, such as desire to please your manager, knowledge of program structure, or interaction with other programs or programmers.

3. What do you consider to be ideal turnaround in your batch system? What do you consider to be ideal access to terminals in your on-line system? What does your manager think about these issues?

4. Give an example of behavioral adaptation to system features, using yourself as the subject.

5. Which is better for programming, on-line or batch?

6. What other views of a program would you like to have supplied by your operating system and compiler? Explain how these views could help you, giving specific examples for each.

7. What do you think of documentation work? What do you think of

people who do a good job of documentation? What would have to be changed to make you do a good job of documentation?

BIBLIOGRAPHY

Rosenthal, Robert, On the Social Psychology of the Psychological Experiment, *American Scientist,* June 1963.
Rosenthal has pioneered in studying the observational biases that creep into experimentation, especially because of expectations on the part of the experimenter. The parallels with debugging are obvious, so that programmers should be able to translate the results in this article directly into their own work practices.

Parzen, Emanuel, *Modern Probability Theory and Its Applications,* New York, Wiley, 1960.
On the matter of the influence of *a priori* probability on the confidence in the results of a particular test, see, for example, pp. 119-120. In general, programmers would benefit from thinking of debugging as a probabilistic process, and Parzen's book would be a good starting place.

Weinberg, G. M., *PL/I Programming—A Manual of Style,* New York, McGraw-Hill, 1970.
For a discussion of the advantages of proper language and proper program structure in program testing, see Chapter 4.

Berkeley, Edmund C., The Personality of the Interactive Programmed Computer, *Computers and Automation,* Dec. 1965, pp. 42-46.
This article is a bit superficial, but raises the interesting question of the "personality" which a system presents to the user. As Sackman has shown, the attitude a user has toward a system influences his performance in using that system, and also that the user's respect for the system grows with increased familiarity. No doubt the personality of the system plays a part in this acceptance, and users could be tested for their perception of the personality of different systems, in order to try to determine which personalities programmers like to work with.

Sackman, Harold, *Man-Computer Problem Solving: Experimental Evaluation of Time-Sharing and Batch Processing,* Princeton, N.J., Auerbach Publishers, 1970.
As the subtitle suggests, and as we have previously indicated, this book summarizes the work to date in this field, and is essential prerequisite reading for anyone about to compare operating systems.

Stange, G. H., The Initial Effects of the Installation of Two Remote Computer Access Systems.
Unpublished class report.

Salsbury, R. G., Ideal Turnaround—An Opinion Survey.
Unpublished class report.

Heiss, William J., and Frederick Schwartz, Positional versus Keywood Coding.
These unpublished class reports provided learning experiences for all involved, and demonstrate that useful work in this field can be done without going off the deep end.

Rosin, Robert F., Supervisory and Monitor Systems, *Computing Surveys,* **1,** No. 1 (March 1969).
In little more than a dozen pages, Rosin manages to make clear the general out-

lines and important issues in operating systems. By taking an historical view, he is able to show how each successive generation of operating system design was more or less intended to patch up the problems left over from the previous generation. One is led to speculate on the way operating systems of the future will look as they begin to patch up the psychological holes left by present systems.

London, Ralph L., Bibliography on Proving the Correctness of Computer Programs, *Machine Intelligence,* **5,** New York, American Elsevier, 1970.
The dream of all debuggers is to someday be able to have the machine prove whether or not a program is correct. A great deal of work is being done on this problem, although it is certainly unsolvable in general. None of the work done to date has any real practical application to debugging, but reading some of these papers will definitely have an effect on the debugger. No definitive summary of work has been written, or can yet be written, so this bibliography will have to suffice.

Weinberg, G. M., and G. L. Gresset, An Experiment in Automatic Verification of Programs, *Communications of the ACM,* **6,** 10 (October 1963), pp. 610-613.
In this early study, the authors tried to show how error detection properties of a compiler depend upon the error environment in which they are used, and they made a number of suggestions for improvement of error-detection performance in an actual environment. Few of these suggestions have been carried out in any major compiler.

Irons, E. T., An Error Correcting Parse Algorithm, *Communications of the ACM,* **6,** 11 (November 1963), pp. 669-673.

LaFrance, Jacques, Optimization of Error Recovery in Syntax-Directed Parsing Algorithms, *ACM SIGPLAN Notices,* **5,** No. 12 (December 1970), pp. 2-17.
Irons' paper represents the earliest, and LaFrance's one of the most recent, on the subject of automatic *correction* of syntax errors by compilers. Underlying any "correction" scheme must be a concept of "closeness" which dictates that construction is to be tried if an error is detected. Workers in this field would like to have a concept of "closeness" which is independent of the psychology of the user, but this seems to be a vain hope. At the very beginning, at least, the major progress will be made by classifying the most frequently made errors taken from actual studies of working programmers using that language and system and then providing special routines to unscramble these errors. For instance, in the PL/C compiler developed at Cornell University, a major step in correcting and successfully compiling PL/I programs is made simply by limiting the user to comments and strings that do not run from one card to the next. This limits the scope of propagation of an error and greatly increases the chances of a proper correction or at least a more meaningful compilation so that everything can be corrected in one more run. Only after the major psychological causes of error have been eliminated by these *ad hoc* methods should we be forced to resort to more elegant methods as suggested in these papers.

Teitelman, W., PILOT: A Step Toward Man-Computer Symbiosis (Doctoral Dissertation, M.I.T.), Cambridge, Mass., June 1966.
The PILOT system is a tool written in LISP for assisting LISP programmers with the job of modifying programs. It contains many interesting features, but it is not clear just how helpful this system is to programmers who habitually use it—or how useful it is compared with simple error detection. Studies along this line would be useful.

Stockham, Thomas G., Jr., Some Methods of Graphical Debugging, *Proceedings of the IBM Scientific Computing Symposium on Man-Machine Communication,* 1966.

Stockham reviews the use of CRT devices for dynamic debugging, tracing its history back to 1958, at least. He bemoans the fact that these early experiments did not evolve into common practice, a failure which he attributes to a "variety of technical and economic reasons." But it could be that lacking any real behavioral data on the *value* of these systems, there was no motivation to overcome the technical and economic reasons. Certainly there is sufficient economic potential in the cost of poor debugging to justify a big technical push, if we can but demonstrate the rewards.

Mills, Harlan D., Syntax-Directed Documentation for PL360, *Communications of the ACM,* **13,** 4 (April 1970).

Mills presents a rather ambitious scheme for extracting the material for documentation as a part of the interaction process with the computer when the program is being written, then making the documentation available through computer processing at a later time. This approach seems to get to the heart of the matter in two ways—it does not seem to require highly motivated people to produce the documentation, nor does it seem to require masses of printed documentation through which one must wade unassisted. In one sense, though, it is the typical computer user's approach to the problem—"let's see if we can make the machine do it." This is an idea that deserves testing, first to see if it really produces documentation that can be used, and then to see if that is what we really want.

Klerer, M., and J. May, *Reference Manual,* Revised ed., Dobbs Ferry, N.Y., Columbia University Hudson Labs., July 1965.

This is the two-page document with which the user starts his exploration of the Klerer-May system. The entire document together with the one-page appendix, is reprinted in Sammet's "Programming Languages" (See Bibliography at the end of the previous chapter).

Leeds, H. D., and G. M. Weinberg, *Computer Programming Fundamentals/Based on the IBM System/360,* New York, McGraw-Hill, 1970.

In this book, you will find a more extensive discussion of documentation of programs than is habitual in programming texts. One chapter deals with flow diagramming, another with writeups, and other aspects of documentation are discussed throughout in connection with related topics. Still, it is far from the complete or last word on the subject.

PART 5

EPILOGUE

R eaders who reach the end of a book are entitled to some praise from the author, since they have paid him the greatest compliment an author can receive. Yet those readers who do reach the end are probably in less need of rewards than the dropout, for it would seem impossible to go all the way through any book without receiving the reward of learning. Perhaps it is possible to go through this book without being touched, although as one reviewer commented, "One comes away with the feeling of having spent a pleasant but somewhat 'wasted' afternoon of reading, and as the old joke goes, 'it ain't till you try to turn your head that you realize how sharp the razor was.' " Although I would have been happier with a less violent metaphor, the remark captures what the book has tried to do. My students have had the same reaction. A typical remark made a year after attending a seminar is: "It was pleasant enough talking about those things, but then I began to see what was going on at the office. Wow!"

The most important thing that this student learned was not any particular behavioral science result or the name of so-and-so's law to parrot back on a test. What he learned was that he had been carrying around with him all his life a well-equipped machine for observing behavior—but that it had never been used very much. As an anonymous sign at the computing center put it:

> The human mind ordinarily operates at only ten percent of its capacity—the rest is overhead for the operating system.

So rather than be concerned so much about that computer operating system, the reader who has really been touched by this book will start to work on the operating system he carries around in his own central processing unit—his head. That will be his reward.

But if we make our own operating systems more efficient, if we observe ourselves and our surroundings more carefully, and if this efficiency and observation lead us to be more productive programmers, of what use is it? The stories of the three wishes send us a message from many cultures, and from the ancient past: "If you get your fondest wish, what then?" If, by psychological, sociological, and anthropological investigation or by simple heightened awareness we become better programmers, to what work shall we turn our talents? For if something is not worth doing, it is certainly not worth doing right.

Is what we are doing with computers worth doing? Is what *you* are doing with computers worth doing? Because computers are such fascinating beasts, because programming is such a game, such a joy, we who program computers are in danger of becoming the unwitting pawns of those who would use our toys for not-so-playful ends. Can there be any doubt that if Hitler had computers at his command, one of the first application would have been keeping closer track on Jews and Gypsies so that all who should have gone to the ovens did go to the ovens? Can there by any doubt that if Pilate had computers, they would have been used to keep the information from informers, the better to crucify those that were crying out for crucifixion by their heretical zeal? Can there be any doubt that somewhere in our country today some human beings are using computers as just another, finer weapon in their arsenal of ways to subjugate other human beings to their wishes—to their conception of the proper life of man?

And having said all that, can there be any doubt that such people—now as in 1939 or at the dawn of the Christian era—find many willing hands and brains to carry out their work in return for fun and profit? Or that some of those willing hands will have held this book, to the profit of their employers?

Many years ago, just a few years after I wrote my first book with Herb Leeds, I read an article describing experiments in which monkeys were subjected to various doses of poison gases, evidently to see how long it took them to die. The work was done in a laboratory for chemical warfare research, with the intent, no doubt, of extrapolating it to human beings. Thirty-six innocent monkeys, as I recall, met their deaths in this gruesome way so that someday, perhaps, thirty-six million people could meet their deaths even more efficiently. The article remained in my mind for months afterward, and indeed it has remained there to this day. By pure coincidence, I suppose, I was accosted at a meeting by a nice young man who had gone out of his way to tell me how much he had learned from our book, how much it had helped him to become a better programmer. I asked him what sort of work he did, and he replied that he worked at a laboratory for chemical warfare research.

Afterward, I tried to rationalize my way out of my depression by imagining that it was a *different* laboratory, which it might have been, or that *he* never worked on the monkey experiment, which might also have been true. But I knew that somewhere, someone who had learned from me was participating in such experiments and worse. I knew that I shared the responsibility—that writing a book is not merely teaching means to unknown and unimagined ends. For a long time I could not write, perhaps for that reason, or perhaps for others. But, eventually, my ego got the better of me and I began again, determined to try making my books unusable to any but the pure at heart.

To a certain extent, this book may have achieved that goal, for the idea of the programmer as a human being is not going to appeal to certain types of people, and they will neither finish the book nor profit from it. But it is naive, I now realize, to expect that bad systems cannot be built by people with good hearts. Otherwise, why would I encounter so many bad systems when almost all of the people I meet are wonderful? No, something else is needed, something not within the power of an author to give to a reader. As Malraux once said, "It is the work of a lifetime to make a man." A book can be but a tiny part of that work—the rest is up to you, and the work will never be finished.

Having said all that, I do not shrink from personal responsibility for what I have done in writing this book. We stand at the brink of a new age, an age made possible by the revolution that is embodied in the computer. Standing on the brink, we could totter either way—to a golden age of liberty or a dark age of tyranny, either of which would surpass anything the world has ever known. Perhaps no individual's efforts will make any difference in the result, but we must never cease trying, for then the result is sure to be tyranny. This book is my effort against the tyranny, the enslavement of men by other men and by their own ignorance. Would that it not be adopted by the forces of tyranny themselves, as no doubt it will be. Lacking that hope, I can only hope that its use to the other forces will, in the balance, be greater.

INDEX